Endorsement

Ross is a man of great boldness and a willingness to step out of the boat for the sake of the lost. Ross is willing to risk being misunderstood and even rejected, if it might possibly mean someone encounters God's love. People matter deeply to Ross because he has God's heart for them.

In this book, Ross writes with incredible maturity of insight and a correct and thorough handling of biblical truth. A solid foundation is expertly laid and the writing style is so engaging that you want to read more. You know you are listening to one who has walked the walk, not to one who only knows the theory.

Ross puts well-known and often-quoted scriptures into the correct context that results in many "Ah-ha" moments. I easily understood what Ross was writing, yet it was profound and empowering. The result of this book will be that many do not want to miss the kairos moments that fill our days. I believe that the truth found in this book will empower a generation to be part of God's pre-ordained end-time harvest! I believe that the market place is waiting for the sons and daughters of God to be revealed through their love and obedience.

Steve McCracken
Prophet
David McCracken Ministries

In the times I have met with Ross, I have witnessed his passion for the raising up of ministers in the market place. He is one that lives it and his book is a testimonial for others wishing to be more effective in market place ministry. The book is well written and engaging. It also offers practical insights into how we can each be more aware and effective in making Christ known to those in our world. I thoroughly recommend it.

Professor Stephen Fogarty
President: Alphacrucis College

I have been in full-time ministry for almost 30 years and one of my great passions is helping people understand that 'ministry' is not confined to the four walls of the church. Indeed, the vast majority of people will never be employed by or hold an office in the church, but their calling is just as vital for the advancement of God's Kingdom on earth.

Ross Walker has spent his life in market place ministry and this book contains sound wisdom and powerful testimonies of what God can do through those who are surrendered to Him, whatever their vocation. It will inspire and equip you to be all that you are purposed to be!

Neil Smith
PlanetBusiness Pastor
Planetshakers Church

I met Ross on the 2017 Believe mission trip to PNG and his book reflects the many stories and principles we have shared in our close friendship since. The book combines teaching with testimony to help the reader understand what is required of them by God and how to make it a part of each day in the workplace. It is encouraging because it is practical and implementable but also challenges us at the same time in our daily living and prayer life so we can be effective in our ministry.

Michael Eadie
Director of ACS Financial Group, Director Believe Global,
Board Advisory to International Christian Embassy Jerusalem,
GM Commercial for a large industrial group.

This book is the inspiring testimony of Ross Walker, a market place Christian who has influenced the lives of so many people over many years. It shows what can happen when we are open to the activity of the Holy Spirit in all areas of our lives, not just on Sundays.

Ross reflects insightfully on Scripture as he tells his story of coming to Christian faith, and many other remarkable stories. It is a story soaked in prayer and the reading of Scripture. While we may be in different places to Ross (my place is primarily academic writing and teaching) and yours could be very different, we can all learn from Ross's experiences in the business world.

So many of our churches neglect the market place where the majority of Christians spend most of their time, and if you are looking for inspiration and ideas for living out your faith beyond Sunday this is a book for you. I pray that you will be blessed by reading this book as I have.

Paul Oslington
Professor of Economics and Theology, Alphacrucis College, Sydney.
Honorary Research Professor, Australian Centre
for Christianity and Culture, Canberra.
Resident Member for 2020, Centre of Theological Inquiry, Princeton.

Ross Walker is someone whose love for others is completely authentic. He lives out kindness and genuine compassion in a way that is rare. Most of us want to embody the love of Jesus – Ross has a lifetime of experience in putting love into practice in his daily life.

His life story has been an encouragement to me, and I am sure that it will encourage and inspire many others.

Janet Dickson, *BA (Hons), Dip Ed*
Co-author Searching for Paradise

MARKET PLACE
MINISTRY

Touching the Lost by His Spirit

ROSS WALKER

Ark House Press
PO Box 1722, Port Orchard, WA 98366 USA
PO Box 1321, Mona Vale NSW 1660 Australia
PO Box 318 334, West Harbour, Auckland 0661 New Zealand
arkhousepress.com

Scripture quotations are primarily from:
The Holy Bible, New International Version (niv) © 1973, 1978, 1984, 2011 by Biblica, Inc.™ Used by permission. All rights reserved worldwide.
Also quoted are the following translations:
The World English Bible™ (web)
The Holy Bible, King James Version (KJV)
New American Standard Bible (nasb) © 1960, 1977, 1995 by the Lockman Foundation. Used by permission.
The Amplified Bible (AMP) © 1965, 1987 by Zondervan Publishing House.
The Amplified New Testament © 1958, 1987 by the Lockman Foundation.
Holy Bible, New Living Translation (NLT) © 1996, 2004 by Tyndale Charitable Trust. Used by permission of Tyndale House Publishers. All rights reserved.
Holman Christian Standard Bible (HCSB) Copyright © 1999, 2000, 2002, 2003 by Holman Bible Publishers, Nashville, Tennessee. All rights reserved.
The Holy Bible, Berean Study Bible (BSB) Copyright ©2016, 2018 by Bible Hub Used by permission. All rights reserved worldwide.
God's Word (GW), © 1995 by God's Word to the Nations Bible Society.
Some Scripture quotations reflect the author's paraphrase.
The names of some people mentioned in this book have been changed for reasons of privacy.
Italics in Scripture quotations are the author's emphasis.

Cataloguing in Publication Data:
Title: Market Place Ministry
ISBN: 978-0-6489380-9-5 (pbk)
Subjects: Business; Ministry;
Other Authors/Contributors: Walker, Ross

Design by initiateagency.com

Foreword

Most books are full of thoughts, ideas, theories and philosophies but occasionally a book is written that is an absolute mirror reflection of the author's life. Ross Walker is a close friend, a member of our evangelistic ministry board and team member on several major International campaigns.

I have come to know him as a strong committed family man, a very successful businessman with huge vision and understanding of wealth building.

I have watched and learnt much from his enormous people skills and mentoring strength. I have constantly observed a Christian man whose grasp of God's word could see him successfully lecturing in any Bible college in our country. However, the thing that has inspired me most significantly is his burning passion for "market place" ministry.

Every day he prepares to minister the love of Jesus to the people he works with and meets in the line of business. His trusted integrity, strong work ethic and real love and sensitivity to people opens the door constantly from executives to janitors for sharing of the reality of Christ.

People are drawn to Ross's warm openness and genuine love and care for people. This comes through in every page of this book. Every day he hungers for the operation of the spiritual gifts and I love regularly hearing of remarkable supernatural events that see not just individuals but whole families turning to Christ.

Now Ross has recorded many of these wonderful stories that will truly inspire you in this significant book. This book is a unique handbook that will impact people in every area of business. It is not just for the CEO or Managing Director but is equally full of wisdom for the employee or student on work experience. It covers practical keys and guides to many aspects of life.

Some years ago I read a book that had a serious impact on my life. It was "How to win friends and influence people" by Dale Carnegie. It had a big impact on my understanding and development of people skills.

This book on "Market Place Ministry" in the same way opened my eyes afresh to the huge supernatural opportunities that await us every day. It is a brilliant, practical and anointed book full of wonderful testimonies and practical biblical teaching that will take your Christian walk to another level.

It is an honour to not only recommend the book and write the foreword but to confidently say that this book will challenge, motivate and take you to a new place of impact in whatever walk of life you pursue.

Evangelist Tim Hall (Dip T, D.D),
Founder and Director Tim Hall International Ministries Inc.

Acknowledgements

I want to wholeheartedly thank my dear friend and colleague Neil Scott who greatly encouraged and acted as a sounding board in the early days and throughout the writing this book. Neil you were and continue to be an inspiration to me and to say thank you is at best an understatement.

To Paul Oslington thank you for your review and insightful commentary. This was of great assistance to me in the writing and shaping of the draft copy into a book.

Janet Dickson is a very special and talented lady who provided 1st level editorial for this book. Thanks for your candid comments and editing efforts. You personally inspired me to dig deeper into God and to unpack a number of areas that added significant value to the book.

To a number of my close friends who read and gave feedback on early chapters of the book and inspired me through encouraging words such as "This is a story that needs to be told"!

Lastly and most importantly, I want to thank Jesus Christ, my Lord and Saviour. He is my constant inspiration and is indeed the author and finisher of my faith (Heb 12:2).

X

Contents

1

Discovering Our Call

I would like to dedicate this book to Tony Wyman—a friend and colleague. Most importantly, I had the honor of being part of his decision to accept Jesus Christ as his Lord and Savior.

Tony went to be with the Lord several years ago, but God-ordained meetings that we had over a period of several years left an indelible impact upon my life and ministry. They reinforced my belief that there's a cry within the heart of every person to know more about God, and that if we make ourselves available, we can be part of God's revelation of Himself to that person.

What an honor and privilege it is to be an ambassador of Jesus Christ to those who are on life's journey and who are yet to find answers to the questions of life.

As we go through these chapters, I want to challenge your thinking, your mindset, and your understanding of the Scriptures to see how they can be easily applied to everyday situations of life within the market place.

I intend to explain what the Lord has revealed to me about touching the lost and to point out some easy ways for this to happen.

I use a number of key Scriptures and their real-life application on a daily basis to reach those who are needing direction on life's journey. I remember always that it's the Lord's will that none should perish, but that all should repent and come to the knowledge of Christ.

We need to remember the response of Jesus to the multitudes: "When Jesus saw the crowds, he had compassion on them, because they were harassed and helpless, like sheep without a shepherd" (Matthew 9:36). In my experience, many business people—whether company owners, managers, or employees—are in a similar state and greatly in need of being reconnected to God.

When Jesus saw these crowds, He also said to His disciples, "The harvest is plentiful but the workers are few. Ask the Lord of the harvest, therefore, to send out workers into his harvest field" (Matthew 9:37-38).

For the purpose of this book, I've defined market place ministry as a calling to go into our nation's workplaces and market places to make a difference by bringing the ministry of Jesus Christ to all of those involved in commerce and trade. Furthermore, I firmly believe that if we can touch company owners, managers, and key decision-makers within any business, we can impact the entire workforce, because change always happens from the top down.

A Business Leader Encounters Jesus

Think of the time Jesus met Zacchaeus (the story is told in Luke 19:1-9). The things we know about Zacchaeus are that he was very wealthy, he was a chief tax collector, and he was short in stature.

Zacchaeus heard that Jesus was coming his way, but the crowd was so great he had to climb a sycamore-fig tree just to get a glimpse of Jesus. This in itself was an act of humility, because sycamore-fig trees were so common in their day that they were actually despised in Jewish culture.

When Jesus stopped at the spot and looked up into the tree, He uttered the words, "Zacchaeus, come down immediately, I must stay at your house today" (Luke 9:5). The heart of Zacchaeus to get things right with God and his fellow man was about to be revealed.

Later that day at his house, Zacchaeus publicly offered to give half of his possessions to the poor and to repay those he might have ripped off—to give them four times the amount he'd wrongly taken, which was the restitution set by law (Exodus 22:1).

Regardless of how Zacchaeus is viewed by biblical commentators, I would like you to spare a thought as to how his workplace (and those tax collectors he oversaw) would have been impacted from that time onward in their daily activities. When you take the time to ponder this, you can get a glimpse of the change that Jesus Christ can bring to a wealthy businessman or businesswomen who reconnects with God.

After this confession of faith, Jesus said to him, "Today salvation has come to this house, because this man, too, is a son of Abraham. For the Son of Man came to seek and to save what was lost" (Luke 19:9). In saying this, Jesus was actually conferring salvation upon Zacchaeus' entire household and affirming him publicly as a son of the covenant of blessing.

Before this encounter, Zacchaeus was lost and without hope. After he met Jesus, he discovered the greatest treasure available to mankind—salvation and entry into the kingdom of God. Suddenly his wealth and the things he'd formerly trusted in no longer mattered. Zacchaeus had found his Savior, and his life now took on new meaning as he recognized the eternal value of the most important decision he would ever make.

One thing that we can be absolutely sure of is that this encounter with the Messiah would have also had an immediate and lasting impact upon his peers and his workplace.

When we're inspired to share the Word of God with anyone either by sowing seed or reaping a harvest and seeing lives radically transformed for the kingdom of God, we're partaking of God's plan outlined in the Great Commission.

I love sharing the Word and love of God and seeing it touching lives wherever I go, but doing so within the market place is my passion. From taxi driver to CEO, I feel obligated to share the good news of the gospel with all, so that all may come to the knowledge of the truth about God.

In my early years of market place ministry, I didn't always see a great deal of significance in my God encounters because I viewed such occurrences as simply walking in obedience to God. However, over time, I began to recognize from the sheer frequency of such meetings, and from my continual speaking into the lives of businessmen and women, that it was God who was bringing people across my path on a regular basis for ministry purposes.

I'm currently in regular contact with many business people, and I'm always looking for opportunities to share with them the good news about Jesus Christ. I see my roles as a management consultant and project manager as a fabulous opportunity that allows me the freedom to be an ambassador for Christ.

Jesus loved people and so must we, if we want to be like him.

One thing that I love about our Lord is that He always saw the potential in people. He looked beyond a person's current position in life and showed the way for them to be reconnected with God's kingdom. To fulfill the purposes of God for our own life, we need to do the same out of a genuine love and concern for the lost.

When I'm introduced to someone new by one of my business colleagues, it's often the case that they know about my faith in God before they know anything else about me. I'm both honored and humbled by that.

My "God Encounter" with Tony

Tony Wyman was an outstanding person whom I encountered on my life's journey. I helped him on his way, and he helped me also by allowing me to speak into his life and to make a difference for the kingdom of God.

Tony came to my office door one day and asked if he could have a moment of my time. I invited him in and motioned for him to take a seat. I asked, "How can I help?"

Tony came right out with it and said, "Does it ever get too much for you?"

Tony was a very intelligent man. He was a highly qualified civil engineer who had a reputation within the department as being extremely bright, a strategic thinker, and someone never to be taken lightly. To have someone of his caliber ask me this question was unusual, to say the least.

I looked at him for a moment and asked what he was referring to.

Tony was never one to beat around the bush, so he came out with a string of observations:

- "You run the most sought-after section for anyone to work in this division."
- "You have more professional staff and resources than just about any other area."
- "You have a portfolio and responsibility that's enormous."
- "You are driving policy development for the entire division."
- "Your budget makes mine look sick."

Then he restated his question: "Do you ever feel that the pressure of it all gets too much?"

Without trying to answer, I said, "Can I buy you lunch?" He accepted immediately.

Tony could see the blessings of God on my life and career as a senior manager in the Department of Transport, and he simply wanted to know what made me tick. I'd been promoted six times in seven years and was probably one of the fastest rising managers in the history of the department. Although Tony wouldn't have seen this as the blessings of God at the time, he knew there was something different about me, and he wanted to know more.

So off we went to lunch, where I said, "You asked if it ever gets too much for me. *Every day of the week.* But when it does, I get before my Father in heaven, and I ask Him for help. I have this view of life that if you really believe in something, you should never give up. You should pursue it with all your might and trust that God is with you and directing your paths."

I continued, "I don't know how many times staff have told me things like 'You'll never be able to get this policy reform approved—it's been tried before and failed.' I would never argue, but instead I respond with comments such as 'We'll see.' And then I would take it to my Father in prayer." I told Tony that almost every time I made a comment of this kind, it would be followed by another comment several months later: "I don't know how you ever managed to get that thing approved." And I would simply smile and thank my Father in heaven who had paved the way for me.

During that lunchtime conversation, I felt led by the Spirit of God to tell Tony about my life's journey and how my own encounter with God had shaped my beliefs and values in our workplace. I explained to Tony that honoring God in the workplace was of paramount importance to me. I also gave glory to God and made Tony aware that any apparent success I'd enjoyed was due to a strong work ethic and my faith in God.

Tony listened intently during our conversation. It must have impacted him, because he wanted to meet again soon to further discuss the things I'd spoken about.

That was essentially the beginning of many God-ordained discussions, and I venture to say that it was a crossroads experience for Tony. I began praying for Tony that he might know the Lord Jesus as his Savior and be reconnected to God.

In due course, Tony informed me that his wife had come from a Salvation Army background, and that until now he hadn't experienced any great level of interest in the things of God.

Regrettably, our education system trains people to think in terms of science, logic, and reason as the means to answer all of life's questions. In reality, although these things are absolutely necessary for our daily lives, to use them without reference to the Creator is as futile as having the ingredients without a recipe or the pieces of a jigsaw without a border to act as a frame of reference.

In the course of time, Tony began to see that faith was the missing piece that was needed to make sense of his life and purpose on earth.

Principles for Market Place Ministry

Through this encounter with Tony, as well as many other experiences with men and women in the market place, I began to understand my calling to market place ministry, and I determined to live by the following basic principles:

- Ask the Lord to guide me daily and look for the Holy Spirit's promptings and insight about how and where to sow seed (the Word of God).
- Demonstrate consistent Christian behavior and love toward others. (This is my testimony.)
- Be prepared to stand up against incredible odds and pressures when the need arises.

- Display integrity, honesty, and openness in all my dealings, while making sure I always tell the truth.
- Present my life as a consistent witness of the God in whom I trust, letting my life mirror my beliefs and values.
- Be prepared to acknowledge God as the source when success comes my way.

Although this sets a high standard, and there are times when I've fallen short myself, these principles which I live by touched the life of Tony Wyman and challenged him about his own life and his need for salvation.

At times we have setbacks and have to face tragic circumstances, including within our own families. But we should never be deterred from knowing and understanding that God holds the keys to life.

I truly believe what Jesus Christ declared about His disciples: "You are the light of the world.... Let your light shine before men, that they may see your good deeds and praise your Father in heaven" (Matthew 5:14-16). When we obey the Scriptures and let our light shine before men, we create an atmosphere for the Holy Spirit to do His work, and we're actually cultivating the presence of God in our everyday lives. This opens the door to the most exciting God encounters we could ever imagine. When we choose to live and honor God in this way, we can find ourselves on the edge of adventure at any time.

In my own journey, the blessings of God have followed into my life and family, as well as in success in the business world and market place. This is the light that first attracted Tony Wyman and has touched countless colleagues in the market place over the last four decades.

I thank God for showing me the light that day in April 1980. For I was truly blind to the things of God, but He opened my eyes to see things I could never have even imagined. For this I'm eternally grateful, and I give all the glory to Him for all that I am and all that I ever hope to be.

I look forward to catching up with Tony Wyman one day in eternity. He's one of my heroes of the faith, and his memory has encouraged me to write about my adventures in market place ministry.

2

Salt and Light

When Jesus spoke about godly behavior, He often used metaphors such as salt and light to describe true believers in God. He declared His disciples to be both "the salt of the earth" and "the light of the world" (Matthew 5:13-14). When those words are viewed in their biblical context, *salt* refers to our ability to influence others, while *light* typically refers to our witness or testimony before others, which is meant to be a reflection of our relationship with God.

Within this context, Christian believers have a marvelous opportunity to become ambassadors for Jesus Christ on a daily basis in their market places. Our salt and light as believers will become evident to everyone we meet when we live out our faith through godly and sincere lifestyles.

In today's world, business owners are always looking for leaders and managers who display character traits such as integrity, trustworthiness, loyalty, honesty, and conscientiousness. Such people are highly principled and display strong ethics in the market place. After all, if you were looking for someone to entrust with the stewardship of your business, wouldn't you be looking for such a person?

From a quality management perspective, I've observed that these character qualities are generally exhibited by employees who maintain a high level of "ownership" of the business. It's also my professional observation that in many workplaces, very few qualify.

To establish a point of difference in the market place as an ambassador for Jesus Christ, we need first and foremost to consistently perform our work tasks in an exemplary manner, whatever our chosen occupation may be.

This goes way beyond our basic skill set or trade, or our educational or professional qualifications; it touches on areas such as creativity, passion, general attitude toward work, sensitivity to others, ability to manage and foster good working relationships, being a team player, and being seen as a go-to person for help or assistance. It also requires that we possess a level of maturity and perspective on life that other people aspire to.

We also need to exude strong character qualities and values, and a lifestyle consistent with our faith—at work, at home, or elsewhere in the community, including at church.

We need to lead by example and to step up to the mark on a consistent basis when this is required of us, knowing that most things of significance in life will require a level of sacrifice that goes beyond the norm.

Kingdom Truths and Principles

This reminds me of what Jesus preached in the Sermon on the Mount (recorded in Matthew 5–7), which was essentially a series of short, themed messages which spoke about specific topics highly relevant to life in Israel at the time.

These messages were essentially a way of Jesus setting the record straight on how the law given through Moses was meant to be interpreted and lived out by faith on a daily basis by His followers.

When Jesus spoke to the crowds, He gave many of them a first-time understanding of the original purpose of the law—its spirit and intent. He pointed out that many of the religious leaders in His day were following the letter of the law rather than the spirit of the law. In doing so, Jesus was effectively likening their behavior to being little more than hypocrisy and exploitation of their position as the religious leaders of the people of God.

To support His claim, Jesus cited numerous examples (several of them mentioned later in this book) where the religious leaders had used technicalities, loopholes, and ambiguous language to avoid having to perform their priestly duties with mercy, justice, and righteousness (consistent with the spirit of the law) rather than simply offering sacrifices (the letter of the law).

For those who were prepared to listen, Jesus explained how Moses was being quoted unfairly and out of context, not reflecting God's original intention.

The explanation given by Jesus had the effect of showing up the superficial interpretations of the religious leaders and their use of the Scriptures for their own advantage and convenience.

Following such statements from Jesus, there's little doubt that many things the people hadn't fully understood began to make sense, because Jesus spoke with great authority and passion while he demonstrated what the kingdom of God was really like.

Although the Pharisees didn't like the contrasts being made by Jesus, there was little they could offer in rebuttal, because He also performed signs, wonders, and miracles which bore witness to kingdom truths. The nature and frequency of these miracles and wonders had never been witnessed before on earth.

Jesus taught His disciples many kingdom principles that Christian believers are meant to live by while on life's journey. If we follow these enduring principles, a natural consequence is that we become salt and light to those around us—because the principles Jesus taught are the ways of God, which alone can lead to abundant life.

In the midst of the Sermon on the Mount, Jesus made what appeared to be an unusual statement to His disciples: "If someone forces you to go one mile, go with him two miles" (Matthew 5:41). To fully understand this statement, we need to understand its context, and that Jesus was speaking at a time when Israel was under Roman occupation.

Most likely, Jesus was referring to a common practice at the time in which Roman soldiers forced people into slave labor rather than undertaking the more laborious tasks themselves. We see an example of this when Jesus became too weak to carry His cross on His way to Calvary, and Roman soldiers forced Simon from Cyrene to carry it for Him (Luke 23:26).

In my experience, most people don't enjoy being forced into tasks that appear demeaning and unreasonable, especially when these are demanded by a hard taskmaster trying to offload their own work onto someone else. When this happens in a workplace, it's essentially an abuse of power, authority, and control. Typically, the perpetrators of this kind of behavior are frequent offenders and well known to other staff as people to avoid.

Most of us with a reasonable work history will have encountered such people in the market place. When this happens, our most natural reaction is to exert our rights and resist this form of abuse as much as humanly possible.

So what does it mean when Jesus says that if we're forced by someone to go one mile, we should go two miles with that person? Why would Jesus ask us to go the extra mile when the situation is obviously one of abuse?

If you meditate for a while on what Jesus said, it's probably not too far removed from something the apostle Paul quoted from Proverbs: "If your enemy is hungry feed him, or if he is thirsty give him a drink, for in doing so you will heap burning coals upon his head. Do not be overcome by evil, but overcome evil with good" (Romans 12:20-21, quoting Proverbs 25:21-22).

When this Scripture is read from a Western mindset, the burning coals are often interpreted as a means of bringing guilt or shame on the enemy (as a form of revenge) so they might have a change of mind about the treatment they've been dishing out. But when understood from an Eastern mindset (as illustrated, for example, in *Light Through an Eastern Window* by Bishop K. C. Pillai of India, originally published in 1963), this passage takes on a totally different meaning. Instead of revenge, the underlying principle is that of blessing your enemy.

In simple terms, this is the same principle of overcoming evil by doing good, as expressed in Romans 12 and Proverbs 25. In fact, the saying may have originated from the way in which coals of fire (for cooking and warmth) were carried from one household to another in village life in Israel. One woman who had the flint would rise first and build the fire, then a boy would take the burning coals—on a piece of pottery balanced on top of his head—to other households to start their own fires. This is a pleasant task for the boy, for when the morning is cold, he becomes warmed by the coals as he goes about his rounds.

The "heaping up of coals" was thus meant to be sign of blessing, to make it easier to light the home fire. The more coals, the easier it was to get the home fire started.

The simple message behind such stories is that if you want to win over your enemy, bless them by doing good.

When we're abused, the flesh cries out for revenge. But we must remember that the Spirit of God always seeks to redeem the situation. The Holy Spirit seeks redemption, not revenge.

Although we're often unaware of it, we rub shoulders on a daily basis with many people who've been seriously scarred by adverse life experiences. I'm quite sure that we've all met people who carry around heavy loads of resentment, anxiety, insecurity, emotional turmoil, depression, hatred, and bad attitudes.

Some of these people will reveal this side of their entire life story within the first few minutes of a conversation. They'll tell you how they were so badly wronged and hurt all those years ago. Their past has become a stumbling block to their future as they're plagued with misgivings and heartbreak over events that can never be undone. They may build up all kinds of defenses and put up walls so no one can get close to them.

At the end of the day, these people are mostly avoided like the plague. Within church and secular circles alike, such people have often been labeled as chronic time-wasters; no matter how much time you spend with them, show them hospitality, attempt to share in fellowship with them, pray for them, counsel them, or minister to them, they're camped on yesterday's experience and have no real desire to move on. They live in a world of regret. And although they can't see it, their past has become a massive stumbling block for their future.

To the rational mind, it's totally illogical to imagine that if we keep replaying the same bad experience again and again, it can somehow change the past. But for many who are camped on yesterday's experience, that's their present reality.

Biblically speaking, we're meant to learn from the past and use it as a tutor to help make a better future for ourselves and for those around us. As ambassadors for Christ, we're called to be initiators of change by breaking the cycle of revenge and payback that the world seems to thrive on. This cycle keeps people trapped by unresolved conflict and offers little or no peace to the soul of man.

The kingdom principle here that Jesus taught is simply to bless the offending party when we're wronged. Although the temptation is always there to take our own revenge, God's purposes will never be achieved for our own lives or for the person who has wronged us unless we actively and consciously seek to break this cycle.

When Jesus told His disciples, "If your enemy asks you to go one mile be prepared to go two miles" (Matthew 5:41), He was really talking about meeting a need and going well beyond the immediate situation to the point that even our enemy might be challenged and possibly convicted of his unfair behavior in light of the generosity being displayed by a disciple.

Such redemptive behavior simply doesn't happen in the natural realm, but from a kingdom perspective it is simple obedience to the teaching of Jesus to "love your enemies, do good to those who hate you, bless those who curse you, pray for those who ill-treat you" (Luke 6:27-28). All four of those elements—to love, to do good, to bless, and to pray for those who oppose us—require proactivity on our part as believers in order to break the revenge cycle.

The "royal law" (James 2:8) calls for us to respond using the supernatural realm by recognizing that as we obey the Word of God, it creates an opportunity for Holy Spirit to do His redemptive work, which includes changing the heart attitude and behavior of the offender.

Jesus was known as a friend of sinners and of tax gatherers. He didn't run from such people, although their deeds were evil; He simply showed them a better way by behaving in a manner that reflected His close relationship with His Father. He became salt and light to those He rubbed shoulders with, and He allowed the Holy Spirit to bring conviction of sin, especially when He revealed the kingdom of God through His teaching accompanied by frequent signs, wonders, and miracles.

He did things and spoke about things that hadn't been heard or witnessed by mankind throughout the ages. And all it took was a mustard seed of faith, and the kingdom of God could be unleashed with power into a person's life.

In the same way, we need to be salt and light in our market places to demonstrate the love and power of God to people at every opportunity. We need to call upon the Father to show Himself strong in our midst by performing signs, wonders, and miracles in the same manner as He did for His Son (John 14:12).

One of our greatest challenges in life should be to let people consistently see the Spirit of Christ living in us. We must never lose sight of the truth that for many people, their daily interaction with us will be the closest they've ever come to a church. We need to make the most of every opportunity by bringing the kingdom of God to them.

How Do We Begin Our Journey?

So how do we start out on our life's journey into market place ministry?

Consider carefully the parable Jesus gave about "talents," which can be found in Matthew 25:14-30. The underlying message of this parable is simple: It doesn't matter where we're positioned in life in terms of talents, skills, gifts, and abilities. The real question is simply this: Are we wisely using the talents we've been given?

In the business context, it doesn't matter where we sit in terms of rank or position within an organization. The question still remains: Are we wisely using the talents we've been given?

Interestingly, one key point from this parable is particularly simple and yet profound: They who are faithful and trustworthy with little will also be faithful and trustworthy with much (Luke 16:10). If we embrace this fundamental kingdom principle in our life's journey, we'll realize that our Lord is simply asking us to give of our very best in every situation. When we do so, our faithfulness and diligence will shine forth to those around us and bring glory to God. To reach our potential, God asks us for nothing more and nothing less.

As Christian believers, one of the most amazing ways to let our light shine before others is to simply apply this principle of faithfulness in using our talents on an everyday basis in the market place. When we consistently give of our best and wisely use our talents, skills, gifts, and abilities, we're moving toward a place of higher ownership within the business. This in itself will provide a genuine point of difference from others who don't hold to the same convictions.

We also need to show a genuine interest in our work and realize that our secular work and our ministry (or worship) are synonymous in God's eyes. Jesus didn't put on a pious façade on the Sabbath and then behave like the rest of the world for the remainder of the week. Nor should we.

One of the main reasons that the universal church has been ridiculed so much by society in recent years is simply that many people who profess to have faith in God do not live a consistently godly lifestyle. For this very reason, Jesus describes the church congregation at a place called Laodicea as "lukewarm" (Revelation 3:16). The people in this church had boasted of being rich, of having acquired wealth and needing nothing. But the Lord described the them as "wretched, pitiful, poor, blind, and naked" (Revelation 3:17). Their lukewarm behavior was bringing reproach on the church, because their faith wasn't sincere.

This is probably one of the strongest messages to our generation about people who practice Sunday Christianity. By trying to have a foot in both camps—the kingdom of this world and the kingdom of God—many people may be walking a dangerous tightrope without even knowing it.

God's instruction to Sunday Christians is clear: "Be earnest and repent" (Revelation 3:19), or face the consequences of being rejected from entering the kingdom. This involves a changed way of thinking based on real convictions of the heart, then living a consistent lifestyle in accordance with the Scriptures.

If God views our work as our ministry, then our market place becomes the place where we have the greatest opportunity to minister on a daily basis outside our home. We also need to realize that making a difference in the market place is a significant part of our testimony before God and men, and that God is watching our comings and goings on a daily basis. Nothing goes unnoticed.

When things don't go our way, who do we turn to? Does it get ugly? Does it involve raised voices or other behavior that's unbecoming of a believer who's truly trusting in God?

We need to realize that God holds the answers to all things, and that there's another realm far greater than the one we see with our eyes.

Finally, we need to realize that often our responses to unfavorable situations will display who we really are—and what we really believe—to those around us.

From a market place ministry perspective, I would like to go a step further and pose this question: Do you see your market place as a valid mission field for the Lord? This is our next topic of discussion.

3

What Is Your Mission Field?

In concluding the last chapter I asked if you see your market place as a valid mission field for the Lord. I would like to be so bold as to suggest that Jesus saw *every* market place as a valid mission field for spreading the gospel.

The Great Commission that was given to all believers can be literally interpreted as: "Go into all *your* world and preach the gospel" (Matthew 28:18-20; Mark 16:15-18).

If you think about the life of Jesus, He had already been fulfilling the Great Commission during His three years of ministry as He simply went about from place to place engaging with people on a daily basis and sharing the message of the kingdom. It didn't matter where He was or who He met along the way; He didn't hold back in explaining and revealing what God (whom He called His Father) and the kingdom of heaven were really like.

He shared with anyone who would listen and taught with such great authority that those around him were totally captivated by His message. He spoke of things that hadn't been uttered since the beginning of time. He did things that previously had been attributed to only the greatest of the prophets, and He even surpassed the prophets in doing things no one had imagined to be possible.

There were times when people nearby were convicted of sin merely by being in His presence, yet He never spoke a single word to condemn the hungry, the lost, the lonely, the desperate, the outcast, the helpless, or the hopeless. He truly was the Holy One of God to His generation.

As Jesus went from place to place, people began to witness first hand what John the Baptist had spoken: "Prepare the way for the Lord" (Luke 3:4). The kingdom of God was forcefully advancing upon the darkness which had engulfed their generation.

His ministry was accompanied by signs, wonders, and miracles, as the Father was bearing witness to His ministry by confirming the words spoken by the prophets about the promised Messiah.

As the momentum of His ministry increased, Jesus began to teach and empower His disciples to minister as well. Jesus was literally bringing heaven to earth and revealing the true nature of His and our Father. The picture He painted of the Father was so different from the religious teachers that people were constantly amazed and in awe of His teaching. There's little doubt that those who listened to the teachings of Jesus of Nazareth soon began to question the interpretation of the law under which their families had been living for generations.

As time went by, Jesus revealed more and more of the kingdom of God to His disciples as He began to engage actively in disarming the enemy of souls—Satan himself—and his demonic realm. Jesus revealed that the kingdom of heaven is constantly at war with the kingdom of darkness, because light and darkness cannot co-exist.

To those who would listen and accept His teaching, Jesus lifted the veil that hung over their hearts and minds as He went into His world and gave light to the lost. To their astonishment, any notion of a distant, impersonal, and judgmental God was replaced with the revelation of the Father being a loving God who longed to have close, intimate relationship with His people.

Interestingly, if you study the world's religions and cults, the picture most of them paint of their so-called god or prophet is of someone distant and impersonal, and their beliefs are typically fear-based—which is exactly the belief system that Satan thrives on.

Jesus often spoke in parables that revealed spiritual truths and principles about life values and relationships. However, toward the end of His earthly ministry, He spoke about His Father being ready not only to forgive but also highly desiring to reconnect with His children, regardless of their lot in life.

During His ministry years, Jesus often spoke about His heavenly Father and their close relationship and He regularly set aside times for prayer and communication with His Father.

Jesus also spoke about things that were of greatest importance to His Father—for that time as well as for future generations. In particular, the Father's desire for intimacy and closeness of relationship with His children was probably the number one reason the Father sent the Son—to show the only way to the Father.

This was in stark contrast to the lifeless, external, impersonal religious teaching and traditions of His day.

Jesus, Friend of Sinners

Perhaps the thing that most upset the religious leaders of that day was that Jesus chose to be known as a friend of tax gatherers and sinners. The theology of the religious leaders simply didn't contemplate the thought of a holy person or supposed prophet associating with such people.

The religious leaders probably thought of Jesus's ministry to "tax gatherers and sinners" as being like Absalom gathering followers from the rabble and uneducated in order to bolster his popularity in the lead-up to the coup against his father, King David (as told in 2 Samuel 15–18—and we all know how that story ended). Although Jesus mixed with people from all walks of life, He frequently spent time with people who were despised, downtrodden, or social outcasts.

When the prophet Isaiah spoke of the Messiah, he said, "A battered or bruised reed He will not break off" and "A smoldering wick He will not extinguish" (Isaiah 42:1-4; Matthew 12:20). These pictures best describe the helpless and the desperate of society. This is why Jesus went out of his way to engage with prostitutes, murderers, thieves, lepers, and people who were blind, deaf, dumb, crippled, lame, or with bodily conditions that rendered them unclean and cut them off from fellowship with others.

Jesus was prepared to speak to the demon possessed and even to the dead, offering life and liberty as people put their trust in Him. He purposefully spoke to these people because they had no voice or influence in society—but God saw them all as family.

This created more than a few problems for the religious leaders, because Jesus not only performed undeniable miracles, but also performed a number of these miraculous signs on the Sabbath day—when no "work" of this kind (so it was thought) was permitted under the law of Moses as interpreted by the rabbis of that day. By the time Christ's earthly ministry commenced, rabbis had so narrowly prescribed the definition of allowable work on the Sabbath day that Jesus found Himself embroiled in an ongoing religious controversy. His every move was being watched by the religious hierarchy who were now faced with a serious dilemma:

- The miracles He openly performed were undeniable and witnessed by all in attendance.

- His teaching about the common and accepted practice of people being allowed to untie an ox to allow it to feed on the Sabbath was contrasted to a "daughter of Abraham" (that is, a daughter of the covenant) being freed from her infirmity on the Sabbath (Luke 13:16).

- Their religious teaching was not only hypocritical when compared to their other actions on the Sabbath, but it had wrongly interpreted the covenant promises made by *Jehovah Rapha* ("the Lord who heals you," Exodus 15:26— "For I am the Lord that heals you"). But the Scriptures made no mention about healing being confined to a particular day of the week.

- The teachers of the law felt humiliated when the people glorified God because of the miracles that had taken place through the ministry of Jesus, and the religious teachers had no explanation for this other than to accuse Jesus of being aligned with the prince of demons—none other than Satan himself (Mark 3:22; Matthew 9:34, 10:25, 12:24; Luke 11:15).

- Jesus redefined allowable work on the Sabbath as doing good on the Sabbath day (Mark 3:4; Matthew 12:12; Luke 6:9). This principle-based teaching was truly liberating to the Jews, who were beginning to rediscover the true intention of the Abrahamic covenant, which predated the law of Moses and stood in direct contrast to the teachings of their day.

- Jesus was revealing that the rabbinical teaching had misinterpreted the true meaning of the Sabbath, as He taught that the Sabbath was made for man, not man for the Sabbath. His words taught or implied that the Sabbath is a purposeful time for human beings to restore their soul and reflect upon their relationship with God—the Sabbath was not just about the enforcement of doing no work (Mark 2:27).

Hated and Despised Professions

When Jesus spoke words of hope into the lives of people who were hated by the religious leaders because of their profession and its associated life-style—such as tax gatherers and prostitutes—these people were changed, because God always looks at our potential; He doesn't condemn us because of our past or profession.

In the Gospel of Matthew, we see a picture of Jesus entering the temple courts, and while He was teaching, the chief priests and the elders came to Him and asked, "By what authority are you doing these things? And who gave you this authority?" (Matthew 21:23).

Jesus responded by asking them a question about where they thought John the Baptist's authority had come from. Jesus knew that John had come preaching a message of righteousness, which caused many sinners to forsake their sinful ways and turn to God. The chief priests and elders were fully aware of this, yet they refused to believe John's message.

After they considered the question Jesus asked, the priests and elders responded, "We don't know." Then Jesus said, "Neither will I tell you by what authority I am doing these things."

Despite responding in this manner, Jesus didn't leave their question totally unanswered. Instead of directly confronting their misguided beliefs, He used two parables which not only displayed amazing prophetic insight, but also meant that His questioners couldn't attack Him directly. Since these were parables, they couldn't be taken literally as direct criticism of anyone, though it was obvious to the listeners that the parables were about the religious leaders and teachers of the law.

The parables Jesus spoke on this occasion included one about two sons (in Matthew 21:28-32) and another about wicked tenants (21:33-46).

Arising from the parable of the two sons was a key question that Jesus asked: "Which of the two did the will of his father?" His listeners answered, "The first." Jesus then confronted them with this:

> Most certainly I tell you that the tax collectors and
> the prostitutes are entering into the kingdom of
> God before you. For John came to you in the way
> of righteousness, and you didn't believe him, but the
> tax collectors and the prostitutes believed him. When
> you saw it, you didn't even repent afterward, that
> you might believe him. (Matthew 21:31-32 WEB)

His message to the Pharisees was clear. When John showed the way of righteousness to those whose lifestyle had previously prevented a relationship with God, they repented and wanted to enter the kingdom, and they embraced the salvation brought to them through the gospel. This was reflected in the first son spoken of in the parable Jesus told.

The second son, who represented the Pharisees, had always professed their ready and willing obedience, and they claimed to be waiting for the kingdom of God to come. Yet they did not receive it when it came, but rather chose to continue making hypocritical professions of faith, which would eventually mean their ejection from God's kingdom.

This is exactly what Jesus was referring to in the second parable about the wicked tenants. Jesus concluded this parable (which was unmistakably directed toward the Pharisees), with these words: "Therefore I tell you that the kingdom of God will be taken from you and given to a people who will produce its fruit" (Matthew 21:43). With these words, Jesus was foreshadowing salvation coming to the Gentiles—who would receive it and bring forth fruit to the glory of God.

A Word of Caution to Our Generation

Scroll forward to Matthew 25, and you'll find a parable about ten virgins—five of them foolish, and five of them wise. This parable lies within teachings of Jesus that are often referred to as end-time parables, relating specifically to the time immediately before the return of Christ to earth. The parable about the virgins is spoken prophetically to the church as a stern warning that many churchgoers or Sunday Christians with all their religious trappings will be shut out of heaven, because they won't be ready or willing when Christ returns to claim His bride.

In the same way that the Pharisees were not ready, many who profess to be followers of Jesus Christ will be shut out of the kingdom of heaven because they have no personal relationship with God.

Just as Jesus accused the religious leaders in His day of being blind guides of the blind, some teachers today who are responsible for the souls of their listeners are also at risk of being shut out of God's kingdom if they fail to teach the whole counsel of God.

The social, popularist gospel is not one that Christ ever preached, yet it's becoming all too common these days. This is a gospel that avoids mentioning sin or repentance and seeks to be so inclusive that it more readily embraces the sentiments of the world rather than the commands of God.

Jesus foretold that people would begin to walk away from sound doctrine and gather around them teachers who would effectively tell them what they want to hear. The popularist gospel is one that strokes the ego rather than challenging the heart of mankind.

Jesus called them false teachers because their teachings aren't based on faith and the Word of God. Paul warns us about why these false teachers find wide acceptance:

> For the time will come when people will not put
> up with sound doctrine. Instead, to suit their own
> desires, they will gather around them a great number
> of teachers to say what their itching ears want to
> hear. They will turn their ears away from the truth
> and turn aside to myths. (2 Timothy 4:3-4 NIV)

We must never forget that the promises of God were not given to a particular race of people, but to people prepared to walk by faith. This is one of the fundamental mistakes that was made by the nation of Israel in interpreting the Scriptures.

People cannot be physically born into the kingdom of God. They need to be born again of the Spirit to enter the kingdom of God. If you read in John 3 the conversation Jesus had with Nicodemus, a great teacher of Israel, you can gain insight into the teachings of Jesus on this subject, especially in John 3:3.

The walk-by-faith journey doesn't start with an infant. No matter what doctrines or traditions a church might hold or teach, a baby simply doesn't have the understanding or capacity to repent. The faith journey starts when a person old enough to understand right and wrong chooses to believe in the Lord Jesus Christ as Savior and makes a public profession of their faith (Romans 10:9-10; 1 Timothy 6:12). While the decision to believe in Jesus Christ as our Lord and Savior is an event, the Scriptures are clear that our salvation needs to be outworked through doing good deeds and pursuing a lifestyle of holiness and wholesomeness that brings glory to God (Philippians 2:12-16).

This is a daily process known as sanctification, which continues for the remainder of our life on earth. With great certainty I can declare that Jesus had no notion in His mind of part-time or Sunday Christians when He commanded all believers to take up their cross daily and follow Him (Luke 9:23).

The wonderful thing about God is that whenever He asks us to do something, He always has a plan for that something to be achieved.

God has empowered believers to live holy lives, dedicated to His service and being conformed to His likeness through the sanctifying (or purifying) work of the Holy Spirit (2 Thessalonians 2:13).

Setting the Record Straight

Whereas the teaching of Jesus won the approval of sinners and tax gatherers that saw many of them saved, His teaching mostly offended the religious leaders of His day.

The priesthood in those days was somewhat corrupt, and Jesus didn't hesitate to point out their hypocrisy. He often contrasted the religious teaching of His day with the law of God (as it was originally intended) and highlighted the differences. The Sermon on the Mount (Matthew 5–7) contains several such contrasts presented by Jesus, which generally take this form: "*You have heard it said…but I say unto you…*" as in these verses:

> You have heard it said, "Love God but hate your
> enemies." But I say unto you, "Love your enemies
> and pray for them." (Matthew 5:43-44)

A key task of Jesus's ministry was to set the record straight about what the Father and the kingdom of God was really like. For example, Jesus went to great lengths to explain to the scribes and Pharisees how their laws contradicted the Word of God, and He exposed the true motivation behind their teaching:

> You have let go of the commands of God and are
> holding on to human traditions.... You have a fine
> way of setting aside the commands of God in order to
> observe your own traditions! For *Moses said,* "Honor
> your father and mother," and, "Anyone who curses
> their father or mother is to be put to death." *But you
> say* that if anyone declares that what might have been
> used to help their father or mother is Corban [that
> is, devoted to God]—then you no longer let them do
> anything for their father or mother. (Mark 7:8-12)

Whereas the commandment was to honor one's parents in their later years (by looking after and supporting them), this teaching was basically saying that no help would be given, since whatever money and resources were available had been set aside for the work of God. Jesus went on to say, "Thus you nullify the word of God by your tradition that you have handed down. *And you do many things like that*" (7:13).

Jesus used Old Testament prophecy to describe the corrupt priesthood of His day:

> Isaiah was right when he prophesied about you
> hypocrites; as it is written: "These people honor
> me with their lips, but their hearts are far from
> me. They worship me in vain; their teachings
> are merely human rules." (Mark 7:6-7)

And in Matthew 23, the seven "woes" that Jesus spoke against the scribes and Pharisees provide a painfully sharp warning as Jesus confronts the dead, lifeless religion that was so pervasive in His day.

When Jesus corrected their religious teaching with the real meaning of Scripture, this often humiliated the religious leaders, since they couldn't match His wisdom—which was further vindicated as many tax gatherers and sinners turned to the Savior and commenced their faith journey.

Relentless Pursuit

Jesus knew the truth that mankind's connection with the Father had been lost in the garden in Eden and that mankind was becoming increasingly lost and captive to sin—in the same manner in which our society is becoming increasingly fragmented over time. But Jesus also knew the purpose of His mission on earth. He was the One who'd been sent to reclaim the keys to the kingdom.

When Jesus reclaimed those keys (Revelation 1:18) through His resurrection, the way was opened for lost humanity to be reconnected with the Father.

Jesus literally came to set captive humanity free.

It didn't matter to Him if a person's past life had caused them to be labeled or stigmatized by society; He knew that all people had fallen short of the glory of God and needed to be redeemed. He was the promised Messiah spoken of by the prophets of old, and He knew His message of redemption would not be popular with the religious leaders of His day who held the reins of power within Judaism. Yet He relentlessly pursued the will of the Father all the way to the cross of Calvary, because He knew the Lamb of God had to be offered up as the only sacrifice that could take away the sins of the world (John 1:29).

This act of sacrifice and obedience by God's one and only Son would open the way for mankind to be reconnected to the Father—as was true in the garden before sin entered the world.

Later in this book we'll look more fully at the gospel message contained in the Scriptures. This message is what I call the gospel panorama, and it simply explains the truth of the gospel in a manner that's easy to share with others. It can be understood by little children as well as by the wise and learned—if there's even the slightest glimmer of faith.

4

The Fields Are Ripe

One day when Jesus was with His disciples, He made this statement: "Do you not say, 'Four months more and then the harvest'? I tell you, open your eyes and look at the fields! They are ripe for harvest" (John 4:35). I can assure you that Jesus was talking *not* about a crop of ripe grain, but about the call God had placed upon the lives of His disciples to become fishers of men (Mark 1:17).

Jesus made this statement about the harvest soon after He revealed Himself as the Messiah to a woman beside a well near her hometown of Sychar in Samaria (John 4:5-42). This Messianic revelation sparked a spiritual revival in Sychar. It was a truly unique encounter because it's the only time mentioned in Scripture where Jesus reveals Himself as the Messiah to someone outside His disciples, and in a manner solely of His own volition.

How did this woman respond? First, she perceived Jesus to be a prophet. Then His revelation of being Himself the Messiah became such a faith-filled encounter for her that she later ran into town and told the people, "Come see a man who told me everything I ever did. Could this be the Christ?"

Open Your Eyes

These responses of faith and belief overwhelmed Jesus with joy to the point that when His disciples returned from town and offered him food, He wasn't hungry, but instead responded, "My food is to do the will of him who sent me and to finish his work"; it was then that He told them, "Open your eyes and look at the fields! They are ripe for harvest" (4:34-35). Jesus was making a declarative command for His disciples to exercise faith and to open their eyes to see the multitudes of souls ready to be brought into the kingdom of God—*right now.* Jesus was declaring to His disciples that they should see the multitudes of people as being like sheep without a shepherd, and needing to be gathered into the kingdom of God.

Jesus made a similar statement when sending out seventy-two disciples to minister in the surrounding towns. He told them, "The harvest is plentiful, but the workers are few. Ask the Lord of the harvest to send out workers into His harvest field" (Luke 10:2).

Both in John 4 and in Luke 10, Jesus was asking His disciples to visualize the plentiful harvest of souls that lay before them and to see every soul as a potential candidate for the kingdom of God. Jesus also told His disciples to pray, asking His Father—who is Lord of the harvest—to send out workers into His harvest field so that souls can be added to the kingdom of God in fulfillment of His Father's will.

A short time later the seventy-two returned with joy and reported to Jesus all that happened. They were full of joy as they said, "Lord, even the demons submit to us in your name" (Luke 10:17).

In response, Jesus immediately refocused their attention toward the importance of having their names written in heaven, because Jesus gave highest priority to the salvation of souls.

In fact, Jesus actively encouraged His disciples not to get too carried away with warfare in the spiritual realm, because He'd never considered Satan to be anything but a defeated foe from the time that deceiver was thrust out of heaven (Luke 10:18).

As the seventy-two returned and reported all that had happened, Scripture records that Jesus was "full of joy through the Holy Spirit" as He spoke to His Father: "I praise you, Father, Lord of heaven and earth, because you have hidden these things from the wise and learned, and revealed them to little children. Yes, Father, for this was your good pleasure." He then said privately to His disciples, "Blessed are the eyes that see what you see. For I tell you that many prophets and kings wanted to see what you see but did not see it and to hear what you hear but did not hear it" (Luke 10:21-24).

The Savior's joy was being made complete because His disciples had received a revelation of their heavenly calling and had acted upon that revelation by forcefully advancing the kingdom of God. Their eyes were seeing the harvest (John 4:36), and their ears were being attentive to the leading of the Holy Spirit as co-workers to bring in that harvest, as they went out into local villages and towns to spread the gospel message.

The sending out of the seventy-two was effectively a prelude or a "type" of the Great Commission which would be given to the early church a few years later—to go into all the world and make disciples, empowered by the Holy Spirit.

In this time in which we live, I sincerely believe that one of the most valid prayers we can make is this: "Lord, open my eyes to see and my ears to hear all that you would show me and say to me about the people I meet today, Amen."

I think that somehow His church needs to understand that it has been given revelation far beyond that given to prophets and kings of bygone eras, and that we need to open our eyes and ears and be prepared to exercise faith and obedience by acting upon what we receive from the Lord.

The "sending out" exemplified through the above Scriptures is now the church's primary mission, better known as the Great Commission: to build the kingdom of God. It was given to early church believers, and it hasn't changed one iota since the time of Christ.

Although the command to go and make disciples (Matthew 28:19) should be a walk of faith and obedience by Christian believers, many do not take up the challenge. They choose to live far below their potential in terms of advancing the kingdom of God. This is particularly true in relation to ministry within the market place. In fact, many within Christendom regard the market place as one of the few frontiers into which the gospel message has failed to make serious inroads, and it's often perceived by believers to be "too hard."

Perhaps, like the early disciples (John 4:35), many believers simply don't see the harvest of souls right before their eyes within their market places.

I'm fully aware of the need to be sensitive and to first build relationship with co-workers, but in my view, this should be a given for believers. However, I've seen that more often than not many believers prefer to keep a low profile—particularly in their workplace—for various reasons:

- *Lack of knowledge:* Some people may feel quite inadequate in terms of their ability to respond to questions that might be asked of them, if they reveal themselves as a messenger of the gospel.
- *Fear of rejection:* Some people may be concerned about the possibility of being rejected or perceived in a negative manner by their co-workers because of their faith.
- *Fear of persecution:* Some may be concerned that taking a stand for Jesus may negatively impact their career prospects.
- *Fear of exposure:* Others may realize that the message they would like to bring is not consistent with their lifestyle or past behavior, and they would prefer not to be labeled as a hypocrite.

- *Matters of integrity:* Added to this, we should always be aware of the need to honor our employer, by using our working time in an appropriate manner.

These and possibly a host of other reasons are seen as deterrents to many believers from sharing their faith in the workplace, the market place, and in the wider community.

I don't want to trivialize any doubts or misgivings that believers may hold about their ability to effectively communicate the gospel message. However, my big-picture perspective is that many believers simply don't see the harvest field of souls that are before them in their market places.

How Do We See the Lost?

How do we see the lost—specifically in relation to our market places? I've heard negative statements from believers like these:

- "I've tried talking with so-and-so before—but they'll never change."
- "These people are so anti-God, or anti-anything to do with the gospel."
- "They never stop giving me a hard time about my faith; and any time the church gets mentioned in a negative way in the media, they point it out to me."

I'm sure we could all add to that list. In my view, such defensive statements are made because we keep looking at the circumstances in the natural realm rather than turning to God in prayer—in the spiritual realm, where Jesus told us the answer lies.

When Jesus encountered difficulty or was on the precipice of a great breakthrough or revival, He often spent the night in prayer, seeking the face of His Father for guidance and empowerment for the coming encounter.

Perhaps we often see the task of evangelizing our market place as too difficult, and we take the easier options (such as going "undercover" or on the defensive, or seeing ourselves as a victim suffering for the gospel cause) rather than following in our Savior's footsteps and asking the Lord of the harvest for guidance and empowerment as we attempt to do great things for God.

To put this into perspective, if we keep looking into the natural realm, this task will always appear too difficult.

The apostle Paul encountered far more intense battles (often a matter of life and death) than we now face, and yet Paul is still regarded as one of the greatest and most effective cross-cultural soul-winners of all time. Like Jesus, Paul spent much of his time in market places, yet Paul makes it clear that there are strongholds of the enemy that need to be destroyed in the spiritual realm before there will ever be a breakthrough in our market place (or the natural realm).

Paul described these spiritual battles in this way:

> For though we walk in the flesh, we do not war after
> the flesh [for the weapons of our warfare are not
> carnal, but mighty through God to the pulling down
> of strongholds], casting down imaginations and every
> high thing that exalteth itself against the knowledge
> of God, and bringing into captivity every thought to
> the obedience of Christ. (2 Corinthians 10:3-5 KJV)

The *New Living Translation* sheds more light on these strongholds by revealing that they relate to human reasoning and the false arguments of the enemy that the "god of this world" has used to keep unbelievers locked up in darkness: "We use God's mighty weapons, not worldly weapons, to knock down the strongholds of human reasoning and to destroy false arguments" (2 Corinthians 10:4 NLT).

The apostle Paul emphasizes that first of all these spiritual strongholds need to be broken by believing prayer; only then will we see a decisive breakthrough in the lives of our co-workers.

It's interesting to note something John Wesley once said (in *A Plain Account of Christian Perfection*) about evangelism: "God does nothing on the earth save in answer to believing prayer."

Believing prayer involves actively engaging with our heavenly Father so we can be transformed by the renewing of our mind, or in the spirit of our mind (Romans 12:2; Ephesians 4:23). In so doing, we can gain an understanding or discernment of His will and guidance for any given situation.

Therein lies the secret to a breakthrough in the lives of those around us. We first need to prevail in prayer (preparing the way), and then live the exemplary life of faith to which we've been called.

My encouragement to all believers is simply this: After you experience a prevailing prayer encounter with God, be ever ready and prepared to meet someone whom the Father may bring across your path later that day or soon after.

I can remember occasions when up to three times in one day I've shared my testimony with someone—from the taxi driver on the way to the airport, on through to the CEO, both of whom equally needed to know Jesus Christ as Lord and Savior. While each encounter we experience is likely to be different, when we aren't harvesting souls for the kingdom we should be sowing seed. Within the market places I visit, I can speak from experience when I say that God encounters have happened to me on so many occasions that it's quite overwhelming.

By laying a foundation of believing prayer, we effectively pave the way for His kingdom to come and His will to be rolled out as we go into our market places on a daily basis. If you don't believe me, lay a "fleece" (see Judges 6:36-40) before God and see what happens. But make sure that within your prevailing prayer, you ask God for a breakthrough in your situation, specifically bringing people's names before the Lord as an act of faith.

Faith in Action

During my days of employment within the Queensland government, at one stage I was working in an office with about twelve other men. At the time my job allowed use of a government car for travel between home and work. On my way to work, I used to pick up a colleague named Andrew who worked in the same office.

Andrew had a Roman Catholic background and was recently divorced. He was also a very nervous person and had been prescribed valium medication by his doctors to settle his nerves.

Andrew's story was one of a failed marriage, regret, and brokenness, and my heart certainly went out to the guy. It didn't take long for me to share my testimony with him and how Jesus Christ had touched my life.

We often had conversations on the way to and from work, and at times we worked on common projects in the office. On one occasion at work, I noticed that Andrew was sitting across the desk from the manager and appeared to be getting a roasting. Andrew was visibly upset by what had happened and was quiet as we traveled home that day.

The next morning as we were going to work, Andrew opened up to me that he was upset because he felt he was being unfairly singled out by the manager, and quite frankly, he was not in a good state of mind.

I asked Andrew for a few more details about what had happened. I then explained to him that for everything we see in the natural realm, there's also a spiritual realm that we don't see.

I then asked Andrew whether he felt he'd done the right thing in the situation. He confirmed that he felt he had. I told Andrew that I agreed with him. I then took what some may consider a brave step, but I felt led by the Holy Spirit; I told Andrew I was going to pray against the spiritual forces that were influencing the manager's behavior in a negative manner toward him, and I was going to believe God for a total change of heart and attitude by the manager.

Andrew looked somewhat dumbfounded that I would make a claim like that, but he replied, "You go for it."

That night I went to prayer, particularly spiritual warfare. In addition to 2 Corinthians 10:3-5 (quoted above), I used the following passages as the basis for my believing prayer:

> Finally, be strong in the Lord and in his mighty power.
> Put on the full armor of God, so that you can take your
> stand against the devil's schemes. For our struggle is not
> against flesh and blood, but against the rulers, against
> the authorities, against the powers of this dark world and
> against the spiritual forces of evil in the heavenly realms.

> Therefore put on the full armor of God, so that when
> the day of evil comes, you may be able to stand your
> ground, and after you have done everything, to stand.
> Stand firm then, with the belt of truth buckled around
> your waist, with the breastplate of righteousness in place,
> and with your feet fitted with the readiness that comes
> from the gospel of peace. In addition to all this, take up
> the shield of faith, with which you can extinguish all
> the flaming arrows of the evil one. Take the helmet of
> salvation and the sword of the Spirit, which is the word

of God. And pray in the Spirit on all occasions with all kinds of prayers and requests. (Ephesians 6:10-18)

Again I say to you, that if two of you agree on earth about anything that they may ask, it shall be done for them by My Father who is in heaven. For where two or three have gathered together in My name, I am there in their midst. (Matthew 18:19-20)

I prayed until I'd received assurance from the Holy Spirit that there had been a breakthrough, because I sincerely believed that there were spiritual forces of wickedness at work in Andrew's situation. Moreover, I believed that their power to negatively influence the behavior of the manager toward Andrew needed to be bound and rendered powerless.

I confirmed with Andrew on the way to work the next day that I'd prayed for his situation, and I told him that God was going to show Himself strong in Andrew's life from that time forward.

Later that day, I noticed the manager speaking with Andrew. They seemed to talk for quite a long time.

When we got into the car to go home, Andrew greeted me with a smile and said, "I don't know what you prayed last night, but don't stop." Andrew was absolutely blown away by the change in the manager's attitude toward him from the previous conversation.

This change of situation came about simply because I'd stood in the gap and interceded for Andrew's situation and bound the spirits of wickedness and the strongholds of the enemy that were influencing the situation.

One thing I know for sure is that Andrew had an encounter with God's grace that day, and he was never quite the same after that.

In my market place ministry experience, this type of situation happens from time to time, and God has always been prepared to show Himself strong to demonstrate His grace to anyone who would reach out for help. All we need to do is ask.

A Challenge

I encourage you to look into these Scriptures, if you aren't already aware of them. And I encourage you to lay a fleece before God to open the heart of someone you care about. Keep praying until you receive a breakthrough.

Then watch and see—and be amazed at what the Lord will do in both the life of your friend and your own life, because this act of grace in sharing the gospel has now become part of your own testimony.

5

The God of All Mercy

One day, Jesus called Matthew, a tax collector, out of his workplace to become His disciple. Later that day, Jesus went to Matthew's house for dinner. Matthew 9:9-13 records that many tax collectors and "sinners" also came and ate with Jesus and His disciples.

From a ministry perspective, it's so important to be aware of the immediate peer group of someone making a commitment to the Lord. These are the people who will most notice the lifestyle change in anyone who's born again. They become part of the ripe harvest field surrounding this new believer, just like those who were impacted by the testimony of the woman at the well (John 4:39).

Jesus understood this truth, so He immediately wanted to hang out with Matthew's fellow tax collectors and friends. Jesus also wanted His disciples to get used to the idea that sinners need to be saved—not avoided, which was obviously the mindset of the Pharisees.

> When the Pharisees saw this, they asked His
> disciples: "Why does your teacher eat with tax
> collectors and 'sinners'?" (Matthew 9:11).

> Jesus overheard their question and replied, "It is
> not the healthy who need a doctor, but the sick.
> But go and learn what this means: 'I desire mercy,
> not sacrifice.' For I have not come to call the
> righteous, but sinners" (Matthew 9:12-14).

Jesus was quoting something written by the prophet Hosea. Here's how this verse (Hosea 6:6) is rendered in three different English translations:

> For I desire mercy, not sacrifice, and I want
> you to recognize me as God instead of
> bringing me burnt offerings. (NIV)

> For I desired mercy, and not sacrifice; and the
> knowledge of God more than burnt offerings. (KJV)

> For I desire and delight in dutiful steadfast love and
> goodness, not sacrifice, and the knowledge of and
> acquaintance with God more than burnt offerings. (AMP)

Jesus was telling the religious leaders of his day that they needed to understand the spirit and intent of the law, for if they understood this, they would have known why He was reaching out to "sinners." It was because sinners need a Savior.

These words Jesus quoted reveal God's desire for intimate, personal relationship with His people rather than our ritualistic uttering of words and our performance of religious deeds (and calling it worship), which was commonplace in the belief system of the Pharisees.

To put this into perspective, we need to understand that God does desire sacrifice, for He instituted sacrifice immediately after Adam and Eve sinned. But even more He desires loving-kindness and mercy, because these reflect the close, intimate relationship God has always desired with His creation (Luke 10:25-29).

Although Jesus always showed respect for the law and the sacrificial offerings it required as part of temple worship, He also knew that the lack of mercy shown by Israel's religious leaders over countless generations had brought about a serious spiritual decline for the children of Israel.

This is the very reason the Messiah (the Good Shepherd) was sent first to gather "the lost sheep of Israel." It's no wonder then that Jesus described the multitudes who flocked to Him as "sheep without a shepherd" (Matthew 9:36). They came to Him, and at various times they listened to His teaching for days on end. During those times, He healed their sick and indelibly touched their souls with words of life He'd learned from His Father.

So What Had Changed?

After all, Jesus was using the same book of the law and the prophets as the religious leaders had always used for centuries, yet everything around Him was changing dramatically.

Within the purposes and plans of God, the current happenings were spoken into being about six hundred years before the ministry of Christ began, when God gave the following word of prophecy to the prophet Jeremiah:

> The days are coming, declares the LORD, when I will
> make a new covenant with the people of Israel and with
> the people of Judah. It will not be like the covenant

I made with their ancestors when I took them by the
hand to lead them out of Egypt, because they broke my
covenant, though I was a husband to them, declares the
LORD. This is the covenant I will make with the people
of Israel after that time, declares the LORD. I will put
my law in their minds ["inward parts," KJV] and write it
on their hearts. I will be their God, and they will be my
people. No longer will they teach their neighbor, or say
to one another, "Know the LORD," because they will all
know me, from the least of them to the greatest, declares
the LORD. For I will forgive their wickedness and will
remember their sins no more. (Jeremiah 31:31-34)

By these words, the prophet was foretelling that God was about to make
a new covenant with Israel and Judah.

Under this new covenant, people would no longer need to be continually reminded about the things of God by their neighbors or kinfolk, or by
wearing phylacteries (small leather packets containing written scriptures)
or tassels on the corner of their garments. Instead, God was about to speak
His law directly into the minds and hearts of His people.

From the moment John the Baptist commenced his ministry of preparing the way for the Messiah, the system of external, works-based religion
called Judaism was put on notice. The axe was being laid at the foot of the
trees, which had been warned to produce fruit in keeping with repentance
or perish (Matthew 3:10).

For centuries, Judaism had produced little fruit. Now it was about to
make way for the fresh and vibrant spiritual life that God would bring
forth, with the times of refreshing that Israel craved (Acts 3:20).

John the Baptist announced the coming of the Messiah when he said: "Look, the Lamb of God, who takes away the sin of the world!" (John 1:29). John came with a baptism of repentance that not only prepared the way for the Messiah to be revealed but also for the veil of the law to be lifted off the hearts and minds of all mankind, that they might receive grace and truth through Jesus Christ (John 1:17).

Now was the time for the word of Jeremiah the prophet to come to pass. A definite shift was about to happen in the spiritual climate of Israel.

Kairos and *Chronos*

The law and the prophets had all looked forward and spoken about this moment in time, waiting patiently for the alignment of God's time-clock (*kairos*) with earth's time (*chronos*), so that all that had been spoken would be fulfilled.

Chronos simply means time as we measure it by a watch or calendar, and it is governed by the earth's rotation around the sun.

Kairos refers to any specific, God-ordained periods throughout history that represent a "right time," an "opportune or seasonable time," or an "appointed season" (Titus 1:3) for something to happen. *Kairos* is measured in terms of eternity, which is God's dimension, and it isn't limited to past, present, or future.

Many promises were fulfilled on the very day Jesus arrived on the earth as the One destined to be Savior of the world. He pierced His way into creation at just the right *kairos* time, slicing through *chronos* with the cry of a baby in a manger.

The moment Jesus chose to give up His spirit on the cross at Calvary was another *kairos* moment: "For while we were still helpless, at *the right time*, Christ died for the ungodly" (Romans 5:6).

Kairos moments—which I like to refer to as God encounters—allow us to get a glimpse into eternity to see the way God works, because when God shows up, all things become possible.

There's nothing more exciting than personally experiencing one of these *kairos* moments. They're often inexplicable in terms of timing, but for all intents and purposes they could never have been planned and executed more perfectly, even with advance notice. They involve an exchange in the supernatural, when God's will and His ways cut into our daily journey through life, and we experience a God encounter at just the right time.

Ushering In the Dispensation of Grace

Malachi was the last prophet to speak into the life of Israel, some four hundred years prior to the New Testament era. Malachi spoke prophetically about a *kairos* moment when he foretold that Elijah would come to prepare the way for the Messiah.

Israel was in a state of serious spiritual decline when John the Baptist—coming in the spirit and power of Elijah (Luke 1:17)—burst onto the scene. John was closely followed by Jesus of Nazareth, the promised Messiah.

From the time of His being commissioned to perform His earthly ministry at age thirty, Jesus became heaven's change agent to set things right on the earth. One of the first things that needed attention was a number of key teachings of the religious leaders, especially where the traditions of the elders were held in higher regard than the commands of God. For example:

- The Pharisees were giving higher status to sacrifices than to mercy, justice, and righteousness (Matthew 9:12-14).
- Divorce was being sanctioned for any reason, whereas according to Scripture, marital unfaithfulness was the only reason which permitted (but did not demand) the breaking of one's marriage vows.

- Allowable work on the Sabbath had been so constrained by the religious leaders that the original intent of the Sabbath had been lost.
- Judaism had not only failed to embrace the "God of all nations" aspect of the Abrahamic covenant, but it had also actively discouraged worship by Gentiles through commercialization of the sacrifice (as with money changers being allowed into the temple courts).

Under the ministry of Jesus of Nazareth, the pendulum of spiritual life in Israel was about to swing firmly from sacrifice toward mercy.

Jesus unveiled the true meaning of many aspects of the law and the prophets as He spoke with power and authority, and then demonstrated what the kingdom of God was really like through the outworking of undeniable miracles.

Very soon He was equipping, training, and releasing disciples, and they were ministering in the same way He was. But mercy itself dictated that Jesus and His disciples went first to those lost sheep of Israel—and only then beyond.

Although Jesus spent a lot of time with His disciples and followers, He was always looking for that one person who was lost, and He regularly set aside time to minister to those in need.

Jesus's ministry was full of God encounters as He spent time with people who were lost, lonely, needy, desperate, brokenhearted, sick, diseased, or demon possessed, who were on a list that seemed never ending. It was when Jesus encountered these people that some of the greatest miracles in Scripture were recorded. As He felt compassion for the lost, miracles of healing and a host of other miracles were released.

As believers, we also need to be touched by people's infirmities so that the life and healing power of Jesus Christ can be released to flow through us to those around us who are in need.

A Heavenly Strategy

Although introducing any form of new teaching that challenged the status quo was a formidable and somewhat dangerous task (because of the prevailing political and spiritual climate of Israel at the time), Jesus had a heavenly strategy to deal with this situation, one that had been spoken of by another prophet around nine hundred years earlier:

> Jesus spoke all these things to the crowd in parables; he did not say anything to them without using a parable. So was fulfilled what was spoken through the prophet: "I will open my mouth in parables, I will utter things hidden since the creation of the world." (Matthew 13:34-35, quoting Psalm 78:2)

These parables contained both spiritual truth and practical examples taken from daily life in Israel. Even more, the parables spoken by Jesus contained a window of understanding that allowed truth to be revealed, while the latch to open the window required faith to be exercised by the listener.

Jesus used parables for many reasons. One of the primary purposes was to reveal the spirit and intent of the law to the religious leaders of His time. One of the most profound parables of this kind followed immediately after Jesus had the following conversation:

> On one occasion an expert in the law stood up to test Jesus. "Teacher," he asked, "what must I do to inherit eternal life?"
> "What is written in the Law?" he replied. "How do you read it?"

> He answered, "'Love the Lord your God with
> all your heart and with all your soul and with
> all your strength and with all your mind';
> and, 'Love your neighbor as yourself.'"
> "You have answered correctly," Jesus
> replied. "Do this and you will live."
> But he wanted to justify himself, so he asked Jesus,
> "And who is my neighbor?" (Luke 10:25-29)

Every religious leader of the day could have easily recited the verses spoken by this "expert in the law" (the words were from Deuteronomy 6:6 and Leviticus 19:18), but Jesus was about to use a parable to demonstrate that simply following the letter of the law hadn't taught these men anything meaningful about what the Scriptures really meant about loving God or their neighbors.

When Jesus went on to give the parable of the good Samaritan (in Luke 10:30-37), He was really demonstrating what the love of God is really like. The love of God goes out of its way to help a person in need. It creates a bridge of goodwill and grace that can open the heart of the recipient to the things of God, which motivated the act of love and mercy in the first place.

Perhaps this is why Jesus saw a valid harvest field as a one-on-one encounter with any person in need, because every encounter is an opportunity to show mercy and loving-kindness to another person.

One thing that isn't so obvious in this parable is that the good Samaritan was most likely late for his next business meeting—but he chose to show mercy (the spirit of the law) rather than sacrifice (which speaks of the letter of the law). This kind of choice is what Hosea 6:6 is all about.

After speaking this parable, Jesus asked the expert in the law who he thought was a neighbor to the person who'd been robbed, beaten, and left to die. The expert replied, "The one who had mercy on him." Then Jesus told him, "Go and do likewise" (Luke 10:37).

Jesus was making the expert in the law aware that although he could lay claim to having a sound understanding of the Scriptures, unless he really loved God and his neighbor to the point of helping when needs arise, he wasn't really fulfilling the greatest commandments.

The expert in the law would have readily put sacrifice (the letter of the law) above showing mercy (the spirit of the law), for such was the normal practice of his day. He would have readily excused both the priest and the Levite for attending to their religious duties instead of helping the needy (there were other people who could do that). Jesus corrected this misconception by pointing him to an extreme situation involving a neighbor in need, and identifying the person whose actions won the Father's approval.

In the same way, we aren't pleasing God when we seek to excuse ourselves from getting involved while encountering a neighbor in need. We must ask: Are we really our neighbor's friend? Or is our first instinct always to find a reason to excuse ourselves and simply pass by the person in need?

This has to be one of the greatest personal challenges presented in Scripture to every believer seeking to engage in market place ministry or any other ministry, because it embraces the very heartbeat of God.

So who is our neighbor?

The Greek word translated as "neighbor" in Luke 10 is *plēsion,* which literally means the passerby, someone you meet in your daily travels, someone we rub shoulders with—which can also include our next-door neighbors.

Jesus's command to us is to go and show mercy to such people in the same manner as the good Samaritan did.

A Workplace Encounter

A number of years ago I entered a new workplace, and within a short period of time I began sharing my faith and personal testimony with a few of the employees.

Word spread about me being a believer in God, and in good conscience I attempted to live a consistent, faith-filled life in the workplace. I soon encountered a number of other believers, and we established a prayer meeting and fellowship group at the Brisbane City Mission.

One day at work, I was asked by a young lady named Jessica, who worked in close proximity to me, if I had a moment to talk.

I said yes, and I sat in a chair opposite her desk. I cannot recall having previously shared my faith or the gospel message directly with her.

Jessica was an attractive young women in her late twenties. She looked at me and said, "You know that I'm divorced from my husband. Since then I've been with other men, and the relationship hasn't always been platonic. Do you mean to tell me that God could forgive me for this?"

I looked at her, and something in my heart leaped with excitement and joy. I had before me a person who was genuinely seeking to get things right with God. Her conscience was telling her that entertaining this type of relationship with men wasn't right, and she was being convicted of her sin.

At that moment the Holy Spirit quickened a scripture in my mind, and I said, "Jessica, it says in the book of Isaiah, chapter 1, "Though your sins be as scarlet, they shall be white as snow."

As I spoke, tears began to stream down her cheeks, and she began to experience the mercy and forgiveness of God.

This was one of numerous God encounters I had with Jessica. She was touched time and again at our prayer and fellowship meetings as the kingdom of God was established and became a daily reality in her life.

When you or I rub shoulders with someone in need, we have opportunity to be a neighbor. To show mercy, compassion, and love in this manner reflects the true spirit and intent of the Scriptures, which are the very words and breath of our God. While we need to be wise in the sense of being led by the Holy Spirit, it's only when we take up this challenge that we can ever claim to have been a true neighbor to that person.

Jesus wants us to exercise faith by showing mercy—just as the good Samaritan did—and to help the person in need regardless of…

- their religion or lack thereof.
- their skin color, race, or culture.
- where they now live or were born.
- their personal baggage or family situation.
- their sexuality and associated lifestyle.
- their tattoos, piercings, nose rings.
- their hair color or style.
- how they dress or smell.
- their health or mental well-being.
- their financial status.

The reality is this: It's much easier to judge and label people rather than making a choice to love and accept them, despite their differences.

I'll conclude this chapter with the following challenge:
- The Word of God clearly shows that it's God's desire for every person on the earth to be reconnected with Him through His Son, Jesus Christ.
- If we truly believe this, then we need to do something about it and become the salt and light we're called to be and to become a neighbor to those in need.

- If we claim to know the love of Jesus Christ in our lives, we need to do what He says and let His love shine through us for all people to see, and then be ready to give an account for the faith that lives in us.
- Our part in the end-time harvest commences with the very next time we have an opportunity to help someone in need.

Remember that mercy triumphs over judgment in God's eyes—and we always need to be ready to reflect that reality as we seek to bring the kingdom of God into our respective market places.

6

How Did Jesus Connect?

J esus has called all Christian believers to become lighthouses to those around them by modeling godly behavior.

By using metaphors such as "the light of the world" and "the salt of the earth," Jesus made a declaration for all Christian believers to become the change agents in their world to usher in the kingdom of God.

I spoke earlier about the need for believers to make a difference in their market places, and how consistent modeling of Christian beliefs, values, and lifestyle is probably the most significant element of our testimony. We need to understand that an unbeliever is given the opportunity to see what God is really like by the way in which we reflect Jesus Christ in our market places and beyond.

Many people will never go near a church, but they'll often take notice of someone who claims to be a follower of Jesus Christ, even if the main reason is to catch them in some form of hypocrisy.

Don't forget that many people followed Jesus around as he ministered, wanting to expose him as a fraud or trying to find a chink in his armor. However, this didn't deter Jesus in any way, because He had a totally different worldview that saw every crowd of people as a harvest field waiting for the workers to arrive.

This is the ultimate reverse mindset—but it's one-hundred-percent kingdom-of-God thinking.

Think about the Harvest

At this point, I would like to encourage some expansive thinking.

To put this next Scripture into context, Jesus had just been on a preaching circuit involving a number of towns and villages, teaching in their synagogues and proclaiming the good news of the kingdom and healing every kind of sickness and disease.

Then in Matthew 9:36, we read this about Jesus: "When he saw the crowds, he had compassion on them, because they were harassed and helpless, like sheep without a shepherd." Jesus knew only too well the fallen and helpless state of mankind. It was within this context that He entered this world, being born of a virgin, and fulfilling so many prophetic words that had been spoken by the prophets of old.

His mission as Savior was to bring a fresh revelation and understanding of the mercy, compassion, justice, and righteousness of God.

Down through the years since the law of Moses had been decreed to Israel, the understanding of these "weightier provisions of the law" (Matthew 23:23) had been largely lost through religious tradition, dogma, and misinterpretation. But once revived, mercy, compassion, justice, and righteousness would truly reflect the Father's redemptive heart for lost humanity.

Not only did Jesus see the crowds as "harassed and helpless"; He also saw the formidable task ahead, because the workers were few in number—as we see in His immediate words to His disciples upon seeing those crowds: "The harvest is plentiful but the workers are few. Ask the Lord of the harvest, therefore, to send out workers into his harvest field" (9:37-38).

The question I would like to ask all professing Christian believers is this: Do you see the harvest field of souls before you as you go into *your* world on a daily basis? Think about the harvest Jesus spoke about, and ask yourself whether this picture also speaks about people from your market place or workplace, from your extended family, or from your group of friends—some of whom are unbelievers.

God's Real Agenda

Before I go further, I wish to confess that many of my friends are not believers. This is because I know God has put me into their lives for a purpose—to lead them to the Savior, Jesus Christ.

I believe Jesus had this same thought in mind (as we saw earlier) when He ate at the house of Zacchaeus, and also at the house of Matthew. Look at that passage again:

> While Jesus was having dinner at Matthew's house,
> many tax collectors and "sinners" came and ate
> with him and his disciples. When the Pharisees
> saw this, they asked his disciples, "Why does your
> teacher eat with tax collectors and 'sinners'?"
> On hearing this, Jesus said, "It is not the healthy who
> need a doctor, but the sick. But go and learn what this
> means: 'I desire mercy, not sacrifice' For I have not come
> to call the righteous, but sinners." (Matthew 9:10-13)

After Matthew made his decision to follow Jesus, he also wanted his mates to meet the Messiah. Matthew didn't care that the religious leaders labeled him and his mates as tax collectors and sinners, because he'd met the One who'd changed his status in heaven's Book of Life from "lost" to "found"—and all heaven was rejoicing.

Jesus's desire to reach out to sinners was an act of mercy and represented a fundamental challenge to the thinking or religious mindset of His day. It was like a veritable slap in the face of the religious leaders, for it was contrary to both their traditions and their interpretation of the law of Moses as handed down through the generations.

After all, there was a call to come out and be separate (Isaiah 52:11)—and this is what Judaism was promoting, and in essence still promotes to the present day.

While there was an element of truth in the Scripture used to support their theology, it failed to embrace the promise that God had made to Abraham (their patriarch) to make him the father of many nations, not just of the nation of Israel.

The Jews hadn't embraced this concept in their religion, but it was central to God's plan for this world.

To be sure, Judaism is a religion built around one race of people, and the attitude that promotes this concept is known as ethnocentricity. Orthodox Jewish teaching holds that other races of people need to adopt Judaism or a derivative of this for non-Jews to find favor in God's eyes

Yet Jesus didn't entertain ethnocentricity, because He knew that His Father had a heart for all peoples, and although His ministry was initially focused on the lost sheep of Israel, it soon progressed to Samaria and then into Gentile territory. This pattern of ministry radiating outward was simply a precursor to the Great Commission's call to take the gospel message to the ends of the earth.

I would like to suggest that Jesus's focus on Israel first, then Samaria, then Gentiles, was more for the sake of His disciples than anything else. They also needed time to understand and adjust their thinking to see God's real agenda and to break down their own prejudices and religious preconceptions. This was an integral part of their training to become a disciple of Jesus Christ.

In like manner, Christian believers (as spiritual Israel) should not isolate themselves from sinners, because we've been given responsibility through the Great Commission to go into all our world and preach the gospel message.

The reality we face daily is that our world—especially in many Western countries—is becoming increasingly multicultural. This is particularly true of our market places and workplaces where people with specialized skills can be brought in from anywhere in the world.

Although this can pose many challenges to promoting the gospel message in a culturally relevant manner, it also provides the greatest opportunities to reach people groups from many different nations without having to go very far past our own front door.

Insights into Sharing the Gospel

Let's turn now to the words of Jesus and the principles He taught about spreading the gospel message.

Within every workplace and market place, and in every sporting, recreational, social, or interest group—and indeed in almost every family or extended family situation—the people we meet will invariably fit into one of the categories described by Jesus in a parable about a sower and four kinds of soil:

> That same day Jesus went out of the house and sat by the
> lake. Such large crowds gathered around him that he got

into a boat and sat in it, while all the people stood on the shore. Then he told them many things in parables, saying:

> "A farmer went out to sow his seed. As he was scattering the seed, some fell along the path, and the birds came and ate it up. Some fell on rocky places, where it did not have much soil. It sprang up quickly, because the soil was shallow. But when the sun came up, the plants were scorched, and they withered because they had no root. Other seed fell among thorns, which grew up and choked the plants. Still other seed fell on good soil, where it produced a crop—a hundred, sixty, or thirty times what was sown. Whoever has ears, let them hear." (Matthew 13:1-9)

Jesus explained the meaning of this parable to His disciples, as He likened His Word to seed and our hearts to the various kinds of soil:

> When anyone hears the message about the kingdom and does not understand it, the evil one comes and snatches away what was sown in their heart. This is the seed sown along the path. The seed falling on rocky ground refers to someone who hears the word and at once receives it with joy. But since they have no root, they last only a short time. When trouble or persecution comes because of the word, they quickly fall away.

The seed falling among the thorns refers to
someone who hears the word, but the worries
of this life and the deceitfulness of wealth
choke the word, making it unfruitful.
But the seed falling on good soil refers to someone
who hears the word and understands it. This is
the one who produces a crop, yielding a hundred,
sixty, or thirty times what was sown. (13:18-23)

All Christian believers have been called to be witnesses of the grace of God (letting our light shine), while some believers have been specifically called as missionaries and aid workers to go into all the world and preach the gospel message. Regardless of your individual calling, the parable of the sower is a powerful wake-up call for all who consider themselves to be Christian believers.

This parable is all about giving unbelievers the opportunity to engage with God when our message is being shared. It also speaks about the warfare that occurs in the spiritual realm for the souls of men and women in the everyday business of life, when we step out in faith to share our message.

As Christian believers, we're called to be sowers of the Word of God on a continuous basis and to take up our cross daily and follow His example. We may never have recognized or even thought about this, but the Scriptures clearly describe how God uses our message to spread the aroma or fragrance of Christ to every person we encounter. With the explosion of telecommunications in recent years, this can mean reaching out to people just about anywhere in the world within an instant of time.

As we share our message, we become to God the pleasing aroma of Christ among those who are in the valley of decision, as people are making their choice about where they'll spend eternity—a choice that depends on whether they accept or reject Jesus Christ as their Lord and Savior.

The apostle Paul describes it this way:

> But thanks be to God, who always leads us as captives in Christ's triumphal procession and uses us to spread the aroma of the knowledge of him everywhere. For we are to God the pleasing aroma of Christ among those who are being saved and those who are perishing. (2 Corinthians 2:14-15)

Become the Message

All Christian believers are called to be witnesses of their faith in God. To do this effectively, we need to understand the principles that Jesus taught for sharing or communicating the gospel message. This includes the reality that not everyone will be saved—despite the fact that God is not willing that anyone should perish, but that all people should come to repentance (2 Peter 3:9).

So what can the parable of the sower teach us about our everyday life journey?

Picture yourself as the sower of God's Word (your message) when you go out tomorrow into your world. You'll rub shoulders with people from all walks of life, and there will be varying levels of engagement. Unless your experience is greatly different from mine, you'll meet a variety of responses when you attempt to bring any conversation about God into focus.

You then tailor and refine your message according to the responses you receive.

Bringing God into focus may take on many forms, but the primary goal should always be to make our faith in God known to those we meet. By definition, the people we meet on a daily basis are described as our "neighbor" in the parable of the good Samaritan. Jesus also acknowledged that the second greatest commandment (after loving God) is to "love your neighbor as yourself" (Luke 10:30-37; Mark 12:31).

When we allow our light to shine, others are able to observe our faith in action. However, before we can become an effective witness we must recognize that (a) we have a message to deliver, and (b) our life has to *become* that message in order for us to be able to proclaim it in a manner that will be readily received.

In *The Prophetic Life,* David McCracken writes, "We have a message to deliver and a message to become." In other words, the message we deliver must continually impact our lives.

When we consider that all our previous life experiences are preparation for what we're to become in life, we can see that our message is always happening and is being continually represented to everyone who comes into our world.

Our attitudes and responses to life simply add to or subtract from our message, and it's quite clear that these life transactions can greatly influence the people in our world either positively or negatively, depending upon the message we deliver.

In essence, our message is on display through our outward behavior and is a clear manifestation of the fundamental beliefs and values we hold. With this in mind, we always need to be sober-minded and clearly focused when our message is being presented to the people in our world.

We need to remember that Jesus spoke (in Matthew 10:19 and John 12:49) about relying upon the Holy Spirit to give us the words to say and how to say them. When it comes to sharing God's Word, there's no better or easier way to get our message across.

When our message is specifically addressing the questions of salvation and eternity, the following observation is obvious: If the *manner* in which our message is presented (how it's said) isn't sensitive to the listener, we risk alienating them before we can share the *content* of our message (what we have to say). This importance of this cannot be overstated.

When we bring the message of salvation, we need to do so with the clear understanding that its primary focus relates to the question of where the listener will spend eternity. The Scriptures are clear on this question; they declare that eternal life is available only to all those who accept and confess Jesus Christ as their Lord and Savior (Romans 10:9-10). The Scriptures are equally clear that the alternative is death and eternal separation from God, which happens by default when a person chooses to not accept Jesus Christ as their Lord and Savior during their lifetime on earth (Romans 6:23).

Jesus went to great lengths to explain what this meant to His listeners because He fully understood the consequences of an eternity without reference to God. Jesus knew that hell and eternal torment would be the final result—as well as people never being able to live the abundant life on earth that has been promised to all who choose to believe in the Lord Jesus Christ.

At the end of the day, the Scriptures are one-hundred-percent transparent in declaring that our place in eternity is solely a matter of personal choice. The Scriptures also reveal that our personal choice will determine not only where we'll spend eternity, but also whether we'll enjoy an ongoing personal relationship with God for the remainder of our natural life on earth.

In view of the great honor and responsibility that has been given to believers to be witnesses of the gospel (which is the truth about God), our message needs to reflect our devotion to the Lord Jesus Christ, and every opportunity to share our message needs to be approached with sensitivity, prayerfulness, and a genuine desire to make God known to the people in our world.

The apostle Paul says it this way in the book of Colossians:

> Devote yourselves to prayer, being watchful and thankful.... Be wise in the way you act toward outsiders; make the most of every opportunity. Let your conversation be always full of grace, seasoned with salt, so that you may know how to answer everyone. (Colossians 4:2-6)

A Range of Outcomes

The parable of the sower and the soils is primarily about identifying the heart attitudes of people toward our message as we bring the Word and presence of God to the people we meet.

When Jesus delivered this parable, He was speaking to a crowd of people of whom many would have been farmers, and they could readily relate to the story. Even those who weren't farmers could have easily imagined the different types of soils and the outcomes Jesus spoke of. He was engaging with His listeners by finding a topic of conversation that would attract their attention, something from their everyday world that was of significance.

In this parable, Jesus first speaks about four different types of soils into which seed is sown. Those different soil types are these:

1. hard and compacted
2. shallow, with a rocky foundation

3. full of thorns

4. good and fertile

Jesus foretells a different harvest from each of the four soil types, reflecting the extent to which the seed could take root and germinate.

Up to this point, the parable is easy to understand. It makes for a perfectly logical and reasonable outcome for each of the soil types.

However, it's only when Jesus goes on to tell the next part of the story that the true meaning of the parable emerges. He compares earthly seed being planted within the soil of the earth with heavenly seed being planted within the soil of the heart.

The following observations of this parable are clear: In the same way that earthly seed can germinate and reach its full potential *only* when it is planted in the right type of soil—so also for heavenly seed (the Word of God); to achieve its full potential for the kingdom of God, it must be planted into a listener with a receptive heart, where the Word is heard and understood—and then acted upon. The goal with planting heavenly seed is always to maximize the harvest—thirty, sixty, or a hundredfold.

The following table of outcomes may help explain the parable:

	a) SOIL TYPE b) HEART RECEPTIVITY	OUTCOME:
1	a) hard soil (earthly) b) hard heart (spiritual)	a) Soil too hard to allow seed to be planted. No crop. b) No interest or understanding of the message. No crop.
2	a) rocky soil (earthly) b) shallow heart (spiritual)	a) Plant sprouted, but roots didn't form in shallow soil. No crop. b) Initial interest and joy, but message did not take root in the heart. Persecution proves too difficult to pursue the kingdom. No crop.
3	a) thorny soil (earthly) b) cluttered heart (spiritual)	a) Thorns grew up alongside plants and choked them. Unfruitful. b) Interested, but in practice often too busy or otherwise preoccupied with the worries of this life, the deceitfulness of wealth, and desires for other things to yield a harvest for the kingdom. Unfruitful.
4	a) good soil (earthly) b) good heart (spiritual)	a) Ready for production. Produces abundant crop. b) Sincere and open heart, very interested and willing to participate in a harvest for the kingdom. Produces abundant crop.

In my many years of working and ministering in the market place, my careful observation is that the sheer busyness of life often sees business people fall into the third category, even if they have leanings toward the things of God.

What market place people need to realize is that having the Word of God choked out of your life is a result of failing to realize that worries, deceit, and ungodly desires all speak of a life without faith—which ultimately keeps people from reaching their life purpose and destiny in the kingdom of God. By contrast, the message of Jesus is to seek first His kingdom and His righteousness (Matthew 6:33), and He will take care of your business (and your busyness).

From my own market place ministry experience, I have little doubt that Jesus perfectly describes heart responses to the message—ranging from outright rejection to wholehearted acceptance by the listener, as well as everything in between.

So when you're confronted by different levels of heart receptivity, don't be surprised by the responses. Rather be prayerful and ask God for a key to open your neighbor's heart.

I've led people to Jesus from all walks of life. I've led people to Jesus on their death beds, and people miraculously awaking out of comas. I've led people to Jesus in homes, motels, cars, restaurants, workplaces, market places, and churches. And one thing I know for sure is that God never gives up, and neither should we.

Just remember that not everyone Jesus met readily accepted His words, even when they were accompanied by outstanding miracles and a demonstration of the Holy Spirit's power. But Jesus continued His ministry unperturbed, making the most of every opportunity and continuing to sow seed, which others could later harvest.

Have you ever considered how many times Jesus might have walked past the crippled man who was placed daily at the entrance to the gate called Beautiful? I would suggest the answer is many, but it wasn't until the apostles Peter and John had an encounter with this man after the day of Pentecost that he was healed of paralysis (Acts 3:1-10).

We need to recognize that there are times and seasons in people's lives, and we must allow the Holy Spirit to guide us in this regard.

We also need to pray for a key into that person's life at their appointed time for salvation and to use the gifts of the Holy Spirit wherever possible. An excellent starting place for understanding this is 1 Corinthians 12 and 14. (We'll explore this topic in later chapters.)

We're all a work in progress, and everyone is on a journey through life. We're born into a world that's often devoid of any real understanding about God, yet there's much to know and discover if we want to have fellowship with our Creator.

God leaves evidence of His creation all around us—but to truly appreciate this, we need to connect with our Creator.

7

Does Your Light Shine?

I want to highlight again the following declaration made by Jesus to His disciples:

> You are the light of the world. A city on a hill cannot be hidden. Neither do people light a lamp and put it under a basket. Instead, they set it on a lampstand, and it gives light to everyone in the house. In the same way, let your light shine before men, that they may see your good deeds and glorify your Father in heaven. (Matthew 5:14-16)

In these verses, Jesus was simply trying to get the point across that some things aren't meant to be hidden:

- In the *natural* realm, this includes a city built on a hill and a lamp set on a lampstand.
- In the *supernatural* realm, this includes your light shining before men— so they may see your good deeds and glorify our Father in heaven.

A primary reason that Jesus shared these examples was to encourage His disciples to step into God's purposes and plans for their lives. His encouragement was simply to allow their light to shine into the dark places of this world so that lost humanity could see their good deeds as evidence of their faith in action—because real faith is never meant to be hidden.

When I was on my personal journey to connect with God, I worked in an office that had around twelve employees, three of whom were Christians. Sadly, none of them revealed themselves as Christians until after I began sharing my faith as a born-again believer.

I'm aware that some people may take offence at what I'm about to say, but I think it needs to be said as a reality check to those who profess to be Christian believers -- If the only difference between you and everyone else you work with is that:

1. you don't get caught up in dirty jokes or surfing the internet for smut or porn,

2. you don't get caught up in workplace gossip, and

3. you don't swear, gamble, or get drunk or do illegal drugs—then I'm sorry, but I know plenty of nonbelievers who are no different from you.

Furthermore, I would like to suggest that your Christianity should never be defined by negative statements about the things you don't do or approve of, because many outsiders have long ago formed the view that these type of rules effectively kill off every possible joy in life.

But it doesn't stop there, because many outsiders also perceive church in the following terms:

- boring sermons that deliver a load of guilt and shame—offering little more than endless thou-shalt-nots about how to behave in order to be acceptable to the church and to God;

- religious tradition, pomp, and ceremony with little meaning to outsiders;

- old-fashioned, outdated hymns using centuries-old language;

- social views that are totally out of touch with contemporary culture on matters such as homosexuality, same-sex marriage, abortion, contraception, euthanasia, religious education in schools, etc.;

The reason I mention this is that I regularly speak to outsiders about the things of God, and these are some of the most common objections and perceptions held.

Sadly, these perceptions are held not only by outsiders. At times I hear it from people who believe in the Lord but are struggling to be accepted because they don't quite fit into the church mold.

Recent investigations into child sexual abuse have highlighted the disproportionate amount of sexual and other abuse which has taken place within the church, associated ministries, and church-based schools across a range of denominations and religions. The revelations that have come to light have only served to make matters worse, especially when the abuse was often reported and either the victims were not believed, or their trauma was trivialized, or the whole matter was swept under the carpet. Although these investigations probably relate to only a relatively small portion of the body of Christ, when this is added to the earlier objections and perceptions, they reinforce why Christianity doesn't enjoy a particularly good reputation within the wider community.

By way of contrast, our daily life as a Christian is meant to be a strongly positive expression of our faith. If people don't see Christ in us, then our light isn't shining brightly enough, and we need to seriously rethink how we should conduct ourselves and how we're living out the faith we profess to those around us.

This is why Jesus referred to His disciples as the salt of the earth (Matthew 5:13-14). He has called us to be the influencers, not the influenced.

If we ever get to the place where outsiders cannot differentiate between Christians and those around them, it's time to do some serious soul-searching and ask ourselves: Has our light gone out? Has our salt lost its flavor?

Although there's a place for silence while building trust with those around us, Jesus never called us to be silent witnesses. His command was to go into all our world and be a point of difference that clearly shows the pathway to the kingdom of God.

Back to the Market Place

The above analogy applies to every area of our lives, but I'm particularly focusing on the market place and the workplace as ideal settings for our faith to shine.

In our workplace, we need to be reliable to day's end and more. If we're asked to go two miles, then be prepared to go three.

We need to hold on to a matter told to us in confidence and feel honored that management, a supervisor, or even a colleague would entrust the matter to us.

Going the extra mile shows our faith in action and has the potential to distinguish Christians in the workplace. Remember, we're called to be a royal priesthood, a holy nation, a people belonging to our God. From the moment we're born again (John 3:3), we become a new creation in Christ Jesus. Our faith in God becomes the anchor for our soul and as we grow in relationship with God, we become more like Him.

As we read the Word of God it has the capacity to transform our thinking and value systems to reflect the very thoughts of God. Our values system becomes not only a critical point of difference, but also a positive expression of our faith. It's also true that having different values can make a statement of their own in a workplace.

While the above is the goal, I've found that the work ethic of some Christians can leave a lot to be desired, especially when the teachings of Christ aren't being fully embraced.

The following observations, principles, and Scripture references come to mind as I attempt to address the topic of letting our light shine:

- "Whoever can be trusted with very little can also be trusted with much, and whoever is dishonest with very little will also be dishonest with much" (Luke 16:10). This reflects our integrity and work ethic before man and God.

- Always do a great job, not just when the bosses are around. This reflects our conscientiousness and servanthood (Colossians 3:23).

- When I consult for business, I adopt a high level of ownership, as if I was the owner, and I make this abundantly clear to the business owners and managers I work with. The truth is, when the business owners or CEOs understand that this is my personal commitment and the values I hold, they often show a deep level of respect and allow me to help guide them in growing their businesses. Why do I do this? It's simply applying what Jesus said: "In everything, do to others as you would have them do to you" (Matthew 7:12). These words contain their own unique creative power to capture hearts simply by treating others the way we would want to be treated.

- Business owners soon learn that my "agenda" is solely to bring greater blessing to their businesses and their families, and that I'm not ashamed to share the motivation for my faith (especially my testimony) with their entire family and extended family if the opportunity arises.

- Because our relationship is built on friendship and a genuine desire to be a blessing, it isn't surprising that I'm often called when their family members have health or well-being issues.

When we build strong relationships with employers and colleagues, they'll be much more likely to call on us in a moment of crisis, with bridges already in place.

Light Shines Brightly in Dark Places

Life can sometimes take unexpected turns, and showing God's love and compassion in the most difficult of situations is what matters. When this occurs, our light is shining bright in a dark place, and it cannot help but be noticed and felt by those in need.

One night, I was finishing work with a client quite late. The company owner's name was Harry, and as I was packing my bag, Harry said, "I have to go and visit my father-in-law now. He's in hospital and very sick. His condition is life-threatening, and we're really worried about him. They aren't sure if he's going to make it. He has been having severe fevers three or four times each day. They've done every known test and have no idea what's causing it."

As I was about to leave, I extended my hand to Harry. "What is his name?"

"Frank."

While still clasping his hand, I looked him in the eye. "Well, I will be praying for Frank tonight."

"You don't need to do that." Then he smiled, "But I know you, and you'll be praying, won't you?"

"Of course!"

We parted for the evening.

As I went home, I felt compassion and a strong burden for Harry's father-in-law. I began to lay hold of God in intercessory prayer for Frank until well after midnight. I had a few hours of sleep, woke again, and continued praying for a breakthrough.

It was about four A.M. that the breakthrough came. I distinctly heard the Holy Spirit whisper gently in my ear, "The fever has left him; he is well." I thanked God for His healing touch on Frank, and then had a few hours of sleep before doing my devotions and starting work.

Around midmorning I saw Harry again. We spoke briefly about a few work-related matters before I asked, "By the way, how is your father-in-law?"

I'll never forget Harry's smile. "He's well."

"Yes, I know."

Harry looked at me as if to be almost in a state of shock. "How could you possibly know?"

"Because the Holy Spirit told me so at about four o'clock this morning when I was praying for him." At that moment my faith was shining into Harry's world.

Harry looked at me with tears welling up in his eyes. He stretched out his hand to shake mine. "You're simply amazing. I've never met anyone like you."

"My God is amazing," I answered, "and He loves us all. There are no favorites."

Ever since that day, neither Harry nor I can ever be the same, because we've caught a glimpse of God's mercy and His power to heal and touch lives.

I've had several God encounters with Harry and his extended family, and I'm believing that Harry and his entire family will one day come to know Jesus Christ as their Lord and Savior.

In the meantime, it's up to me to prove faithful with the trust I've been given and to continue to be salt and light to all the people God has given me to love and care for.

Insights for Anyone Aspiring to Leadership

Within the household of faith, every great leader has first learned to serve the ministry of another. In the same way, if we're to prosper in our workplace, we first need to serve before we can ever aspire to be respected leaders. It's only by serving faithfully that we gain credibility in the eyes of those around us.

When this kind of servanthood occurs, words such as loyalty, integrity, trustworthiness, faithfulness, good character, and sound judgment all spring to mind. It's only after character qualities are developed that a person has a solid foundation for strong leadership.

Not surprisingly, these character traits are exactly the same type of qualities that the apostle Paul told Titus and Timothy to look for in the leaders of the fledgling New Testament churches. It's also interesting to note Paul's words in 1 Timothy 3:7 that overseers (elders) "must have a good reputation with outsiders." I would suggest that the most likely place where the reputation of prospective overseers are tested is in the workplace or market place.

In practice, it's often the character qualities that we display in the workplace or in our servanthood to the body of Christ that become the foundation for our promotion within church or parachurch ministries. I would also suggest that the workplace and the market place is the venue where many a person's primary gifting is first discovered and then developed.

We know from Scripture that the "gifts and calling of God are without repentance" (Romans 11:29). For real servanthood to occur, the question becomes: To whose authority or dominion are our gifts subject? To the kingdom of God, or otherwise?

If the kingdom of God is our desire, then we need to press in like the apostle Paul. With dogged determination, Paul made it his mission in life to persuade men and women everywhere to accept Jesus Christ as their Savior and wholeheartedly come under the dominion of God's kingdom.

In our workplaces, we need to aspire to the leadership and character qualities of Joseph, as seen in Genesis 37–47. Then we can be overcomers regardless of what may be thrown at us. When it all seems too big for us to handle, we need to continually commit the situation to God in prayer, then let Him guide and direct our paths until we achieve a victorious outcome.

One of the greatest signs of God's favor on your life is fruitfulness. This brings a blessing to your family and friends, your church, and your business. We must never forget that Abraham, the father of faith, was blessed that he might be a blessing to others (Genesis 22:17-18).

In order to achieve this, we need to regularly pray for our businesses and employers to prosper, and we should always be ready to put in a good word for the business when mentioning it to others. Apart from anything else, this means that our job is likely to be safe into the future, because the sowing and reaping principle is involved.

In my experience, far too many people adopt the victim mentality and criticize any negative aspects of their workplace. In contrast, Christians need to adopt a redemptive approach and become a change agent for Jesus Christ in their workplace.

All Christians are called to make a difference in their workplaces. To achieve this, we need to have an outlook on life that is positive, faith-inspired, and filled with hope, both for now and for the future.

At times, this world can be such a dark place. Amid that darkness, Christian believers need to ask the Lord for opportunities to share their faith in Jesus Christ and to be constantly ready to inspire hope into others when the situation arises.

Jesus said, "If I be lifted up, I will draw all men unto me" (John 12:32). Sharing our life's journey and its ultimate purpose is one of the most powerful things we can ever do. Our testimony will always lift up the name of Jesus Christ as our Lord and Savior to those we rub shoulders with on a daily basis.

After all, these are our neighbors.

Introducing Your Friend

Have you ever been to a special event, a function, or a party where a friend introduces you to someone new? In the truest sense, this is exactly what Jesus has asked us all to do. By telling people about our own life journey (which is our testimony), we can't help but introduce people to Jesus.

At this point, I would like you to give some further thought to the parable of the sower. When we share things about Jesus Christ, this is the same as sowing seed for the kingdom of God.

The seed—the Word of God—will always attempt to take root (by faith), and the type of soil (receptivity of the heart) will determine whether a harvest of salvation occurs.

Regardless of whether we're sowing seed or reaping a harvest, I know from my own life journey that we can never be quite the same after we've had an encounter with the Author of life.

As believers in Jesus Christ, we're all called to be witnesses by sharing our faith. As we sow the seed, the Word of God will challenge the hearts of listeners because it contains the very essence of God Himself:

> For the Word of God is living and active. Sharper than
> any double-edged sword, it pierces even to dividing soul

and spirit, joints and marrow. It is able to judge the
thoughts and intentions of the heart. (Hebrews 4:12)

Notice in this verse that it's the Word of God that has its own creative
power to divide soul and spirit and to judge the thoughts and intents of the
heart. All we need to do is speak the Word of God—and allow the Holy
Spirit to do the rest.

But if we don't take up the opportunity to speak the Word of God when
the need arises, we're effectively hiding our light under a basket or a bed.

From a scriptural perspective, I would also like to dispel the myth that
the primary call of believers is to get unsaved people into church so the pastor can do their thing and lead them to Christ. If this is what you've been
led to believe, I would like to suggest that this myth is fundamentally flawed
and shows a serious misunderstanding of the purpose of what's known as
the ascension gift ministries, as described in the book of Ephesians:

> So Christ himself gave the apostles, the prophets,
> the evangelists, the pastors and teachers, *to equip*
> *his people for works of service*, so that the body of
> Christ may be built up until we all reach unity in
> the faith and in the knowledge of the Son of God
> and become mature, attaining to the whole measure
> of the fullness of Christ. (Ephesians 4:11-13)

We see here that the role of ascension gift ministries is to equip or train
believers in how to carry out "works of service" for the building up or edi-
fication of the body of Christ.

The Greek word here for "works of service" is *diakonía,* which means
ministry or active service done with a willing (voluntary) attitude. *Strong's*

Exhaustive Concordance says that "for the believer, *diakonía* (ministry) specifically refers to Spirit-empowered service guided by faith." *The Pulpit Commentary* says that "building up of the body of Christ" as mentioned in Ephesians 4:12 means "increasing the number of believers and promoting the spiritual life of each; carrying on all their work as Christ's servants and with a definite eye to the promotion of the great work which He undertook when He came to seek and to save the lost."

It's apparent from all this that ascension gift ministers should be equipping believers to carry out the Great Commission. This is the means by which the body of Christ is meant to be built up and populated.

However, most equipping of believers within church life generally centers around people being encouraged to live holy and faith-filled lives through inspirational sermons, discipleship classes, undertaking Bible studies, attending home fellowship groups, and possibly engaging in some form of outreach. While these activities are perfectly valid for building up the faith of believers, the reality is that most of these activities do not embrace the Great Commission or lead to church growth.

Planetshakers Church (in Melbourne City), where I fellowship, is one of a number of exceptional churches around Australia that focus heavily on outreach into the community. Sermons often target evangelism-based topics (including powerful testimonies) as a means of encouraging believers to share their faith, and the fruit of this (in terms of church growth and discipleship) has been extraordinary.

However, within many of the more evangelical or fundamentalist churches, evangelistic training isn't generally given any real form of priority as a specialized or dedicated topic. And within mainline churches, it's seldom if ever taught.

The biblical pattern used by the greatest soul-winners throughout history has been the sharing of personal testimony, inextricably linked to an encounter with one or more members of the Godhead.

At every opportunity, the apostle Paul went to great lengths to make people aware of his conversion experience: how he was extremely zealous for God to the point of persecuting members of the fledgling Christian church to their death, and then—on the road to Damascus—how he experienced an encounter with the risen Christ that totally transformed his life. The scales covering Paul's eyes (which speak of religion or spiritual blindness) literally fell off.

Paul's revelation of the Christ was so complete that within days of this encounter, he was refuting the arguments of those who had previously been his greatest supporters. In so doing, Paul became the main target of those who were continuing to persecute Christian believers.

Paul's encounters with people from all walks of life were underpinned by his consuming desire to "become all things to all people so that by all possible means I might save some" (1 Corinthians 9:22). As a result of his previous life of blind religious zealotry, he felt an incredibly great debt to humanity to set the record straight, and to preach the good news that Jesus Christ was the promised Messiah.

When evangelism (or sowing the seed of God's Word) becomes a constant focus of teaching and is practically outworked in the lives of believers, outsiders cannot help but be impacted. If this message is consistently taught and outworked through the body of Christ, it should manifest itself in the form of church growth as unbelievers are introduced to Jesus Christ and have their own personal "Damascus road" encounters.

If you don't sow seed, you don't yield a crop. This law of seedtime and harvest was instituted by God Himself (Genesis 8:22).

When churches aren't growing, maybe it's time for church leaders to have a good look at whether the saints are being equipped and encouraged to share the gospel message.

Sharing Leads to Changed Lives

A number of years ago, I was leading a street ministry outreach in the car park of the community center where we held church on Sunday. This ministry was specifically targeting a group of young people from about twelve to twenty-five years of age who hung around the car park, particularly on Friday and Saturday nights.

When I invited a number of our young people from church to join me, the take-up rate wasn't high, but I gave them the following instructions:

- Be a good listener.
- Be a friend and build relationships.
- Pray beforehand and be ready to share the good news about Jesus Christ.
- If you share the gospel message, leave out Christian clichés like "hallelujah," "glory to God," "praise the Lord," etc., and don't use King James English; it will straightaway alienate this generation that often struggles with simple English.
- If you pray with someone, keep it simple, and especially don't use archaic words like "thee," "thou," and the like.

Probably the easiest way to explain this type of outreach is to testify of a God encounter I had one night, and how I prayed for a young man in serious need to reconnect with God.

Before I met Daniel, he'd been sleeping outside a local bakery off and on for weeks, since it was the only warm place nearby in the middle of winter. Daniel had a heroin addiction and had lived with a number of families for short periods, but was inevitably kicked out of each place for stealing and pawning anything of value to support his drug habit.

I met Daniel on the street at about one A.M. on a Saturday morning. He was a handsome young man. And he was drunk, trying to fight withdrawals from heroin addiction. He was an absolute mess.

"I need help," he told me. "You gotta help me, man."

"Sorry, I can't help you," I responded.

He looked at me as if I was his last hope in life, and it was fading fast. I soon followed up with, "But I know someone who can."

"Who then?"

"God."

Daniel was desperate. "Okay, I want God's help."

"Let's ask Him for help."

We sat in the car talking for a while so I could better understand Daniel's struggles. Then I prayed: "God, I'm here with my friend Daniel, and he's asking for Your help. Daniel has been hurting bad and he's messed up a lot of things along the way. He wants Your help, Lord, and he's sorry for the things he's done. He's hurt himself, his loved ones, and most of all You, but he's asking for Your help. Father, in the name of Jesus Christ, as I now lay hands on Daniel, I ask You to touch his life so that he'll never be the same after this encounter with You, Lord."

As I laid hands on Daniel, the power of the Holy Spirit fell on him, and I saw Daniel's whole body vibrating and lifting out of his seat. His arms were shaking violently and his entire body was being shaken. This went on for about twenty minutes, and I could only describe what I saw as an amazing demonstration of the supernatural power of God at work.

The glory of the Lord had indeed shone on Daniel that night, and I was also incredibly touched by the Holy Spirit. My body was also shaken as I called on the Spirit of the Lord to touch this young man.

Daniel had an encounter with the Most High God that night, an encounter he would never forget. When the Holy Spirit had finished ministering to Daniel, he was completely sober.

We found lodgings for him for the rest of the night.

Daniel was only fifteen years old, and he'd been away from home for around eight weeks. His mother had been worried sick about him, and not surprisingly, he returned home to her the very next day.

When God shows up, the edge of adventure gives way to God's amazing grace. That's what I see in Daniel's story: a situation out of control…total desperation…a prayer for help. Then God's grace abounds…His mercy comes…and another lost one is added to God's family.

The book of Acts ends all too abruptly and appears unfinished. My response to this is that it's still being recorded in the books of heaven through the lives of you and me—just like in Daniel's story.

Never Again the Same

When we introduce Jesus Christ to someone new and they have a true God encounter, they can never again be quite the same person.

When God shows up, He delights to show Himself strong through signs, wonders, and even miracles. If you can't relate to this teaching, I would suggest that you may need a God encounter yourself. Then start spending time with the "sick" who need a doctor, instead of spending all your time with the "righteous," which contributes little to the task of fulfilling the Great Commission.

We simply need to introduce the people we meet to Jesus Christ, because our relationship with Him should be infectious to the point where we, too, will say, "As for us, we cannot help speaking about what we have seen and heard" (Acts 4:20).

The apostles Peter and John spoke those words when they were called before the Sanhedrin to give an account of the healing of a crippled man. The first thing that they did was to attribute this miracle to the resurrected Christ, and to claim that salvation was to be found only in the name of Jesus Christ.

The Jewish leaders had been observing these men: "When they saw the courage of Peter and John…they took note that these men had been with Jesus" (Acts 4:13). Peter and John exuded godliness, spiritual authority, humility, and a readiness to make everyone aware that by their Master's power a lame man had been healed. They simply introduced the religious leaders to the risen Lord, and it was up to Jesus and the Holy Spirit to do the rest.

For people to be drawn into the kingdom, our lives need to continually reflect an ongoing, intimate relationship with the Lord Jesus Christ. This is the only way our light will shine brightly enough to impact this world in favor of the kingdom of God.

We don't all need to be evangelists or missionaries and go to the uttermost ends of the earth for God—because wherever you're living now, there's a harvest of people who need to be introduced to Jesus.

People are everywhere, right at our doorsteps—they're in our shopping centers, our parks and gardens, our lecture halls, our retirement villages, our hospitals, our coffee shops, our sporting events. And they're in what are probably the most untapped places in our cities—our market places and workplaces, where I spend most of my time.

To be involved with market place ministry, you don't have to know everything about Christianity or the Bible; you just need to be in love with Jesus. When you have real love for someone, you can't help but mention them naturally in your conversation.

Be the Friend

I was sitting in my car one day with Harry (whose father-in-law Frank I had prayed for, as mentioned earlier in this chapter) as we listened to the Steve Green song "People Need the Lord." I told Harry of my intention to devote the rest of my life to bringing as many people to Jesus Christ as possible, and that included him and his family, and then to continue our friendship in heaven.

Harry looked at me with tears in his eyes, then said, "Never stop talking to me, my friend."

Just as I was being a friend to Harry, I want to encourage you to be the best friend you could ever be. Simply be ready to introduce others to *your* best friend—the Lord Jesus Christ.

8

How Not to Connect

Constant grumbling and complaining are probably the worst testimony a Christian can ever have in a workplace or market place—and indeed anywhere in life.

I'm sure we've all met plenty of whiners and people who spend a lot of their time complaining, believers as well as unbelievers. In my experience, people avoid having any meaningful contact with perennial whiners, especially in the workplace, simply because they don't want to become embroiled in the associated negativity.

We need to examine and scrutinize the language we use and the self-talk we allow to occur in our presence, remembering that we're always in the presence of the Holy Spirit.

In Philippians 2:12-16 (quoted below from *The Amplified Bible*), Paul gives probably the soundest advice anywhere about how Christians should conduct themselves in their workplace. Paul goes to great lengths in each verse in that passage.

First he encourages believers to work out their salvation in such a manner that their conduct does not offend God or discredit the name of Christ:

> Therefore, my dear ones, as you have always obeyed [my
> suggestions], so now, not only [with the enthusiasm you

would show] in my presence but much more because I
am absent, work out [cultivate, carry out to the goal, and
fully complete] your own salvation with reverence and
awe and trembling [self-distrust, with serious caution,
tenderness of conscience, watchfulness against temptation,
timidly shrinking from whatever might offend God
and discredit the name of Christ]. (Philippians 2:12)

Paul would have us recognize that God's work within us gives us the
power and the desire to carry out His will:

[Not in your own strength], for it is God who is
all the while effectually at work in you [energizing
and creating in you the power and desire], both
to will and to work for His good pleasure and
satisfaction and delight. (Philippians 2:13)

He encourages believers to have a good attitude and work ethic, which
essentially means keeping a check on our words and actions before men
and God. He also encourages us to recognize that grumbling, fault-finding,
and complaining are negative character qualities that are not based on faith,
hope, or love—and as such, they should not be embraced by people who
profess to be Christian believers:

Do all things without grumbling and fault-finding
and complaining [against God] and questioning and
doubting [among yourselves]… (Philippians 2:14)

Paul goes on to encourage us to maintain a credible and consistent testimony before all men and to appear as shining lights—as the go-to people in the midst of a generation that generally knows little about God:

> …that you may show yourselves to be blameless and
> guileless, innocent and uncontaminated, children
> of God without blemish [faultless, unrebukable]
> in the midst of a crooked and wicked generation
> [spiritually perverted and perverse], among whom you
> are seen as bright lights [stars or beacons shining out
> clearly] in the [dark] world… (Philippians 2:15)

The apostle then encourages believers to be ready to offer the gospel message to all men. This is the greatest gift a person could ever be given—and if received, it will have eternal consequences on the coming day of Christ's return:

> …holding out [to the world] and offering [to all
> people] the Word of Life, so that in the day of Christ
> I may have something of which exultantly to rejoice
> and glory in that I did not run my race in vain or
> spend my labor to no purpose. (Philippians 2:16)

From my experience, many workplaces are far from ideal working environments, and the extent to which you can let your light shine may vary considerably. However, we need to be determined to continually pray and entrust our situations to God, and then follow a faith-filled course of action that will ultimately shape our testimony before men and show how brightly our stars are shining.

Lifestyle to Match the Message

I've had both management and workers say to me—as they comment on someone's poor work performance— "And he calls himself a Christian."

We need to understand that outsiders will always be ready to criticize if we wear the Christian label but our lifestyle doesn't match their perception of Christianity. In some cases, their criticism is quite valid. In fact, the unbecoming behavior of some undisciplined Christians can become a source of embarrassment to other believers in the same workplace who are trying to live an exemplary lifestyle.

It's quite interesting that we're often judged by outsiders and even by Christians who are looking through eyeglasses that may have religious filters. When this occurs, we need to be careful that we aren't the ones trying to pick the speck out of someone else's eye while having a log in our own (Matthew 7:2-4).

The Pharisees and teachers of the law missed the purpose and plan for "times of refreshing from the Lord" (Acts 3:18-19) that God had foretold through the prophets; they missed it because of their unwillingness to change their ways, even though the Messiah was ushering in the greatest spiritual awakening in the history of mankind.

Their legalism effectively put the Messiah to death, because the message of truth that He brought—through His intimate relationship with the Father—was based on faith and never on a legalistic set of rules.

When someone raises the topic of Christianity or is criticizing a professing Christian, I try to use that as a starting point for a conversation. While it's important to distance yourself from "bad" behavior, it's also important to gently correct uninformed or narrow-minded religious observations that bear little resemblance to the teachings of Christ.

If we really see ourselves as the redeemed of the Lord, we should be what Demos Shakarian referred to in the title of his bestselling book: *The Happiest People on Earth.*

As Christian believers, our beliefs should reflect these understandings:

- We're no longer bound by the curse of sin and death that results in eternal damnation and separation from God.
- Jesus Christ came to this earth as the "good news" message from His Father.
- This message is that the Father had sent His Son to pay the price for the sins of all mankind by dying on a cross—and that as a result, whoever would believe in Him could have eternal life.
- Before He ascended into heaven, Jesus commissioned all believers to be His witnesses and ambassadors on this earth and to go into all of our world to preach the good news, to make disciples, to baptize them in the name of the Father, Son, and Holy Ghost, and to expect to see signs and wonders following.
- All believers were given authority from Jesus Christ Himself to do these things and to take dominion over creation as God had originally intended.
- We're to pray, "Your will be done on earth, as it is in heaven" with heartfelt conviction that God is with us in whatever we do, for He said, "Never will I leave you, never will I forsake you!" (Hebrews 13:5).

Friends, we need to know what we believe and why—and to be able to share it with conviction. You never know when you may need to give an account of your faith, so be ready at all times, looking for a *kairos* opportunity to come your way.

Ready: In Season and Out

I can remember one night, when I was doing street outreach ministry in Brisbane, and I was in the same car park of the local community center where I'd met the heroin addict Daniel (who I mentioned earlier), and where I used to meet with a number of street kids. Suddenly the most well-known drug dealer in the area arrived in a black limousine. He was sitting in the back, in a wheelchair, behind the chauffeur.

The car pulled up right next to where I was standing, and the dark-tinted electric window rolled down.

"You got two minutes," he said. "Tell me what you believe and why."

What would you say if someone posed that question to you?

Let me tell you that religious jargon goes right out the window when you're confronted with a question of this kind. You have to be real and get right to the point, or you have no chance of influencing people for Jesus Christ.

To say the least, my Holy Spirit-inspired response both shocked and challenged him to the core of his being, because he had massive need in his life, and Jesus held the answer.

Until that day I'd never seen or met this drug dealer, but he knew who I was, and strangely enough I immediately knew who he was without any form of introduction.

Think about these things the next time you enter your workplace or market place and begin looking for *kairos* opportunities or God encounters to take place. I can speak from experience when I say that you never know who might be sitting, standing, walking, eating, chatting, daydreaming, or beside themselves with worry—and they wind up right next to you because God wants to use you to engage with them.

I believe that these God encounters are meant to be a regular part of His purpose and plan for every one of us. There's absolutely no doubt that God is capable of arranging our circumstances for this to occur, for Scripture declares, "The steps of a good man [or woman] are ordered by the Lord" (Psalm 27:23).

The question for professing believers is this: Are we open to these opportunities? Are we willing to make time available? Are we willing to listen to the Holy Spirit for direction, and ready to follow His leading and desire to set the captives free, to bind up the brokenhearted, to love the unlovely, and to help the lost become found?

God has called us to be the good Samaritan to our neighbors. This is how we're meant to do life. We're not to simply hang on until Jesus returns; rather, we're to impact our world to usher in the return of the Lord Jesus Christ.

About Priorities

How can our light shine if we're not making a difference in the lives of those we rub shoulders with daily? How can we become the salt of the earth if we aren't providing compelling evidence of Christ living in us and influencing others toward the kingdom of God?

I'm one of the busiest people I know, but I never neglect my time of daily devotions with the Lord, and the importance of this time escalates when I'm extra busy. I've come to understand that He *does* order my footsteps, and that we've all received an anointing from the Holy One of Israel to do His will.

It's His desire that we be successful in all that we do. And much of what we actually do or achieve in life really comes down to a matter of priorities.

A parable Jesus told about a great banquet (in Luke 14:15-24) is a story about priorities. Those who were invited (representing those claiming to have a relationship with God) found excuses not to attend the banquet, and it caused the banquet host to say, "I tell you, not one of those men who were invited will taste my banquet" (Luke 14:24).

Jesus followed this story with some teaching about the cost of being a disciple and about "good" salt (Luke 14:25-35). This was no coincidence, because Jesus was challenging us about our priorities in life. When He spoke earlier to His disciples about priorities and commitment, He stated this expectation: "If anyone would come after Me, he must deny himself and take up his cross daily and follow Me" (Luke 9:23).

These compelling words deliver a significant personal challenge to every professing believer to follow in the footsteps of Jesus Christ.

What Are Your Default Thoughts?

I've often been asked, "How do I know where my heart is with God?"

When I hear this type of question, I usually ask them about their default thinking, and I say something like this: "The things you consider, ponder, or hold as most important are where we'll spend most of our free time either thinking or doing or both." If your thoughts gravitate toward the kingdom of God, this is a good thing. If they're continually consumed by worldly matters or success (however that may be defined), then our wrong priorities are being revealed.

The apostle Paul spent his early years enveloped with study, ideology, and tireless zeal. He acquired much knowledge and climbed the ranks within his chosen profession as a Pharisee. But listen to the higher perspective he later attained about his meteoric promotions, his influence, and the sense of importance it all once seemed to carry:

But whatever things were gain to me, those things I have
counted as loss for the sake of Christ. More than that,
I count all things to be loss in view of the surpassing
value of knowing Christ Jesus my Lord, for whom I
have suffered the loss of all things, and count them but
rubbish so that I may gain Christ. (Philippians 3:7-8)

Paul knew only too well the importance of valuing his time here on earth, and he unquestionably had this in mind when he told the church at Ephesus, "Be very careful, then, how you live—not as unwise but as wise, making the most of every opportunity ["redeeming the time," KJV], because the days are evil" (Ephesians 5:15-16).

My main focus is the market place, but the apostle's words about making the most of every opportunity should resonate in the hearts and minds of every believer as we journey through life.

It only takes an occasional attendance at a funeral to drive home the reality that our time here on earth is finite. Our days are numbered. So if we want to make the most of every opportunity for the kingdom of God, today is always open to be a day of new beginnings.

The apostle Paul's new beginning started on the road to Damascus when he had an encounter with the risen Christ. After the scales fell off his eyes and he was filled with the Holy Spirit (Acts 9:17-18), Paul went on to be the greatest soul-winner of his day.

Paul's encounter changed the course of his life from that day forward. He never forgot his God encounter, and he freely shared his testimony to all who would listen.

His testimony of conversion is repeatedly recorded—in chapters 9, 22, and 26 of the book of Acts—as a witness to all mankind. Metaphorically, his story speaks about mankind's desire to achieve, to climb the ladder of success and influence, and to reach the heights of whatever our heart might be set upon.

However, Paul's quest was far nobler than any secular occupation because he honestly believed he was following a heavenly calling while he was advancing through the ranks of Judaism. But Paul found his true calling and the real meaning of life only when he had an encounter with Jesus Christ, the risen Lord. After this encounter, Paul could clearly see for the first time God's purpose and plan for his life.

Paul never ceased sharing about his personal encounter with others for the remainder of his life, and upon hearing his testimony, countless others had their spiritual eyes opened as they came to believe in the Savior of the world.

Seeing through Eyes of Faith

We need to see our market places through the eyes of faith, because this vast field of people will offer some of the greatest opportunities for God encounters to take place.

Whether we're on our way to work, or at lunch, or sitting in a board meeting, when we present ourselves as His ambassadors, God delights to show Himself strong. I've experienced some of the most incredible miracles while sitting around boardroom tables by receiving a word of knowledge or of wisdom (1 Corinthians 12:8) that unlocks a difficult or gridlocked situation for God's glory. I speak more about this in Chapter 17.

In business offices, I've witnessed people being miraculously healed either physically or emotionally through prayer. I've also led many people into a born-again experience, and I've spoken many words of life to others. There's no limit to our ministry—if we're prepared to trust God and allow Him to direct our paths.

There have been countless times that I've undertaken hospital visits to pray for and offer comfort to the extended family of CEOs, company staff, or their friends. The opportunity to do so arose simply because I'd taken the time to build a bridge of friendship as an ambassador for Jesus Christ.

Bernie's Story

Not long ago, I visited a friend who was seriously ill in hospital. Bernie was a lovable, larger-than-life character who'd been diagnosed with cancer about six months prior.

When I visited Bernie, he was only the shell of the man I used to work with. He'd lost around thirty kilograms, but his spirit was still strong.

We began to talk. Bernie told me that many people had come to visit—"But they stand at the door and don't know what to say."

I told Bernie, "I have no trouble with that."

He smiled, no doubt wondering what I was about to say. "Hey, Bernie," I said, "I love you, man. You're my friend." Then I began to tell Bernie about a lady named Sue who had come to my wife's birthday party a few weeks prior. As I saw Sue walking along the food line, I happened to comment, "Sue, you don't seem to have much on your plate." She told me she couldn't eat any more than that because she had a kinked bowel. "I'm fed up with doctors," she said. "I've been to them all, and they haven't been able to help me one iota. If I eat any more than this, I wind up in terrible pain. It has driven me crazy for the last three months."

I smiled and asked, "Would you like me to pray for you?"

"Someone told me I should come and see you," she answered. We agreed to catch up toward the end of the party for prayer.

Later, we met in my office, where I began by sharing part of my own Damascus road experience with her. I told her about some of the miraculous things I'd just witnessed on a recent trip with Planetshakers Church to Papua New Guinea.

Sue shared with me that her only Christian education was through Sunday school until she was about ten years of age, but she always believed in God.

I asked Sue if she had faith the size of a mustard seed (Matthew 17:20), because that was all our Lord had said she needed to be healed. She said, "Yes."

I anointed Sue with oil in the name of the Lord Jesus Christ, after explaining that the anointing oil symbolized the power of the Holy Spirit to heal. I began to pray, and a few moments later I simply commanded the kinked bowel to unravel, in the name of Jesus Christ.

When this happened, Sue immediately exclaimed with a loud gasp, "Oh," as she could feel something instantly happen inside her stomach.

We left my office, and for the next thirty minutes before she left the party, Sue told everyone who was still there, "Look at my stomach. I haven't felt like this for months." Over the next few hours, Sue continued to experience this sign and wonder, at the end of which she was totally healed.

Bernie was amazed by this testimony, but then I told him about how, when I next caught up with Sue a few weeks later, she wanted to make her peace with God. It was then that I led her in a prayer to become born again, and I explained to Bernie what this meant.

I then told Bernie, "When I go to heaven, I want as many of my friends to be there with me as possible, and that includes you." I asked Bernie if he would like to pray with me, like I had prayed with Sue.

Bernie immediately said yes. I led him in a prayer to receive Jesus Christ as his Lord and Savior.

I told Bernie that as we were praying, there was a party going on in heaven because the angels are rejoicing before the throne of God that another lost soul had been added to the kingdom of God.

I thank God for this precious time I spent with Bernie, because within two weeks, Bernie's body gave way to cancer and he passed into eternity.

At the time I told Bernie, "You might not fully appreciate the decision you've just made, but you'll know for sure later that this is the most import-ant decision a person can ever make."

When I attended Bernie's funeral, I knew many people there. They worked in the bus and coach industry in which I mainly work, and many already knew that I'd been to visit Bernie and how it had impacted his life.

I'll never forget the words of Bernie's partner, Ann, at the end of the funeral. Ann told me that Bernie kept talking about my visit and how he had made his peace with God. Every night Bernie would ask Ann to read to him from a Planetshakers book called *Eternity*, which friends of mine had left when they visited Bernie a few days after my visit. *Eternity* talks about our decision to follow Christ and where we'll spend eternity.

The Word of God had indeed impacted Bernie, and this precious soul who was lost was now found.

He had been blind, like all of humanity is without Christ—but now he could see.

Hope Restored

Regardless of a person's beliefs or values, the one thing I've come to know is that when the chips are down, people need to have their hope restored. This includes atheists, agnostics, Christian believers, and every-thing in between.

I know that Jesus Christ is the greatest source of abundant life and hope, and He loves all people of all kinds. Through His sacrifice on the cross of Calvary, we're able to bring hope to a dying world.

My heart still sings as I remember the words of sincere gratitude a friend once penned to me after I prayed for his dying dad. My friend was the CEO of a company that I consulted for. He was a hardened atheist, but he deeply loved his dad.

Doctors offered no hope. His dad's condition was terminal. His dad was told to put his house in order.

After I prayed, God answered my request, and his dad was granted another six months of life before finally passing.

My friend was able to spend quality time with his dad, and he knew that God had answered my prayer.

I'm still touched by the memory of all this, but much more by the words of gratitude from my friend—who'd experienced a work of grace in his life, and in his own way was giving glory back to God.

9

The Place of Abiding

As I was drawing the previous chapter to a close, I was encouraged by the Holy Spirit to write about "abiding," and the following words of Jesus figured prominently in His encouragement to me:

If you abide in Me, and My words abide in you, ask
whatever you wish, and it will be done for you. My
Father is glorified by this, that you bear much fruit,
and so prove to be My disciples. (John 15:7-8 NASB)

It's my belief that anyone serious about living a faith-filled life is also keen on bearing fruit for the kingdom of God—fruit that will last and stand the test of time. According to Scripture, this can happen only if we "abide in Him."

A few years ago, our family lived on acreage and had a small orchard with a number of fruit trees. We lived in a subtropical climate, so the trees were prolific in growing and producing fruit during the winter months.

I carefully observed over many years that the best fruit is always found out on a limb, which starts off as a tender shoot and over time grows into a fruit-bearing branch. Toward harvest time, these limbs are often pulled almost vertical toward the ground, hanging down with the weight of the fruit. When you see these limbs straining under the weight of the fruit, the sight brings great joy, because your efforts of husbandry are being rewarded with abundance.

In the same way that abundant fruit is produced in the natural, so it is with the spiritual.

What an incredible picture this paints of the times we step out in faith to do exploits for God—and a soul is saved, a distraught person is encouraged, a broken heart is mended, a serious illness is healed, or a captive is set free. This is why the Savior came to earth—to bring good news.

We need to realize that every time we step out in faith, we're going out on a limb for a heavenly cause, and we're building the kingdom of God. Spiritually, the limb speaks of a place of new growth. The more we go there, the more fruit (fullness) we'll find, and the stronger we'll become to carry the weight of the purpose and plans that God has anointed us to accomplish.

On occasion I've personally witnessed miracles so amazing that I lost my appetite for earthly food, just as Jesus did when He was incredibly touched by the faith of the woman at the well (John 4:31-32).

Oh what joy there must be for our Lord and His angels, looking from the other side of a miracle, when the saints of God step out in faith into the supernatural!

Whenever the Holy Spirit is involved, I always have an expectation of fruit happening and remaining. When we're born again, we cannot help but bear fruit for God, provided we walk in His ways and follow Him with all of our heart. This is known as *abiding* in Him.

In fact, as we encounter God, every provision is made for our life to be transformed—so that the apostle Paul could confidently say, "I have been crucified with Christ, and I no longer live, but Christ lives in me. The life

I live in the body, I live by faith in the Son of God, who loved me and gave Himself up for me" (Galatians 2:20).

Likewise when the writer of the book of Hebrews spoke about Jesus's journey to the cross, he referred to the "joy that was set before Him" (Hebrews 12:2). While we should never forget that Jesus endured the cross to give His life to save ours, I'm confident that the joy being referred to—at least in part—was in knowing that His disciples would one day walk in His footsteps and bring forth abundant fruit by stepping out in faith, empowered by the inner working of the same Holy Spirit who would raise Him from the dead (Ephesians 3:20).

The place of abiding spoken of in John 15:8 is where the evidence of discipleship is bringing forth abundant fruit to the Father's glory. It's also where obedience to the Word of the Lord becomes the norm. It is our coming to the realisation that apart from Him, we can do nothing.

The Deception of Divided Loyalties

Ultimately, divided loyalties are the root cause of those who claim to be subjects of the kingdom but in practice are often too busy or otherwise engaged to be fruitful for the kingdom of God. This speaks of the kind of wasted talents we discussed earlier.

The sad thing is that many people—including many business people—have an incredible capacity to bear the type of fruit that does *not* remain or have eternal benefit.

According to the Scriptures, the only fruit that really matters is that which impacts people's lives for Jesus Christ during our time here on earth, because this fruit can have eternal consequences.

Jesus gave the clearest illustration of abiding in Him through the timeless principle expressed in these words: "If anyone wants to come after Me, he must deny himself and take up his cross ["daily," Luke 9:23] and follow Me. For whoever wants to save his life will lose it, but whoever loses his life for My sake and for the gospel will save it" (Mark 8:34-35).

True discipleship involves a divine exchange—His life for our life. We're to deny ourselves and take up our crosses daily and follow Him.

As disciples, we're meant to impact our world by reproducing fruit after our own kind. This simply means making disciples of other men and women.

Taking Love to a New Level

The place of abiding takes love to a new level, where the commandment to love your neighbor as yourself (Leviticus 19:18) is exchanged with the command from Jesus to "love one another, as I have loved you" (John 15:12).

This progression of demonstrated love to others speaks figuratively of the cross that Jesus told His disciples to take up and follow Him on a daily basis. More than this, the standard by which we're to love our neighbors is lifted from an emphasis on how much we might love ourselves to the place of loving each other as Christ has loved us.

Perhaps more than any other Christian teaching, this command is one of the greatest challenges to every generation, because Jesus effectively redefined how we're meant to love our fellow man. Jesus then revealed the extent of His love—not only by washing His disciples' feet, but also by speaking prophetically into their lives to prepare them for future ministry.

Little did they know that within hours of this conversation, Jesus would become the greatest love gift mankind has ever received. "Greater love has no one than this," Jesus had said, "that he lay down his life for his friends" (John 15:13)—and those words not only set the scene for the cross, but also reset the benchmark for *agapé*, the God kind of love we're called and enabled to demonstrate toward others.

In the market place where many Christians dwell on a weekday basis, there's such a great emphasis on self-promotion that many people find themselves on the corporate treadmill of success, promotion, and networking only to discover—years later—that every level holds an illusion of greater happiness and joy that simply doesn't exist.

Looking back, I've had people tell me that they were much happier when they had little. Regrettably, it often takes a lifetime to discover that having more doesn't make you happy. Giving more is the only thing that really satisfies, because it reflects the very nature and character of God.

I rub shoulders with some very wealthy people as well as some very poor people, and I can assure you that having more (or less) money doesn't automatically equate to higher levels of happiness.

Jesus spoke about this in the parable of the sower when He described a heart that's preoccupied with the worries and cares of this life, the deceitfulness of wealth, and the desire for other things. The subtlety of these competing desires for material things—being preoccupied with anything other than God —is what lures mankind into a false sense of security about achieving greater happiness.

The reality is that most people are still choosing to eat the forbidden fruit of self-dependence that shifts one's focus away from the kingdom of God. This shift in focus toward material things chokes the Word of God, making it unfruitful in people's lives.

The irony of seed being sown among thorns is that they all grow up together, but it's not until harvest time that the verdict of "unfruitful" becomes fully evident. This is a subtle deception, and the result is a failure to achieve God's purposes for one's life.

Contextually, this is similar to the parable of the ten virgins in Matthew 25:1-13. The five foolish virgins found out too late that the Bridegroom (Jesus) would greet them with the revelation, "I tell you the truth, I don't know you" (Matthew 25:12).

This deception is very powerful. Regrettably, many Christians live unfruitful lives because they get so caught up on the treadmill of success, which elevates the things of this world above the things of God.

Jesus warned His followers about this type of deception on many occasions. He knew that subtlety was how mankind was first seduced in the garden in Eden, and we're still fighting against the same enemy of souls—Satan—who's relentless in trying to destroy the work of God wherever he can.

For Christians who are kingdom focused, the remedy to this deception is both obvious and profound. You simply cannot be deceived by some "thing" unless you put your trust in it.

By way of contrast, here is Jesus's perspective on how we should live our lives: "Seek first His kingdom and His righteousness, and *all these things* will be added to you" (Matthew 6:33). In God's upside-down world, it's by seeking first His kingdom that we're blessed and all our needs are met on a daily basis.

Incidentally, "all these things" mentioned here by Jesus are the things that the pagan (nonbelieving) world is running after, instead of making the kingdom of God their priority in life (Matthew 6:25-32).

What Constitutes Real Happiness?

From a market place perspective, the tyranny of time, the deceitfulness of power, and the allurement of prestige and greater wealth all hide under the presumption of increased happiness.

The reality lurking behind this deception is that everything comes at a price.

From corporate executive right through to base-grade workaholic, the immediate cost is to our families and friends. However, it goes much deeper than this, because living with divided loyalties also chips away at our life purpose and personal integrity.

In truth, there's a spiritual void within all mankind that only God can fill, but people will always try to fill it with all kinds of other things that never really satisfy the true longings of the soul.

I've often asked the how-much-is-enough question of wealthy business-men who struggle with these issues, only to find that they generally have to run off to their next business meeting.

From a scriptural perspective, the church of Jesus Christ is planted somewhere between the thorny soil and the good soil described in the parable of the sower. The other two soils simply don't sustain spiritual life.

Regardless of our position, title, rank, or status in life, we all need a moment of truth when we ask ourselves, Where am I in terms of personal fruitfulness for the kingdom of God? If you speak to ministers, they'll generally tell you that the Pareto principle applies to much of church life—that about twenty percent of the people do about eighty percent of the work. If this statement bears any resemblance to truth in terms of church life, then it's hard to imagine what God's people might be doing during the week in terms of evangelistic activity and making disciples in the market place, where many believers spend the majority of their time apart from being at home.

The parable of the sower clearly shows that the spiritual growth of every believer is directly related to the condition of their heart. As such, it's the heart that determines the ability to generate supernatural increase from what is sown into people's lives through the Word of God.

Incidentally, the parable of the sower is one of only seven parables that appear in all three synoptic Gospels (Matthew, Mark, and Luke), and it's the only parable among those seven that draws a correlation between the state of people's hearts and their receptivity to the gospel message.

So Let's Do Some Digging

As with most things of God, the first time something is mentioned in Scripture, it often carries a deeper purpose which is often veiled but can be found if you dig a bit deeper.

Not surprisingly, Genesis—the book of beginnings—offers amazingly similar themes to both the parable of the sower and the place of abiding in Him. For example, when God created man on the sixth day, the first command He gave was to be fruitful and multiply.

Like any good father, God immediately provided food for His family: "I give you every seed-bearing plant on the face of the whole earth and every tree that has fruit with seed in it. They will be yours for food" (Genesis 1:29). When God created mankind, He also provided seed-bearing plants to reproduce after their own kind and provide a continuous supply of food.

The Genesis account reveals that the Lord God planted a garden in Eden and caused all kinds of trees to grow out of the ground to become mankind's food supply. Then He placed Adam in the garden to cultivate it and keep it (Genesis 2:8-9). After this, God gave a command to Adam about what food he should eat and what food was forbidden. Other food was available, but God set a boundary for the good of mankind. In making known His command, God also indicated the consequences of disobedience to it:

> From any tree of the garden you may eat freely;
> but from the tree of the knowledge of good and
> evil you shall not eat, for in the day that you eat
> from it you will surely die. (Genesis 2:16)

Up until this point, the paradise of God was producing fruit and replenishing itself supernaturally, requiring little apparent effort from Adam. Before Adam and Eve entertained the lies of the serpent (Satan), they were without sin and in regular fellowship with their heavenly Father, and they could have lived in this state for eternity (Genesis 3:22) had they not disobeyed the command of God.

It was only after they ate the forbidden fruit, that their eyes were opened and they realized their nakedness and tried to cover themselves. This act of disobedience set the scene for an immediate shift in the spiritual climate in Eden, which led to mankind's expulsion from the garden.

Although this may have appeared harsh, their eviction from Eden was an act of tremendous mercy by God. For had they not been banished from Eden, they could have eaten from the tree of life and been sealed in an unholy state and eternally separated from God.

It's obvious that Adam and Eve, after eating the forbidden fruit, did not die physically but spiritually—they were cut off from God as if dead. In order to redeem mankind, it would take the second Adam (1 Corinthians 15:45) sent from heaven—in the form of the Messiah, Jesus Christ, the Son of God—to bring mankind back into close fellowship with the Lord God.

One consequence of Adam's disobedience was that the law of sin and death came into existence. Man's days were renumbered to seventy years (or more, by the grace of God, following the introduction of the law of Moses), and after physical death everyone is to face judgment and give an account of their life on earth before a holy God (Revelation 20:12-13). This is orthodox Christian theology, and is ageless in its application.

Because of Adam's disobedience, God spoke judgment upon the man:

> Cursed is the ground because of you; in toil you
> will eat of it all the days of your life. Both thorns
> and thistles it shall grow for you; and you will
> eat the plants of the field. (Genesis 3:17-18)

Adam's deception led to the ground being cursed and to mankind being relegated to painful toil for producing his food. Also, the land would produce thorns and thistles as a constant reminder of the horrific consequences of man's disobedience to God, otherwise known as sin.

Jesus used the parable of the sower to demonstrate that seed sown on thorny ground carries the same type of curse (no fruit for the kingdom of God) that comes from disobedience to God's command, and stands in direct opposition to the place of abiding in Him.

The place of "abiding in Him" (John 15:7-8) also contains some amazing parallels to God's intent for mankind at the beginning of creation. Both were intended to be a place of obedience, a place of fruitfulness, and a place where choices determine destiny (Genesis 1–2; John 15:1-8).

While the first Adam made a bad choice and plunged all creation into chaos, the second Adam—Jesus Christ—was sent to break the curse of sin and death through His atoning, sacrificial death on the cross of Calvary.

There's little doubt that Satan's final parting act was to inspire Jesus's captors to weave a crown of thorns (as a reminder of the cursed and fallen state of mankind) to inflict maximum pain and suffering and to mock His claim to authority as the promised Messiah, the Son of God.

Satan had no clue that Jesus of Nazareth would be resurrected from the dead, but this single event not only shifted the spiritual climate of the entire planet, it changed the course of history for all time and eternity.

By conquering death, Jesus set in place a plan for the redemption of mankind. In that plan, people are given power to choose their own destiny, which included belief in the Savior.

When Jesus made the following promise to His disciples, He was also resetting the pattern for all future believers to be able to align themselves with God's original intention for mankind (as revealed at creation):

> If you abide in Me, and My words abide in you, ask
> whatever you wish, and it will be done for you. My
> Father is glorified by this, that you bear much fruit,
> and so prove to be My disciples. (John 15:7-8 NASB)

"Abiding in him" is declared here by Jesus to be first and foremost a place of obedience to God's Word. Emanating from this are both provision and fruitfulness.

Notice that it's the bearing of much fruit that brings glory to the Father, and this is also a sign of discipleship.

Jesus then went a step further by introducing kingdom principles in His teaching which underpinned the spirit and intent of the law. These principles give much needed understanding of God's Word, and at the same time expose the practices of religion being based on external observation of regulations and laws, while internally people's hearts were elsewhere.

Perhaps the most challenging kingdom principle that Jesus introduced involved the alignment of faith and obedience to God's Word through the principle of seeking first God's kingdom and His righteousness (Matthew 6:33). This principle ultimately requires repentance from everything we treasure or value more highly than our love for God. It gives no place to building our own kingdom first and then asking for God's blessing when the treasure of our heart is residing elsewhere.

It's unquestionable from Scripture that we need to be born again to enter through the narrow door (Matthew 13:22-30) into the kingdom of God. The key to open that door requires faith as the central element.

However, due to mankind's fall from grace in the garden in Eden, we're all born into this world spiritually dead and separated from God. Our default state for journeying through this life relies primarily upon logic and reason working together with our five senses.

Faith Is the Key

Regrettably, our default state will often steer us away from the pathway of faith and belief in God, because it makes no sense to an unbeliever to walk by faith and not by sight.

This struggle is somewhat understandable, because our entire education system uses scientific reasoning as the basis for measurement, and the level of academic achievement is typically used as the gauge of success in today's society.

From our early years, just about everything is centered on education and learning outcomes in preparation for adulthood. Our society typically defines adult success by the amount of assets and wealth a person acquires throughout their lifetime—things such as houses, investments, superannuation, and cash in the bank. Also included are the kind of cars a person drives, the schools their children attend, the social groups they mix with, their holiday locations, the restaurants they frequent, the invitations they receive, where they shop, and even the clothes they wear.

But in a parable about a rich fool (in Luke 12:13-21), Jesus made it clear that a man's life does not consist in the abundance of his possessions. In fact, what we accumulate on earth will become someone else's possession as we pass from this life into eternity.

The reality is that we all came into this word with nothing, and we'll all leave the same way. Jesus took this thought to another level when He said, "What does it profit a man to gain the whole world, yet forfeit his soul?" (Mark 8:36). Where we spend eternity will have nothing to do with how much money or possessions we have when we depart from this life, but it will have everything to do with whether or not we have excepted Jesus Christ as our Lord and Savior.

Once a decision is made to believe in Jesus Christ, our reward in heaven will largely depend on how we've used our wealth, resources, talents, gifts, and abilities during our lifetime on earth.

The question will be: Have we been sowing our seed into only this life, or are we laying up for ourselves treasures in heaven as well as building God's kingdom here on earth? In practical terms, the faith being described means seeking God rather than the things of this world in order to have our daily needs met.

Jesus taught His disciples not to run after or worry about the things sought by the pagan world (unbelievers), because our heavenly Father already knows our needs, and if we put our trust in Him, He will reveal Himself as our Provider (Matthew 6:25-34).

Jesus also identified the root cause of mankind's worry about material things as a lack of faith in God. We must believe first and foremost that He exists (Hebrews 11:6), and second that He desires a personal relationship with all mankind (James 4:5)—a desire that has never waned from the time of creation.

Because of God's great mercy, love, and compassion, He sought a way to restore that which had been lost in Eden. He immediately put a plan in place for mankind's redemption, and this became the central theme of all Scripture from the moment the law of sin and death entered the world in the garden in Eden.

This theme has echoed hope to a lost humanity ever since.

The good news is that Jesus Christ paid the ransom price for our redemption through His sacrificial death on the cross. When Jesus rose from the dead, the curse of the law of sin and death was broken, and the same Holy Spirit power that raised Christ from the dead now lives in all those who put their trust in Him.

Because Jesus was raised from the dead, all who believe in Him are able to receive eternal life. This promise is revealed in what's probably the best-known verse in the Bible: "For God so loved the world that He gave His one and only Son that whosoever believes in Him shall not perish but have eternal life" (John 3:16).

All mankind needs to understand that God, who is holy, can do only two things with sin: either judge it, or forgive it. In terms of eternity, our relationship with God while we're here on earth will determine where we'll spend our life beyond the grave. For those who make the choice to believe in Jesus as their Lord and Savior, their sins are forgiven and their future residence in heaven is secure. For those who choose to take their chances and bear their own sin (by not believing in the Savior), Scripture declares that they will spend eternity in hell.

There's no middle ground on this, according to the authorized canon of Scripture. Don't be deceived or misled on this.

God had a plan for the redemption of mankind, and He sent His Son to make sure it happened. Jesus gave His life on the cross in exchange for our life, but this divine exchange requires faith to be activated on our part.

This happens by believing that Jesus is the Son of God, that He died for our sins, and that He rose again. By believing this in our heart and confessing it with our mouth, we're born again.

That's the good news of the gospel message in a nutshell.

Once we commence our faith relationship with God, we're called to discipleship, and we're meant to produce fruit for the kingdom. This is where "abiding in him" can take our faith to new levels. As we walk in faith and obedience to God, He promises to meet our daily needs, and He promises that our life will produce much fruit.

Bearing fruit for the kingdom brings glory to the Father and is evidence that we're His disciples.

10

God Encounters

Think for a moment about the number of stories in the Bible where Jesus or His followers just appeared on the scene, engaged in a conversation—and saw people's lives changed forever.

Let there be no mistake. The God who created the universe ordered the footsteps of those involved, inspired the exchange of words and actions, and took delight when a seed was sown into a person's life so the kingdom of God could be established there. In many instances, the seed immediately took root and the person's life was transformed. Figuratively speaking, the person was harvested into the kingdom.

Across the many encounters recorded in Scripture, the seed often brought with it a challenge to tradition, culture, and religious expectations. The seed also paid no attention to social status, education, or financial prowess. Indeed, it may be said that the seed is the greatest leveler mankind has ever known, because there's only one way for the seed (the Word of God) to take root: through the faith of the hearer.

Christianity teaches that we're all born into this world as sons of Adam, and every person has a spiritual void that only God can fill. The skillful sower recognizes this void and shapes the Word to encourage the hearer to move from a place of dependence on the material (or secular realm) to a place of dependence on the spiritual realm by exercising faith in Jesus Christ.

The moment anyone exercises faith in Jesus Christ, their spirit undergoes a rebirthing process and they're born again and adopted into God's family as a son or daughter (Romans 8:15).

Their Greatest Opportunity

For every inhabitant of our planet, God arranges circumstances so that people from all races, tongues, and nations have an opportunity to reach out and connect with Him at some point during their lifetime. Some people grab hold of this opportunity while others do not. Whatever choice is made, God honors their decision. However, many are unaware that this single decision is the most important they'll ever make, since it holds the key to where they'll spend eternity.

If the choice is made to reject Jesus Christ, the consequence of that decision is to remain a son or daughter of Adam for all eternity—born of the flesh but not of the spirit.

Let there be absolutely no mistake (and I don't want to sugarcoat this part of the message). The decision to reject Jesus Christ means eternal separation from God and spending eternity in hell, a place Jesus described as absolute loneliness, despair, and hopelessness. Jesus also called it a place of "darkness, where there will be weeping and gnashing of teeth" (Matthew 22:13).

We're all born into this world with a propensity to sin which we inherited from Adam, and there's no way to restore our relationship with God other than by recognizing our sin, repenting (turning away from our sin), and seeking God's forgiveness through Jesus Christ.

Biblically speaking, the only way we can spend eternity in heaven with God is to believe in our heart that Jesus is Lord and to confess with our mouth that God raised Him from the dead (Romans 10:9-10) and then follow the teachings of the Word of God. This scripture is often used as the tenet or guiding principle for a prayer of repentance when a person makes a decision of their own free will to commit their life to Jesus Christ.

If you want to get a glimpse of how much God knows about our lives, read Psalm 139. This psalm openly declares God's amazingly intimate knowledge of everything about us—from the time before we were born right through to knowing every word we speak before it leaves our mouth. What an amazing God we serve!

Think on these things as you ponder the following encounters, and pay special attention to how the message was shaped to impact those listening. As you reflect upon the following stories, understand that these God encounters didn't happen by some random act. The people involved were all presented with a seed, and they allowed it to be sown into their lives.

A Burning-Heart Encounter

In Luke 24:13-35 we encounter the story of two men on a journey (from Jerusalem to the village of Emmaus) who met with the resurrected Christ on that road, but who failed at first to recognize Him. Their encounter concluded with the following words spoken by one of the two men who were walking with Jesus: "Were not our hearts burning within us as He spoke with us on the road and opened the Scriptures to us?"

These men recognized Jesus only through the breaking of bread, but even in the lead-up to this moment, they knew there was something incredibly special about the stranger who'd encountered them on the Emmaus road.

Before meeting him, these two men had been agonizing over the events of the last few days in Jerusalem, but they couldn't see the big picture that God had planned and carried out with absolute precision. In their hearts, they were desperately seeking understanding. It was as though all their hopes and dreams had been buried in the tomb where the broken body of Jesus had been laid.

When the "veiled" Jesus came alongside them, the Word of truth was about to be sown into their lives through a massive download of Scripture taken from the Old Testament. This picture had been announced centuries earlier by the prophets, and had been fulfilled through the resurrection of the Lord Jesus Christ. But as yet, the veil of understanding hadn't been lifted from the two men's eyes.

As they walked together along the road to Emmaus, Jesus began to explain to these two men how the shadow of the cross had fallen across every page of the Old Testament. The men listened intently in a desperate attempt to try to make sense of everything that had just happened.

Then Jesus said to them: "How foolish you are, and how slow to believe all that the prophets have spoken! Did not the Messiah have to suffer these things and then enter his glory?" (Luke 24:25-26).

> And beginning with Moses and all the Prophets,
> he explained to them what was said in all the
> Scriptures concerning himself. (24:27)

Luke says that Jesus "explained"—and the Greek word used here conveys a thorough explaining or interpreting, unfolding or expounding the meaning of what is said. While the Scriptures don't provide the exact details of the ensuing conversation, we know that Jesus enlightened these two men about His preexistence and His role throughout the history of mankind.

With the benefit of hindsight and more than two thousand years of biblical study, it's relatively easy for today's Christian believers to understand the following list of appearances, types, or shadows of Jesus Christ throughout the Old Testament. With great certainty, we can postulate that Jesus would have mentioned most or all of these Old Testament realities as pointing to Himself:

- The seed of woman (Genesis 3:15) who will one day crush Satan.
- The ram caught in the thicket that Abraham offered for a burnt offering in the place of his son (Genesis 22:13).
- The Passover lamb, without spot or blemish, offered up for the deliverance of the people of Israel (Exodus 12:22-24).
- The prophet whom Moses said would be greater than himself (Deuteronomy 18:15,18).
- The captain of the Lord's host who met with Joshua (Joshua 5:15).
- The kinsman-redeemer of Ruth's inheritance (Ruth 3–4).
- The scarlet thread hung out the window by Rahab, bringing deliverance to her family and victory to the Israelites (Joshua 2:17-21).
- David, the anointed king of the people, as a picture of Jesus, who was also called the Son of David (1 Samuel 16:13; 2 Samuel 2:4).
- Job the sufferer, who said, "I know my Redeemer lives" (Job 19:15).
- Queen Esther risking her life before the king, as a picture of Christ as the Great High Priest at the right hand of the Father, interceding for His people (Esther 8:3-4).
- The Messiah's appearing many times in the Psalms, most prominently when David describes Him as "my shepherd" (Psalm 23:1).
- Isaiah speaking of the Messiah's miraculous birth (Isaiah 7:14), and speaking also of the Suffering Servant (Isaiah 53:11).
- Jesus as the fourth man in the fiery furnace with Shadrach, Meshach, and Abed-Nego (Daniel 3:19-25).

- Jonah as a picture of Jesus in the tomb for three days, then being raised from the dead to preach a message of repentance (Jonah 1:17, 3:3-10).
- Malachi speaking of Jesus as the sun of righteousness (Malachi 4:2).

This list is only a glimpse at the countless times Jesus Christ appeared as a type or shadow in the Old Testament. So when Jesus lifted the veil off the two men's understanding as they accompanied Him along the twelve kilometers of roadway between Jerusalem and Emmaus, is it any wonder that they confessed, "Were not our hearts burning within us while he talked with us on the road and opened the Scriptures to us?" (Luke 24:32).

They had such a need for understanding and perspective! Then Jesus appeared at precisely the right *kairos* time, and then explained to them everything in the Old Testament Scriptures— "beginning with Moses and all the prophets"—concerning Himself.

He could see the beginning from the end, and now He had opened their minds to the same understanding.

This was no chance encounter. And it speaks of our continual need to rely on God for revelation and understanding of the situations we face on a daily basis, and to be ready for the God encounters He wants to bring across our path.

We need to understand that these encounters typically occur only when we're hungry for the things of God and seek to walk in His footsteps.

God wants to enlarge our perspective to see things the way He does. To achieve this, He has given us the Holy Spirit for fellowship and to speak into our lives on a daily basis—to lead us, guide us, and empower us with His gifts and His desires.

Think for a moment about the incredible testimony of these men whose hearts were burning as He spoke to them, as the shadow of the cross fell upon the Old Testament Scriptures, and then as He finally revealed Himself through the breaking of the bread. This revelation was so great that Luke was inspired by God to include it in the New Testament, to be shared among the nations.

The shadow being cast had one common thread that the wise are always able to grab hold of: *faith* in the Messiah, the Son of God, Jesus Christ.

Are you hungry for the things of God? Are you prepared to step out of your comfort zone, to listen and follow the leading of the Holy Spirit?

If your answer is yes, I encourage you to pray and ask God for opportunities to shape and sow the Word, and also for God encounters, particularly in your market place or workplace, so you can shine brightly for Him.

And never forget: Faith is the key.

Jesus Meets a Woman at a Well

The story of Jesus meeting a woman at a well is told in John 4:3-42. Read that story, then consider the series of events that took place:

- Jesus left Judea to return to Galilee.
- This is the first mention in the New Testament of Jesus or His team traveling into Samaria.
- He arrived at a town called Sychar near Jacob's well about noon, then immediately sent His disciples off into town to buy food.
- Being tired from the journey, He sat down by the well.
- It was about midday, and most likely the weather is hot, so He was thirsty.

The scene is thus set for one of the most amazing God encounters recorded in Scripture. This single encounter ended up bringing an entire town into a spiritual revival.

Jesus began the encounter by breaking with Jewish tradition—first by speaking to a Samaritan, and second by asking a woman who was a stranger for a drink of water (John 4:7).

Her response was most likely one of surprise as well as curiosity when she spoke these words: "How is it that You, being a Jew, ask me for a drink since I am a Samaritan woman?" (John 4:9 NASB).

Remember that although some traditions are timeless and good, Jesus often went out of His way to debunk traditions that robbed people from enjoying God's blessings. Such traditions dictated, "It's always done this way," without the slightest questioning of Why?

Whether it's in the market place or elsewhere, God may ask us to do things that break with the norm or our tradition. The question is, Are we ready and willing to obey?

(Be honest. If we were praying for a blind person, how many of us would really be comfortable if the Holy Spirit said to you, "I want you to spit onto the dust of the ground, make some spittle, and apply it to this person's eyes"?)

There beside the well in Sychar, Jesus chose to whet the Samaritan woman's appetite for spiritual things: "If you knew the gift of God, and who it is that said to you, Give me to drink; you would have asked of him, and he would have given you living water" (John 4:10).

Jesus continued to speak about spiritual things in words that culminate in one of the most revelatory statements in the Bible: "Whosoever drinks of this water shall thirst again. But whosoever drinks of the water that I shall give him shall never thirst; but the water that I shall give him shall be in him a well of water springing up into everlasting life" (John 4:13-14).

The woman responded immediately by saying, "Sir, give me this water, that I thirst not, neither come here to draw" (John 4:15).

We need to realize that mankind is often hungry for spiritual things, a hunger that material things cannot satisfy. King Solomon knew this only too well, for he possessed extensive amounts of shields, horses, wealth, and servants, and had more wives and concubines than any other man in recorded history. But in the end, he looked at his life and attributed all these material things to vanity (Ecclesiastes 1:1).

Jesus often used parables that had a twofold meaning to open the door to further inquiry by those who were serious about wanting a relationship with His Father. Parables and testimonials have the power to change people's thinking. In the market place, I've often used New Testament parables or testimonies of God encounters (my own or other people's) to communicate spiritual truth.

For example, the scales falling from Saul's eyes on the road to Damascus could easily be likened to the paradigm shift that's needed by many older CEOs to fully embrace the technology changes needed for their businesses to be cutting edge into the future. If we can identify something that will challenge another person's thinking or have them question the very things they take for granted in everyday life, more often than not this can give rise to a deeper conversation that sees man as a spiritual being and not just a commodity.

In my own personal encounter with God and the committing of my life to Jesus Christ (which I'll tell about later), it's obvious that I was drawn by the testimony of Leon Patillo in exactly the same way. Leon shared that he had everything money could buy, but there was still something missing.

My own missing piece was the void that only God could fill, through the person of the Lord Jesus Christ coming into my life.

An Amazing Revelation

As the God encounter continued beside the well in Sychar, Jesus came to the point of revealing something about the woman (in John 4:16-18)—a revelation that led to a moment of truth regarding her personal life.

The woman understood immediately that this information could not have been known by natural means, so she immediately confessed: "Sir, I perceive that you are a prophet."

I never cease to be amazed at what the Holy Spirit will reveal to us about people—especially if we ask Him.

A number of years ago we were staying in a caravan park over the Christmas holidays. The spot next to us was occupied by a middle-aged couple who had a young son, probably around ten years of age. I introduced myself and Carmel to them and sought to find out a little of their background.

Harry and Nancy seemed like a nice couple, but there was something about them that I couldn't quite put my finger on. Nancy seemed to want to talk more, but when Harry was around she said little. For several days, Nancy found no opportunity for conversation.

I blended God into our conversations and let them know about our faith in Jesus Christ, but the conversation never went beyond work, children, and the weather. Undeterred, I took the matter to the Lord in prayer, and that night I had a dream about Harry and Nancy.

The next morning, Harry and their son decided to go fishing, which meant that I had a *kairos* opportunity to speak to Nancy by herself.

I invited Nancy into our caravan to join Carmel and me for a cup of tea.

As Nancy was about to sit down, I said "Last night I had a dream about Harry and you, and I would like to share it with you."

Somewhat stunned, Nancy looked at Carmel. "Does he do this often?" she asked. Carmel replied, "Yes. I hate it when he does."

Although an introduction like that does little to inspire your faith, I obtained Nancy's permission, and then told her what I'd been shown by God in the dream. I told her that the Lord had shown me that at one time she and Harry were both devoted and walked in close fellowship with the Lord. In the dream, something had happened in their church, a matter of great upset, and Harry had turned away from the Lord as a result. Although Nancy hadn't turned away from the Lord, I told her that she was now being torn between loyalty to God and to her husband. I then gave her a word from the Lord—saying that He wanted her to return to Him with all her heart.

There was a lot more to it, but that was the gist of the dream and the message.

We all shed many tears that day, and I can testify that Nancy did recommit herself to the Lord. Nancy was touched not just because of what had been spoken; she told me that there was no way I could have known any of what I told her that day. She knew that God was calling her back to Himself, and she was rejoicing in that. Nancy had witnessed God in action in her life through an amazing encounter.

This God encounter happened because I sensed something in my spirit, and dared to inquire further of God.

I could recount many other similar testimonies of how God has revealed things about people at just the right time, particularly in the market place. But the overriding message here is that He wants us to step out in faith and see the power of His Word revealed as people's lives are changed forever.

Too Close to Home

For the woman at the well of Sychar, her discomfort grew as she got deeper into her conversation with Jesus. He was getting too close to home.

She therefore reverted to "religious speak" by telling Jesus, "I know that Messiah is coming (He who is called Christ); when that One comes, He will declare all things to us" (John 4:25). "Religious speak" is so common in our worldly culture today. Rather than address real issues, people try to hide behind a mask of religiosity or spiritual belief and make excuses as to why they should delay their decision about having a serious and intimate relationship with God.

After mentioning the Messiah, the woman at the well heard a response from Jesus that she wasn't planning on. Jesus told her, "I who speak to you am He" (John 4:26).

Once Jesus made this declaration, she had nowhere to hide. With God there is only hot or cold, because lukewarm believers are displeasing God (Revelation 3:14-22).

The woman's response was instant. He had captivated her heart, and she ran into town and told people there, "Come see a man who told me everything I ever did. Could this be the Christ?" Those who heard this also responded immediately: "They came out of the town and made their way toward him" (John 4:29-30).

The result, as we see in John 4:39, was that "many of the Samaritans from that town believed in him because of the woman's testimony, 'He told me everything I ever did.'" We need to understand that nothing is hidden from God. One of the Old Testament names for God is *El Roi*, which means "the God who sees all." He knows all about our past, present, and future.

He also has the ability to send people into our lives so that we may encounter them where they are, at just the right time, to bring much needed revelation—like that which the two men received on the Emmaus road.

God's heart is always to reconnect with His people.

Jesus came into this world to save that which was lost, and this is a vital part of the Great Commission we've been given to carry out until His second coming.

This single encounter between the Messiah and a Samaritan woman set the scene for a spiritual harvest to take place in Sychar. Because God's *kairos* timing is always perfect, this woman's heart was like the good soil. It was ready for a thirty, sixty, or hundredfold crop to be harvested. Whatever God had planned and she responded to in faith would now be accomplished.

An Overriding Message for Future Generations

The very next words of Jesus about what had just happened are as much a challenge to us today as they were that day to His disciples.

Jesus was involved in a deep, life-changing conversation with this woman when his disciples came back from town with some food. Their attitude is simply amazing:

- They question Jesus: "What are you doing talking to a woman, and a Samaritan at that?"
- They could see that He was engaged in conversation with the woman and that she was impacted by what Jesus had to say, yet all they wanted to do was get rid of her.
- This attitude was no different from the disciples' attitude toward the Syro-Phoenician woman whose daughter was demon possessed, when

Jesus also chose to ignore their comments. Instead, when that woman gave a life-changing profession of faith ("Even the dogs eat the children's crumbs under the table"), Jesus responded by working a miracle to set her daughter free (Mark 7:24-30).

I'm sure that many potential God encounters are destroyed by wrong and insensitive attitudes of people—including family and friends—toward the lost and hurting, especially when they approach the situation purely from a judgmental or worldly perspective.

In Touch with the Spiritual

Upon their return to the well outside Sychar, the disciples offered food to Jesus, but He said, "I have food to eat that you know nothing about."

- Jesus was led from above, while His disciples were being led by their stomachs.
- When Jesus saw the reaction of this woman to her Messiah, He was so uplifted in His spirit that any sense of worldly hunger left Him.
- He was filled with the Spirit to the point of overflow, and it is likely that He could barely contain Himself. If you have ever witnessed an absolutely amazing conversion experience, healing, or deliverance, or had an encounter with the Holy Spirit in the miraculous realm, you might get to understand a little of how Jesus may have felt at that moment.
- His hunger for the spiritual far outweighed His natural hunger, to the point that He was not interested in food.
- When Jesus told His disciples, "I have food to eat that you know nothing about," and, "My food is to do the will of Him who sent me and to finish His work" (John 4:32,34), these words were His way of saying these men needed to realize that His mission (and their subsequent

commission) was to get in touch with the spiritual and realize that this would answer all their needs and fulfill their lives in every way possible.

The underlying message Jesus wanted His disciples to grasp is found in His next statement: "Don't you have a saying, 'It's still four months until harvest'? I tell you, open your eyes and look at the fields! They are ripe for harvest" (John 4:35).

When they started the journey from Judea to Galilee and deviated into Samaria, I'm quite sure His disciples were thinking, "Why would the Lord want to go into this God-forsaken place?" Most likely, they wanted to get out of there as quickly as possible, because Jews had no dealings with Samaritans.

In response to this, Jesus told His disciples to open their eyes, because they weren't seeing God's plan of salvation for the Samaritans and the Gentiles. Yet after a few words with a woman who had met and received Jesus as her Messiah, almost the entire population of Sychar was harvested into the kingdom of God.

Jesus's call to His disciples to open their eyes is also a call to every believer. It tells us that there's a harvest of people right in front of us—and most particularly in our market places—who need to be introduced to the Messiah.

If left to their own devices and prejudices, the disciples wouldn't have given this women the time of day. Jesus, however, always went out of His way for the one who became many. And so should we.

In the same way, many believers of our day fail to see that God also has a desire for Jews, Muslims, Jehovah's Witnesses, Mormons, Hindus, Buddhists, people involved in cults, secularists, humanists, agnostics, atheists, academics, intellectuals, and indeed for all creation to be saved and come to the knowledge of Jesus Christ.

We're all on life's journey, and our road may have many intersections, roundabouts, side-roads, and detours. But we need to find the narrow gate and the one-way street that leads to our final destination.

Jesus emphatically described this one-way street in these words: "I am the way, and the truth, and the life; no one comes to the Father but through Me" (John 14:6).

Today, the questions we need to ask ourselves are these:

- Are our eyes open spiritually, or only to the material realm?
- Do we see people all around us who don't know God?
- Are we asking God to use us as part of His end-time harvest, in whatever capacity and with whatever talents and gifts He has given us?

If our response to these questions isn't one of greater desire for the things of God, we need a moment of truth to assess our spiritual temperature on the scale of cold, hot, or lukewarm.

Philip Meets an Ethiopian Businessman

An encounter that the evangelist Philip had with an Ethiopian eunuch (as described in Acts 8:26-39) is best remembered by the response Philip received when he asked the Ethiopian whether he understood the prophecy he was reading from Scripture. He replied, "How can I, unless someone explains it to me?" (Acts 8:31).

The context of this encounter is that Philip had just been involved in an amazing revival in another town in Samaria where crowds of people had been converted to the Christian faith, many paralytics and cripples received healing, and evil spirits came out of many (Acts 8:4-13).

At the height of this revival, the Holy Spirit wanted Philip to meet someone special who could significantly impact the destiny of an entire nation. We read that an angel of the Lord said to Philip, "Get up and go south to the desert road that goes down from Jerusalem to Gaza" (8:26). Although this was desert, Philip obeyed immediately:

> So he started out, and on his way he met an Ethiopian
> eunuch, a court official in charge of the entire treasury
> of Candace, queen of the Ethiopians. He had gone
> to Jerusalem to worship, and on his return was
> sitting in his chariot, reading Isaiah the prophet.
>
> The Spirit said to Philip, "Go over to
> that chariot and stay by it."
>
> So Philip ran up and heard the man reading
> Isaiah the prophet. "Do you understand
> what you are reading?" Philip asked.
>
> "How can I," he said, "unless someone explains it to
> me?" And he invited Philip to come up and sit with
> him. The eunuch was reading this passage of Scripture:
> "He was led like a sheep to the slaughter, and as a lamb
> before the shearer is silent, so He did not open His
> mouth. In His humiliation He was deprived of justice.
> Who can recount His descendants? For His life was
> removed from the earth" [quoting Isaiah 53:78].
>
> "Tell me," said the eunuch, "who is the prophet
> talking about, himself or someone else?" Then
> Philip began with this very Scripture and told him
> the good news about Jesus." (Acts 8:27-35)

Bible scholars have placed the timing of these events at around four to five years after the birth of the early church recorded in Acts 2. Philip was one of seven men who were chosen by the disciples to wait on tables, which released the apostles to the ministry of the Word of God (preaching and teaching) to which they'd been called (Acts 6:1-6). Philip was known among the disciples as someone full of the Spirit and wisdom. All seven of these men were presented to the apostles, who prayed and laid hands on them.

The Greek word used for waiting on tables is *diakoneō* ("to serve"). It means caring for the needs of others in an active, practical way, as the Lord guides. A derivative of this word was used by the apostles when they first began to appoint "deacons" for each assembly, who were effectively ministers in training (1 Timothy 3:8).

To be considered for this role, Philip would have served faithfully for a number of years. He also would have been known as an understudy to the apostles, and would have been thoroughly schooled about the ministry of Christ in the same manner as Stephen, who in Acts 7 had spoken to the Jewish leaders in Jerusalem, which ultimately led to his becoming the first martyr in the New Testament church.

So when the eunuch asked Philip, "Who is the prophet talking about, himself or someone else?" Philip would have been ready to give a good answer. He knew that in Isaiah 53 the prophet was speaking not about himself or another man, but about the Messiah. Although the Messiah's reign had been described in wonderful imagery, He had to suffer before entering into His glory.

Philip would have described the many prophecies fulfilled by Jesus of Nazareth, and how He died on the cross for the salvation of all mankind, and how He rose from the grave and was now exalted to the right hand of

God "as Prince and a Savior, in order to grant repentance and forgiveness of sins to Israel" (Acts 5:31).

The eunuch responded in faith by confessing his belief that Jesus Christ is the Son of God, and he immediately asked for baptism (Acts 5:36-37).

This was one of the most spectacular God encounters mentioned in Scripture. Consider the following:

- An angel gave direction.
- The Holy Spirit guided Philip to go up to the eunuch's chariot and told him to stick to it like glue.
- Philip heard this man reading about the Lamb of God—and he asked him a simple question: Do you know what you're reading?
- An opportunity arose, and starting from that very Scripture, Philip preached Christ to this man.
- The eunuch responded and was immediately baptized.
- Philip was then taken away suddenly, and the eunuch went on his way rejoicing.

The episode ended as mysteriously as it began—with divine guidance and Holy Spirit empowerment. Philip's sudden departure happened through his being miraculously translated (or transported) around fifty kilometers away to the coastal town of Azotus, and there he continued preaching the gospel message before coming to Caesarea.

For experiencing this type of God encounter, the key is to know and hide the Word of God in your heart.

Philip started from the very verse that the Ethiopian was pondering. Philip's recent revival experience was fresh in his mind, and he knew the reality that the Lamb of God who had risen from the dead was the same One whose very words Isaiah had prophesied:

The Spirit of the Lord GOD is on Me,

because the LORD has anointed Me
to preach good news to the poor.
He has sent Me to bind up the brokenhearted,
to proclaim liberty to the captives
and freedom to the prisoners,
to proclaim the year of the LORD's favor
and the day of our God's vengeance. (Isaiah 61:1-2)

Philip knew the reality of the risen Lord. And the power of Holy Spirit was working both in and with him. He knew this reality: "These signs shall follow those who believe" (Mark 16:17). And he went out to do his part in the Great Commission.

What can we take from this story? Friends, if you're hungry for the things of God and willing to pray for keys or openings, the Holy Spirit will bring *kairos* opportunities your way so the Word of God can produce treasures and bring richness to every situation you face.

We need to "dwell in the land and cultivate faithfulness," and God will truly fulfill the desires He has placed in our heart (Psalm 37:3-4 NASB).

The Story Goes On

I could write about many other scenes depicted in the Scriptures. However, it suffices to say that our part in the Great Commission involves our writing the ongoing chronicles of the book of Acts through the way we live our daily lives, and especially through our own God encounters.

As I've said, market place ministry is my passion, but when all is said and done, ministry amounts to little more than being a neighbor to those we meet in our everyday journey through life, and introducing them to our best friend, Jesus Christ.

Is there any greater gift that we could share with our neighbor?

Never forget that Jesus saved the best wine until last. So there's much work yet to do—and the Holy Spirit wants greatly to lead us into God encounters.

All we need to do is ask, pray, prepare, and make ourselves available. The rest is up to God to make the way.

11

Shaping the Word

I n the last chapter, I spoke about Jesus and His disciples engaging in life-changing encounters with everyday people. These people received the Word of God as a seed of faith that went deep into their hearts and took root in good soil.

To deliver an effective message, these skillful sowers shaped the Word in a manner that challenged the mindset of the listener to go beyond logic and reason, into the realm of faith. When this occurred, the listeners positioned themselves for an encounter with God when they believed from their heart.

What can we glean from these examples to help us shape the Word so it touches the heart of the listeners we encounter?

A good starting point is to understand that while the gospel message is relatively simple for believers to understand, it hasn't always been clearly and strongly communicated to a world that's becoming increasing fragmented, messed up, and godless.

Earlier we looked in some detail at the parable Jesus told about the sower and the soils. The following explanatory words Jesus gave about this are worth our closer attention:

> Consider, then, the parable of the sower: When
> anyone hears the message of the kingdom *but does*

not understand it, the evil one comes and snatches
away what was sown in his heart. This is the seed
sown along the path. (Matthew 13:18-19)

Jesus was describing what happens when the message of the kingdom is presented in a manner not easily understood. The consequence is that Satan steals the message before it can take root in the heart.

According to *Strong's Exhaustive Concordance*, the Greek word translated here as "understand" is *suniémi*, which means "to put together, to comprehend; by implication, to act piously—consider, understand, be wise." The *HELPS Word-Studies* take this thought further, indicating that *syníēmi* ("put facts together") means to arrive at a summary or final understanding, complete with life applications. For people's mental comprehension to transform their hearts, they need to be presented with a message they can grasp by putting facts together to come to a final understanding, which is then applied in real-life situations.

The Scriptures reveal that Jesus used parables, stories, and discussions around social issues coupled with signs, wonders, and miracles to build a bridge to connect with people from all walks of life.

Finding a bridge of communication with the people we meet (our neighbors) is what this chapter is about. I wholeheartedly believe that shaping the Word to make it understood by our generation is a significant key to unlocking spiritual renewal across our land.

Shaping the Word simply means saying or doing something to draw someone's attention to the kingdom of God. Often it can take the form of the unexpected or the unfamiliar, but always the intention is to get people to think and put facts together beyond their current circumstance or beliefs about life, and to exercise faith in God through His Son, Jesus Christ.

So let's explore where "shaping the Word" happens in the Scriptures.

Parables

Jesus often shaped the Word through the use of ageless parables. Each parable contained a story, many of which related to both the kingdom of this world and the kingdom of God.

The story would generally contain a dual meaning of obvious and hidden truth to gain the attention of the listener. The listeners were then told, "He who has ears, let him hear" (Mark 4:9). Jesus asked His listeners to use their spiritual ears, not just their natural ears, to hear what the Spirit of God was saying.

Spirit of the Law

Jesus also shaped the Word by rightly applying the spirit and intent of the law to any given situation. He often ventured into the supernatural realm to vindicate what He was saying to onlookers as He demonstrated what the kingdom of God was really like (Luke 13:10-17).

When Jesus was teaching His disciples, He took the law and the prophets and would rightly apply the truth of God's Word. He often spent nights and early mornings in intimate prayer with His Father to ensure that He was correctly applying the Word to every situation.

For example, Jesus would often perform miracles of healing in the synagogue on the Sabbath, in the full knowledge that teachers of the law held a different and distorted view about God's law.

In setting the person free, Jesus opened the congregation's spiritual eyes for them to see that their religious teachers had failed to grasp God's perspective on the rightness of healing a person on the Sabbath.

In the congregation of God's chosen people, such a miraculous healing was both undeniable and attracted everyone's attention. Yet while such incidents appeared to humiliate the Pharisees, their spiritual eyes and their hearts often stayed closed to the possibility that maybe the tradition handed down by the elders had been incorrect or incomplete.

Jesus Knew their Thoughts

Jesus shaped the Word to challenge many practices and prejudices of religious leaders of His day because He "knew their thoughts." Aware of their thoughts, Jesus used the wisdom of God to either correctly interpret Scripture or to rightly judge any given situation.

On one such occasion, a "sinful" woman quietly entered the house of a Pharisee where Jesus was having a meal. Jesus knew exactly what the Pharisee was thinking. He also knew that the Pharisee was blinded by his recognition that "this woman is a sinner," which made it impossible for him to see her acts of repentance.

Using the wisdom of God rather than confronting this prejudice head-on, Jesus told the Pharisee (whose name was Simon) a brief parable about forgiveness (in Luke 7:41-43): "Two men were debtors to a certain moneylender. One owed him five hundred denarii, and the other fifty. When they were unable to repay him, he forgave both of them." Jesus then asked Simon, "Which one, then, will love him more?"

Simon answered, "I suppose the one who was forgiven more."

Jesus told him, "You have judged correctly." Jesus was then able to compare and contrast forgiveness of debt with forgiveness of sin. In essence, the parable allowed the Pharisee to put all of the facts together to make a right judgment about the forgiveness of debt.

Jesus conferred the same judgment upon the sinful woman in their presence by declaring to her, "Your sins are forgiven" (Luke 7:48). Wisdom is always vindicated by the deeds that follow (Matthew 11:19).

Does this still happen today?

I can speak from personal experience when I say that speaking to someone while knowing their very thoughts is not only incredibly confronting, but it also gains the total attention of the listener. I've had this happen within a workplace setting, and I can tell you that it has the power to change the atmosphere in an instant. This is especially the case when you can look someone in the eye and say, "God just revealed this to me as we have been speaking."

From a scriptural perspective, I believe this is akin to a situation Paul describes—when a word of prophecy is spoken in the presence of "unbelievers or people who don't understand these things," but they are then "convicted of sin and judged by what you say. As they listen, their secret thoughts will be exposed, and they will fall to their knees and worship God, declaring, 'God is truly here among you.'" (1 Corinthians 14:24-25 NLT).

Jesus Could See Faith

Among His listeners, Jesus recognized both great faith (Matthew 8:10) and little faith (Matthew 6:30), and He spoke words of direction and destiny into the lives of people displaying either.

When the Word is spoken and there's an atmosphere of faith and desperation that's so real it can actually be seen, you already have the listener's attention, and a miracle is just waiting to happen.

Miraculous Signs

Jesus shaped the Word by allowing everyday people to see miraculous signs, especially when He was moved by heartfelt compassion for people in desperate need (John 11:35-43). This is one of the most visual means of gaining a person's attention, since the outcomes are indisputable.

Before Jesus raised Martha's brother Lazarus from the dead, He said to her, "I am the resurrection and the life" (John 11:25). He then asked if she believed this.

In many ways, this was not an unusual question by Jesus, because belief in the resurrection of the righteous was a long-held tenet of Judaism. However, the "I Am" was both purposeful and able to be demonstrate resurrection truth. For when Jesus asked for the stone to be rolled away from the entrance to the tomb of Lazarus, things were about to take on a completely unexpected supernatural aspect.

Jesus asked Martha, "Did I not tell you that if you believed, you would see the glory of God?" (John 11:40). He then proceeded to raise Lazarus from the dead.

Take note of the various facets of this situation: a close friend's death, desperation, heartbreak, tragedy, God's unmistakable *kairos* timing, extraordinary compassion, revealed truth, a flicker of faith. Then the situation ignites, and a miracle follows—with every emotion imaginable on display—and the glory of God is revealed—while all of creation takes note.

We must never forget that the God we worship is the God of the supernatural. With Him all things are possible, and nothing is impossible.

In a moment of time, everything can change. Things we'd given up on—our long-forgotten hopes and dreams—suddenly take on new meaning as the God of all hope breathes new life into our present reality.

Imagine for a moment how Mary and Martha felt when they were confronted with these words from Jesus: "Take off the grave clothes and let him go" (John 11:44). Lazarus, their brother, had been raised from the dead!

There's a lesson for us in all this, because Jesus deliberately delayed His return to Bethany, knowing full well what He was intending to do.

When we put this story into perspective, it was meant not only for the two sisters and those offering them comfort, but also for every generation since that day needing to see the glory of God revealed in their lives.

I want to encourage you to never forget the words of Jesus to Martha, when you confront your next seemingly impossible situation. Whether it happens in the workplace, market place, family, church, social circles, or wherever— "All things are possible to him who believes!" (Mark 9:23).

Letting your work colleague or neighbor know that you care enough to pray for (or visit) their loved one, relative, or friend is often a catalyst for change in their lives.

Jesus is still the One who restores hope when every earthly voice screams that the situation is impossible.

God's Word

Jesus knew God's Word thoroughly and often linked any given situation with the mind and will of God.

When situations were apparently out of control or needed the will of God to be known with certainty, Jesus used the Word of God as the heavenly conduit to restore divine order to the situation (Luke 4:1-13).

In some instances, the Word of God brought power and authority; in others it brought revelation or wisdom. Whatever the need, the Father's will was being accomplished on earth as it is in heaven.

Jesus embodied what it was like to have a close relationship with His Father. Whenever a situation arose where someone needed God's help, He simply called upon heaven's resources and then moved in the power and authority that God had made available to Him through the Holy Spirit.

It may seem amazing to some, but Jesus left all believers with the following promise before His earthly ministry ended: "Truly, truly, I say to you, he who believes in Me, the works that I do, he will do also; and greater works than these he will do; because I go to the Father" (John 14:12 NASB).

The question for all professing believers in our day is simply this: Are we walking in the timeless promise made available through this declaration, or are we settling for something far below heaven's best?

The Cry for Workers in the Market Place

Our nation's workplaces and market places are full of busy and time-poor people who need to encounter God.

Yet I wonder how many of God's people are so tied up with the "worries and cares of this world and the deceitfulness of riches" (Mark 4:18-19) that the good seed being sown into their lives has been choked, rendering their lives unfruitful for the kingdom of God.

The Greek word for "choked" (*sympnigó*) means to "press in on" as well as "choke." It operates in people having wrong identifications. The consequence of aligning with sin cuts a person off from Christ's provisions (His life-supply) and leaves them inoperative—stalled and spiritually suffocated (as explained in the *HELPS Word-Studies*).

The parable of the sower is just as real to the workplaces of today as it would have been to Zacchaeus when he encountered Jesus for the first time and his heart was laid bare.

The parable of the good Samaritan was a word about another business-man who took time to help someone in desperate need.

I want to encourage you to believe enough in the promise Jesus made in John 14:12 that you make it a point of personal prayer to ask for God encounters to take place within your market place or workplace among colleagues, associates, visitors, and nearby businesses. Then be prepared to take time to speak into people's lives with the assurance that God will take care of your business.

Within the wider context of society, this also applies to your neighbors, friends, and social network, as well as the passersby or strangers we meet. When it comes to the passersby or the stranger, never forget that you could even be entertaining angels without knowing it; so make the most of every opportunity (Hebrews 13:2).

I've had some incredible God encounters with strangers I'd never seen before, and in many cases have never seen again. I know for sure that God brought our paths together for a reason, and in every instance I was able to share the gospel message that could impart life to the listener.

Finally, when it comes to the issues of life and death, there's no place for a silent gospel. People could easily observe the godly life of Jesus and His disciples at any time, but Jesus and those disciples were always proclaiming the gospel message whenever they went.

We need to do the same.

Controversies

Jesus picked up on smart comments like "And who is my neighbor?" and He used a parable to illustrate what being a neighbor was really like (Luke 10:25-37). I'm confident that this response from Jesus was not what the Pharisee wanted to hear—most particularly the notion that appearing to be on a religious mission does not justify leaving an injured man to die on the roadside.

Without uttering the words, Jesus was asking the Pharisee to learn from the parable that a real neighbor would show mercy.

These lessons were often delivered in a public place and attracted the attention of onlookers, who would be led to reassess what they actually believed about the things being spoken and why.

In many market places and workplaces, smart comments, cynicism, and controversies are often the norm when it comes to any discussion about sex, religion, or politics. Shaping the Word within these and other topics can often pose a serious challenge to believers, so it's important to be well schooled in terms of the Word of God, as well as having a well-thought-out response to these and other topics.

After many years of public and private sector engagement, I've had many conversations indicating where people have been incredibly misinformed—especially about religion. And when the truth is revealed, it can actually become a lightbulb moment.

Praying for godly wisdom (James 1:5) and seeking wise counsel are also great keys to unlocking these challenges.

Social Justice

Jesus was ready to confront issues of the day in a heavily male-dominated society—issues such as women being demeaned through divorce for any reason, when God has ordained that "the two shall become one flesh" (Genesis 2:24). Jesus took the view that only through marital infidelity could the marriage bond be broken.

Perhaps the most confronting example of this was the public display of a woman caught in the act of adultery, who was brought into the temple courts to interrupt Jesus while He was in a teaching session (John 8:1-11). The woman was made to stand before Jesus and His disciples by a group of religious zealots who were calling for the death penalty.

Jesus had their full attention when He gave this command: "If any of you is without sin, let him be the first to throw a stone at her" (John 8:7).

This was truly a moment when heaven came to earth and the law of the conscience overrode any sense of legalism.

Mercy indeed triumphed over judgment that day as Jesus uttered these words to the woman: "Then neither do I condemn you. Go now and leave your life of sin" (John 8:11).

Unlike her accusers, Jesus was without sin and could have lawfully thrown a stone at her, but His call was to redeem a lost and wayward humanity.

Ready to Offer Encouragement at All Times

In our nation's workplaces and governments where internal politics and struggles over power, authority, and control often lead to compromised decision-making and hypocrisy, it's easy to become cynical and judgmental.

Just like Jesus did with the woman caught in the act of adultery, we need to be ready to show mercy whenever a lost soul needs direction, and to speak a word of righteousness into the breach.

This applies as much to the politician and the CEO as it does to the janitor or clerk. They all need to hear the Word of God if they're going to be impacted by the message that gives life.

I've shared my testimony with many politicians, CEOs, and senior executives, right through to the janitor and the taxi driver. Many are crying out for truth and peace in their lives and in the lives of their families and loved ones. However, despite their best endeavors, many are simply looking in all the wrong places.

The answer I give is simple and yet profound.

First, I never miss an opportunity to share my testimony of the encounter I had with Jesus Christ. Second, I use this as the basis to ask them about their own lives and their relationship with God. This is a key to soul-winning, and I take my inspiration from the apostle Paul.

Gifts of the Holy Spirit

To reveal His authority and the power of God that existed in His life, Jesus used every available gift of the Spirit mentioned in 1 Corinthians 12 (except the gifts of tongues and interpretation, which weren't given until the day of Pentecost as recorded in Acts 2).

Spiritual gifts (1 Corinthians 14:1) are freely available, and believers are encouraged to earnestly desire them. Spiritual gifts are primarily given to the church (the *ecclesia,* meaning literally "called out ones") for the common good (1 Corinthians 12:7).

These gifts are generally exercised in places where two or more are gathered, and the attention of those directly involved in the exercise of the gift and onlookers is inevitable, because these gifts operate in the supernatural realm and carry the power and authority of God.

In my experience, there's a sense of awe and excitement when these gifts are operating, especially what are known as the vocal gifts, which are able to "lay bare the secrets of the heart" (1 Corinthians 14:24-25).

The Great Commission that Jesus gave to believers is to "go into all our world…and preach the good news…. And signs and wonders will accompany those who believe" (Mark 16:15-17). Spiritual gifts are a God-given means of empowering those who believe to move in the supernatural realm so that both believers and unbelievers can be touched by the light of the gospel message.

One of the most exciting ways Christian believers can exercise their faith in God is through the gifts of the Holy Spirit. What better opportunity can we have than to pray and believe God for these gifts to be manifested as we go off daily into our market places? These gifts will be covered in more detail in Chapters 16-18.

History and Culture

The apostle Paul often spent time studying the history and culture of the people to whom he preached. He was looking for evidence of past God encounters as a means to connect with local communities.

When Paul was in Athens (Acts 17), he searched until he found an altar inscribed to an "unknown God," an altar that had been preserved from an encounter the people of Athens had with God some six hundred years prior to Paul's visit. That original encounter is a spine-tingling story (as told in *Eternity in their Hearts* by Don Richardson), one which centers on a prophet called Epimenides, who was called to Athens to lead its plague-infested people into an incredible encounter with the living God.

In the workplace setting where the subject of religion is often held up to ridicule, it has been my experience that a topic that has been well researched and openly discussed can often dispel the myths and misguided statements that would otherwise add fuel to the fire of condemnation upon the church.

Indeed, I've often used this story about Paul's visit to Athens to share the good news with people of Greek origin.

Testimony

When Paul was on a heavenly cause, he was absolutely fearless as an apostle, teacher, preacher, and miracle worker, but most importantly as a servant of God.

Paul's regular practice when pioneering new works was to attend the local synagogue and give his testimony, followed by his sharing from the Old Testament that Jesus was the promised Messiah (Acts 9:20-21; 17:2; 19:8-9).

History reveals that this practice certainly received the attention of the local Jewish worshipers and God-fearing Gentile worshipers, often galvanizing their beliefs to the point that many made the decision to believe in Jesus Christ as Lord and Savior.

Paul's testimony was compelling because he sincerely believed that in killing off followers of "the Way," he had been carrying out a heavenly cause (Acts 22:1-21). After his personal encounter with the risen Lord on the road to Damascus, Saul adopted the name Paul, and he was never the same.

Do you have a testimony ready to share about your own personal encounter with Jesus Christ?

I share my testimony in Chapter 15 of this book, and I also share it at every possible opportunity with both unbelievers and believers as a source of encouragement to people who are on the journey of life and looking for direction. My testimony has touched the hearts of many people, especially those in the market places and workplaces I visit.

History reveals that if I can share my story and gain a person's attention even for only a few moments in time, it can have eternal consequences.

I'm sure that there is an endless variety of means for gaining the attention of the people in our world. Most importantly, we need to pray and ask

God to bring people across our paths and to grant the opportunity to share the gospel message and our personal testimony.

At the end of the day, it is God who opens the heart of unbelievers, and He responds to the slightest flicker of faith—a battered or bruised reed, or a smoldering wick (Matthew 12:20).

Truly, there is none like our God!

12

More about Shaping the Word

L et's consider further how we can "shape the Word" to help our generation encounter God.

Learn from Good Examples

Jesus was the master communicator, and He called upon heaven's resources frequently. He was consistently in touch with His Father through a strong prayer life, and He was led daily by the Holy Spirit.

We've looked at many of the methods Jesus and the apostles used to propel the gospel message to their generation, and it turned their world upside down. Throughout the Scriptures, Jesus encourages us to do likewise, and to realize that He has given us authority and commissioned us to do the same things and even greater things than He did (John 14:12).

We need to realize and personalize the fact that the same power God used to conquer the grave—by raising Jesus from the dead—now lives in us (Ephesians 1:18-21).

The methods used by Jesus and His apostles are just as relevant today in our nation's market places and workplaces as they are in any other evangelical endeavors of the church of Jesus Christ.

People need to know about Jesus—and who will tell them, if we don't? So when you see a situation of need in your workplace or market place, especially among stressed out staff, think about pursuing these goals:

1. Start out by just being a friend.
2. Always keep a listening ear and commit the situation to God in prayer.
3. Ask God for keys that will allow you to speak into or unlock the situation, and for the opportunity to do just that.
4. When the opportunity arises, exercise faith and believe God for the right words to say and the right way to say them. Be enabled by the leading of the Holy Spirit to reveal the things that God has shown you.
5. Remember to always give thanks to the Lord.

The only question that remains is: Will you take up the mantle for this generation?

Be Yourself, and Leave Religious Trappings Behind

The Word of God has ready appeal to the God-given conscience of mankind. When we speak about Jesus Christ and the Bible being the Word of God, we shouldn't try to cloak it in religious jargon, clichés, or tradition—especially when we're speaking to the younger generation. "Religious speak" and tradition generally only serve to stifle the things of God.

So be yourself, and speak in everyday language that people can understand and relate to.

Jesus did this—and so should we.

Understand that Outcomes Are More Important Than Methods

Religion and tradition will often try to limit the way in which God finds expression to just a few of their preferred methods or practices. While these may achieve a measure of success, we should never try to put God in a box, because there may be many different pathways to achieve the same or better outcomes.

We need to learn to elevate outcomes above methods in our priorities, and begin to look for fruit among the leaves rather than wondering if we're looking at the right tree. Something can have all the trappings, but unless it bears fruit that remains, it is cursed (John 15:16).

Being led by the Holy Spirit is absolutely crucial when it comes to understanding outcomes that are going to impact the listener.

It's helpful on this point to consider the story in 2 Kings 5 of the healing from leprosy of Naaman, a Syrian army commander. It's one of the most profound miracles of healing in the Old Testament. The fingerprints of God are all over this story, as He set up a God encounter with Naaman through a captured servant girl who spoke out in faith to her captors about the prophet of God.

Naaman was a highly successful army commander, and highly thought of by his master, the king of Aram (Syria)—but the leprosy he'd contracted was no respecter of persons, and neither is God.

Our expectations of how God might or might not do something are not what matters. We simply need to follow His leading and be obedient to what He tells us to do.

Naaman's main objection in this story was to the method proposed by the prophet Elisha to heal him of leprosy (2 Kings 5:11). As soon as

Naaman learned his lesson and took a step of faith by humbling himself and obeying the word of the prophet, healing flowed—and he confessed his belief in the God of Israel as the one true God (2 Kings 5:15). Within a few moments, Naaman came to understand that God's ways are so much higher than our ways, and that there's only one way to enter into the supernatural realm: through faith in God alone.

In the same manner, we also need to understand that God's ways and His agenda are always far greater than anything we could ever think or even imagine. He is the Master of multitasking, far beyond anything the age of technology could fathom or dream.

We simply need to let God be God in our daily situations and follow His leading. Be assured: The Holy Spirit doesn't need our help—just our cooperation.

The apostle Paul said, "I will use all means possible to win the lost." To the Jews he became a Jew, to the Gentiles he became a Gentile. He learned to weep or to laugh or to comfort those in need, all in order to win them for Christ (1 Corinthians 9:19-23).

We need to be prepared to do the same and look for the Naaman's in our world.

For a Fresh Look at Your Market Place

In today's business world, Naaman's leprosy could easily be replaced by leaders who demonstrate behaviors such as pride, arrogance, haughtiness, power, authority, control, manipulation, deception, misrepresentation, coercion, collusion, greed, avarice, lack of honor and integrity, and loving money more than colleagues. Such business and political leaders who see themselves as untouchable, not answerable, not wanting to be accountable, always blaming others rather than taking responsibility—these are the very ones Jesus came to redeem.

I'm sure you can easily add to this list based on your own life experiences.

Although Naaman was a star performer on the battlefield of life, his leprosy problem (which speaks of our fallen nature) could only be dealt with through an encounter with the living God.

As soon as Naaman experienced his encounter with God, his spiritual eyes were opened, and he pledged allegiance to the one true God (2 Kings 5:13-18).

I want to tell you from many years of experience working in the business world that this world is full of people like Naaman who need to encounter God.

Think about this the next time you're mistreated, or your efforts aren't valued in your workplace. When this happens, it's so easy to retreat into your shell and adopt the victim mentality (*Why me?*) rather than seeing the situation as a challenge and an opportunity for a God encounter with the offending party.

The reality is that God is always working things together for the good of those who love Him, and even in the midst of the most severe trials, something good can always come (Romans 8:28; Genesis 50:20).

Imagine for a moment how the young Israelite girl might have felt when she was abducted from her family by bands of raiders from Aram, then forced into the servitude of Naaman's wife (2 Kings 5:2). She'd done nothing wrong, yet seemingly she was being punished in one of the most horrendous ways known to mankind—abduction into slavery. She could have easily said, "Why me, God?" and embraced a sense of abandonment. Instead, she chose to cling to her faith in the knowledge that God was watching her every move.

Little did she (or anyone else) know that God was about to hatch another plan which would lead not only to the healing of her master, but also—and most importantly—to Naaman pledging his allegiance to the King of kings (2 Kings 5:15).

God's *kairos* time-clock was so perfect that He just happened to arrange for this servant girl to be abducted at precisely the same time Naaman was going through his personal ordeal with leprosy. When the servant girl found out about the leprous condition of her new master, her faith came to the fore as she told her mistress, "If only my master would see the prophet who is in Samaria! He would heal him of his leprosy" (2 Kings 5:3).

Her words seem to contain the same faith-based sentiment that Martha, another servant, spoke to her Lord just prior to seeing her brother Lazarus raised from the dead: "Lord, if You had been here, my brother would not have died. But even now I know that God will give You whatever You ask Him" (John 11:21-22).

Naaman must have been so desperate to find healing that when he heard the words of faith spoken by the young Israelite servant girl, he went to the king of Aram and was granted permission to seek healing in Israel.

How miraculous was that in itself!

Is Our Focus on the Method or the Healer?

When Naaman arrived at the house of Elisha with his horses and chariots, the greeting he received was nothing like he expected—because God must first deal with the heart of man, before a relationship can ever develop.

> Elisha sent a messenger to him, saying, "Go and
> wash in the Jordan seven times, and your flesh will be
> restored to you and you will be clean." (2 Kings 5:10)

Amid all his pomp, grandeur, and sense of self-importance, Naaman must have felt terribly let down by the greeting from this great prophet of Israel. Receiving a greeting only from a messenger and not from the famous prophet himself would have surely offended his sense of pride.

To add insult to injury, Naaman was told by the messenger to "go and wash in the river Jordan," and Naaman no doubt asked, "Why seven times?" Little did Naaman realize that the faith it took to bring him to Israel also works hand-in-hand with humility, for "God opposes the proud, but gives grace to the humble" (1 Peter 5:5).

The pride of this great warrior first had to be dealt with before he could ever come into relationship with the God of Israel and receive his healing. Look at how this man responded to the prophet's words:

> Naaman was furious and went away and said, "Behold,
> I thought, He will surely come out to me and stand and
> call on the name of the LORD his God, and wave his hand
> over the place and cure the leper. Are not Abanah and
> Pharpar, the rivers of Damascus, better than all the waters
> of Israel? Could I not wash in them and be clean?" So
> he turned and went away in a rage. (2 Kings 5:11-12)

Left to himself, Naaman would never have received his healing that day because of his anger with the God of Israel.

By way of background, the Arameans were idol worshipers and had treated the Israelites badly for many years. So when one of their nation's greatest military leaders was led by faith to seek healing from the God of Israel, the scene was set for a God encounter of monumental proportions.

The story doesn't end with Naaman's anger, because his servants came to the rescue and offered him words that would breathe life and healing into both his present reality and his eternal destiny. They said to him, "My father, had the prophet told you to do some great thing, would you not have done it? How much more then, when he says to you, 'Wash, and be clean'?"

Naaman submitted at last. "He went down and dipped himself seven times in the Jordan, according to the word of the man of God; and his flesh was restored like the flesh of a little child, and he was clean" (2 Kings 5:13-14).

I would like to put forward a few thoughts regarding the workplace that might shed some light on this story.

- As a management consultant with more than twenty-five years of market place experience, I'm fully aware that employees (servants) often know a lot more about humility than CEOs and senior executives (kings or commanders, as it were, in the story of Naaman).
- Initially, it was the faith of a young Israelite girl that inspired Naaman to seek healing in Israel. This speaks of the employee who's least likely to be listened to who nevertheless provides answers to some of the business's greatest needs.
- It speaks also about the message of faith being able to give life and hope when the situation seems hopeless. (Naaman had no doubt asked the God of Rimmon for healing, but it wasn't forthcoming.)
- It also speaks about God opposing proud managers while giving grace to humble employees (servants) by giving them wisdom and understanding way beyond their years (James 1:5).

- Finally, it was the faith of Naaman's servants that encouraged him to take the step of humility that led to his healing and salvation. Naaman's servants knew only too well the simplicity of obeying their master's commands in the knowledge that he would be well pleased with them. By looking through the eyes of faith, they simply recognized that Naaman could also be healed of leprosy if he simply obeyed the voice of the God of Israel, the Master of everything—after the pattern of their own servanthood to their master Naaman.

The rest is history, but one important acknowledgment was yet to be made. When Naaman finally addressed Elisha after his healing, he spoke these words: "For your servant will no longer offer burnt offering nor will he sacrifice to other gods, but to the LORD" (2 Kings 5:17). Naaman recognized that to please his Lord, he must take the place of a servant and recognize that faith must work together with humility and obedience for the Master's reward to be forthcoming.

Within the workplace setting, it's often the case that when poor decision-making occurs, middle and lower management can see the writing on the wall long before senior executives are aware that there's even an issue.

For example, provided there's opportunity for consultation to occur before the release of important business directives, senior executive management can often glean valuable insights from lower level management, and refinements can be put in place to make directives operationally workable. In the absence of meaningful consultation, there's always the potential for the business to go into damage control through the issue of retractions, clarifications, etc. A little humility can often reap dividends.

The above example also speaks of having a common set of core values including character traits such as honesty, loyalty, integrity, truthfulness, honor, trust, valuing people, customer-first culture, collaborative and team-orientated processes, and the like. These core values need to be prominent and set the minimum standard of behavior in any business for its potential to ever be realized.

Finally, servanthood is always the key to success in any business venture. The way in which we serve our customers determines our level of success in the business world, because servanthood is a principle of the kingdom of God.

This isn't surprising, because servanthood is also the precursor to promotion within the kingdom of God.

Follow the Leading of the Holy Spirit

The New Testament is full of encounters where the leading of the Holy Spirit was central to the ministry and thinking of the disciples. It started with the Lord Himself: "Jesus, full of the Holy Spirit, left the Jordan and was led by the Spirit into the wilderness" (Luke 4:1).

When people were given ministry responsibility in the New Testament epistles, "being full of the Holy Spirit and faith" was consistently mentioned as a mandatory requirement for the task (Acts 6:5; 6:8; 7:55-60; 11:24).

The apostle Paul went as far as linking our sonship with being led by the Spirit of God: "For all who are led by the Spirit of God are sons of God" (Romans 8:14).

The disciples clearly understood that the ministry of Jesus (one place at a time, one person at a time) had been replaced by the ministry of the omnipresent Holy Spirit who could simultaneously live in the hearts of all believers.

In the same way that the Father sent the Son (1 John 4:4), the Son then sent the Holy Spirit, according to the Father's promise (Luke 24:49) to empower all believers to be witnesses in carrying the gospel message to all nations (Acts 1:8), until the culmination of the ages when Jesus will return to earth (Matthew 24:26-31).

This is Christianity 101.

Position Yourself by Living a Consistent Godly Life

For Christian believers to impact the kingdom of this world, we must consistently live out our faith daily and shine in what is often a dark place.

Look at two declarations Jesus gave to His disciples:

> You are the light of the world. A city on a hill cannot be hidden. Neither do people light a lamp and put it under a basket. Instead, they set it on a lampstand, and it gives light to everyone in the house. In the same way, let your light shine before men, that they may see your good deeds and glorify your Father in heaven. (Matthew 5:14-16)

> If anyone would come after Me, he must deny himself and take up his cross daily and follow Me. (Luke 9:23)

These words speak about being a shining light and about denying ourselves. The reality is that you cannot have one without the other.

For our light to shine, we need to do the things no one else is prepared to do, and this means putting the needs of others in front of our own. It means…

• going the extra mile when the other person's load is heavy.

- spending time with someone who's hurting, to feel their pain and be touched by their infirmities, and to offer to pray for them.
- being the neighbor who shows up to help and is prepared to show mercy rather than judgment.
- being the one who goes to visit a sick friend at home or hospital, and who takes time to pray for that person.

When Jesus speaks about the final judgment of mankind, His words speak volumes about how we should conduct ourselves during our time on earth and the rewards that will follow for those prepared to take up the challenge (Matthew 25:34-36,40).

Every action to bless another person's need is recognized by the King in the coming kingdom. However, good deeds come about as a result of seeds being sown into people's lives in the present age—seeds that allow them to see God's mercy and wisdom in action.

> Who is wise and understanding among you? Let him
> show it by his good conduct, by deeds done in the
> humility that comes from wisdom. (James 3:13)

Make Peace with Your Past

As I was writing this chapter, the Holy Spirit spoke to my heart and revealed that while we have unresolved conflict in our lives, we cannot give ourselves fully to the work of the kingdom. We need to find a place of peace with our past in order to encounter the future God has planned for us. Whether it's in our marriage, our family, our market place or workplace, our social network, or our church group, if we're to carry out kingdom business we cannot afford to have energy drain happening all over the place because of ongoing conflicts in our lives.

To put this into perspective, is it any wonder that the Lord Jesus instituted holy communion as the great circuit-breaker for believers? This sacrament was always intended to include a time of personal reflection whereby we examine our lives so that sin issues, which are often underpinned by unresolved conflicts, can be brought out into the open and dealt with.

Real—and Fulfilling

The biblical stories and principles presented in these last two chapters are ones I draw upon regularly to shape the Word to believers and unbelievers alike in the market place, and also to my wider community. The Word of God is rich with examples of people being drawn to God through encounters that are often unexpected, stirring up a desire to know more.

In an age where stereotyping has become common and there are many misconceptions about the church, it's often refreshing to challenge people's thinking and to lead them into an encounter with God. The market place has traditionally been regarded by many in ministry as one of the most difficult fields for the sower and reaper to work in. I wish to challenge this belief, because God has led me on a different journey—and I happen to see the hand of God touching lives in my market place on a daily basis. How real and fulfilling it is to live out my faith (despite my flaws) before my loving and holy God!

And what an honor and a privilege it is to be part of God's plan to save the lost!

13

Back to the Market Place

One of the most serious flaws in the thinking of Western culture is the notion that we should separate our secular and spiritual lives.

Critics of the gospel message often say, "Keep it for Sunday"—a schedule that effectively means "when we're not around to listen." It's as if our culture dictates that we compartmentalize our belief systems in the same way we may hold opinions on any number of other topics, so as not to offend others. This is one of the underlying reasons that political correctness has gained momentum in recent years. Yet in attempting to please (or appease) everyone, we also risk losing a great deal including our identity.

While some people might hold to this belief, I can confidently say that Jesus lived out his faith on a daily basis and never made any attempt to polarize or hide His views about any topic. In essence, Jesus Christ is the personification of the old computer term WYSIWYG—What you see is what you get.

Jesus didn't claim to be the Son of God only on the Sabbath, and then live like a son of the devil for the remainder of the week. His relationship with God His Father underpinned His faith, values, beliefs, character, hope, and ultimately His will.

His belief system so permeated His life that it guided Him through the darkest hours of every trial and tribulation as well as the temptations associated with His times of extreme popularity, when pride could have easily caused Him grief.

Those who aspire to be wise in the Lord will know that maturity in God's eyes means that we follow in the path of His Son, who not only walked by faith but had to learn obedience through the things He suffered (Hebrews 5:8). It's for this reason that spiritual maturity needs to be manifest daily in the market place or workplace through our actions and behavior to make an impact for Jesus Christ. It's simply not enough to claim the higher moral ground on the basis of our faith and spirituality unless we're above reproach in the outworking of that claim over our life.

Are We Above Reproach in Our Work Ethic?

Based on my personal observations and direct feedback that I've received over many years of involvement in the market place, I've listed below a number of matters for the consideration of all professing believers.

Without wishing to be perceived as a veritable John the Baptist bringing to light a checklist of possible misdeeds by those who consider themselves Christians, I would simply say that as professing believers, we need to assess our work performance on a regular basis. It's easy to be blinded by our own faults and to treat any criticism as suffering for the sake of Christ.

Moreover, in spite of our thoughts on these matters, it's other people's perceptions about how we perform our daily work tasks that underpin both our reputation and our testimony in the workplace or the market place, and indeed, in society in general.

The matters listed below are in no particular order of importance, nor are they meant to be exhaustive in their content, but they all concern failing to be above reproach in our work ethic.

Low Productivity

In terms of work output and or quality of work, if a person's reputation is one of low productivity, this is counterproductive to the achievement of a good testimony.

As a result, we need to receive regular feedback through performance reviews, while also giving feedback to others if we're a business owner or manager.

Without a doubt, Christian believers should give their very best at all times, using their God-given talents, skills, gifts, and abilities to be a blessing to those they work and associate with.

Being prepared to go the extra mile with a cheerful attitude should be the norm for all believers, because this reflects the very nature and heart of God to the lost and broken world in which we live. When you're asked to go the extra mile, how do you respond, and how is your attitude?

This is where our light needs to shine in what might be a dark place for most people.

Taking Shortcuts

In the long run, the practice of always trying to take shortcuts will often end up costing the business money and lost opportunities.

Be careful, if this is your tendency, because with both God and mankind there are no real shortcuts to gaining experience and maturity. It takes both hard work and perseverance.

Performance reviews need to be taken seriously if this character trait is identified.

When you're asked to perform a certain task and the risk of success is likely to be related to how the task is undertaken, you should always err on the side of caution rather than compromise during execution.

Ask yourself: If this was my business, how would I expect the task to be undertaken?

Once this is settled, then you need to follow your convictions and honor your employer with a clear conscience.

Wasting Time

Wasting time can take on many forms:

- standing around talking about non-work-related matters for extended periods;
- speaking on the phone for extended discussion on private matters;
- spending extended periods on the internet in matters not directly related to work (such as social media, games, etc.);
- taking overlong breaks;
- disappearing for a while to another area of the workplace for a chat, instead of being at work;

These may sound trivial, but I'm personally aware of instances where significant amounts of time are robbed from employers on a daily basis as a result of smoking or drug addictions as well as excessive toilet breaks, which can in some cases be accompanied by other activities such as on-line gambling.

In my own experience, this type of behavior is most prevalent in the public service, where staff management practices are often poorly policed and disciplinary action is often viewed as more trouble than it's worth because of the excessive red tape involved.

If you're involved in any of these types of behaviors, consider the following:

- When you think no one is watching, just remember that God is both omnipresent and omniscient—nothing escapes His attention.
- When we consider that all promotion comes from the Lord, how then should we behave in the day and hour in which we live?

Regardless of our attempts to justify our behavior, we're really robbing our employer and effectively dishonoring the God we claim to serve when this occurs. Once again, we need to ask ourselves: If this was my business, would I consider this acceptable behavior?

Remember that your testimony before both God and man is at stake.

Pushing the Envelope for Time Off

In most workplaces, a small number of employees may consistently push for time off. When this occurs frequently, with little notice to the employer (to allow alternative arrangements to be put in place), it's undoubtedly an abuse of the employment relationship.

Apart from putting unnecessary stress on the employer and the staff directly affected by one's absence, it's highly damaging to the reputation or testimony of the person involved.

Jesus told His disciples, "Do to others as you would have them do to you" (Luke 6:31). When this verse is read in context, it takes on even greater significance, because the surrounding verses are all about loving your enemies. In other words, we set the tone of how we want to be treated simply by the way we treat others.

It's up to professing believers to be proactive in the workplace and set the bar for how they want to be treated. This is exactly what "doing unto others" means. If you want to be treated in a certain way, then make sure you're treating others that way, and ensure that any undesirable behavior isn't something you regularly engage in.

Abusing Sick/Personal Leave Privileges

Sick or personal leave was originally intended to be a privilege taken when a person was genuinely sick or when a member of their immediate family required care.

In today's world, personal leave (which now includes sick leave) has become so exploited through "sickees" that modern workplace agreements will often embrace a certain number of days where leave can be taken "without reason" simply to curtail this type of abuse.

From a Christian perspective, anyone who takes days off to do "whatever" is essentially abusing this privilege and dishonoring God before their employer.

Others may take a different view in this matter. However, I would like to encourage you to consider this from the perspective of your employer. It's foremost a matter of conscience. We need to remember that telling the truth on the leave form is what matters to God. Our reliability, integrity, and trustworthiness is what matters in these situations.

What we can get away with "legally" is never a substitute for upholding the spirit of the law, because this type of abuse negatively impacts our testimony before both God and man, especially our employer.

The apostle Paul had a general principle which he applied in his teaching: "If a person is not prepared to work, then he shouldn't eat" (2 Thessalonians 3:10). In the spirit of that principle, if someone wants to take sick leave when they're not sick, they don't deserve to get paid.

Quite apart from the fact that the person has lied to their employer about the reasons for their absence, *El Roi*—the all-seeing, omniscient God—is watching.

A person's testimony in the workplace and market place is most at risk with this kind of abuse. Employers have said to me, "So-and-so is a good bloke and his work is good—but you know, every time he works up a sick day, he takes it off. What he doesn't realize is that the next time the business takes a dive, he'll be the first to get laid off."

The question I pose is this: If you were his employer, wouldn't you make the same judgment?

Cheating on Time Sheets

At times I've observed cheating on time sheets in the private sector, but in my experience, this is most common among public servants, some of whom appear to adopt the following attitudes:

- "No one will know."
- "The timesheets never get checked properly anyway."
- "Who cares?"

However, in violating their conscience, people conveniently suppress the truth that God knows.

Remember what Jesus says: "They that are trustworthy [or faithful] with little can also be trusted with much" (Luke 16:10).

This type of behavior damages a person's testimony, as fellow workers come to know who's cheating on their timesheets. If this happens on the timesheet of a professing believer, their credibility is shot to pieces—especially if they're seeking to take the higher moral ground on other issues such as integrity, truth, honor, and the like.

The devil wants believers to compromise their faith, values, and beliefs, because this renders their witness powerless and undermines their God-given authority.

Compromise is one of the most powerful tools the enemy uses to ensnare the human race, and Christians are not exempt. When Satan took Jesus to the three places of temptation at the beginning of his earthly ministry (Luke 4:1-13), his main aim was to get Jesus to compromise what He knew to be true and to settle for less than God's plan for His life. Jesus resisted Satan's plan each time, because He understood God's Word and was not prepared to deviate.

However, Luke 4:13 also says that after this time of temptation, Satan left Jesus "until an opportune time." With this in mind, it's no wonder that the apostle Peter, who had personally been buffeted by Satan through his denial of Jesus, warns us: "Be of sober spirit, be on the alert. Your adversary, the devil, prowls around like a roaring lion, seeking someone to devour" (1 Peter 5:8).

Satan's primary work on earth is to steal and kill and destroy—but Jesus came that we may have life and have it abundantly (John 10:10). Never forget that Jesus is the Lion of the tribe of Judah, and He came to destroy the works of the evil one.

All through the ages of the Adamic line, Satan has used every opportunity to compromise the faith of believers. He also tries to destroy and entangle anyone who might even be a candidate for the kingdom. From presidents to paupers, Satan is on a mission to destroy the human race and to take as many people to hell as he possibly can, so he can rule and reign over them.

What price do you put on your integrity? This is really a matter of the heart. Are a few minutes on a timesheet so important that you're willing to trade your integrity and even your testimony before God and man?

Not Being Trusted to Work without Supervision

Employers often find it difficult when key employees and support workers cannot be trusted to do their best unless they're constantly under supervision.

I've personally witnessed this, and I've heard many employers comment about particular staff who are good at what they do, but who must be watched closely or else they slack off, or their productivity drops off terribly when left on their own.

The various excuses for this behavior display a lack of honor toward your employer, who's providing the means to feed your family. This behavior is also a poor testimony before your fellow workers, and it's unbecoming of a person who professes Christianity. At the end of the day, such behavior is akin to theft.

And remember: God is watching.

Once again, this is really a matter of personal integrity. By not working hard unless the boss is around, a person's honesty is being tested and our testimony before both God and man is compromised.

Consider these Scriptures:

> God is not mocked, whatsoever a man sows,
> that also shall he reap. (Galatians 6:7)

> Don't work only while being watched, in order
> to please men, but as slaves of Christ, do God's
> will from your heart. (Ephesians 6:6 HCSB)

Financial Compromise in the Workplace

In addition to the more obvious things like cheating, lying, and stealing, there are many other forms of financial compromise related to the work place. Let's look at some of the more prominent ones.

Abusing the Cash Economy

In Australia, the cash economy includes the practice of not charging legal taxes on goods and services in exchange for being paid in cash, which is then not declared for taxation purposes.

Interestingly, Satan offered Jesus power and riches if he would only bow down and worship him (Matthew 4:8).

Jesus said, "Render unto Caesar what is due to Caesar" (Luke 20:25). In other words, pay your taxes.

Scripture also talks about how God hates it when people accept bribes to pervert just outcomes (Deuteronomy 16:19).

The truth of the matter is that if we make or accept cash payments, someone else (as well as Satan), has always got something "on us."

Apart from the fact that our God-given conscience should be troubling us, we're breaking the laws of the country we live in, as well as the law of God.

I've been offered cash payment or been asked to pay in cash on many occasions. I always refuse for the reasons outlined above.

It may appear to be a better deal for us to accept cash, but remember that God is watching, and it's better to trust God for our provision than to be compromised financially, since the enemy of souls is always looking for a reason to accuse you and me before the Father.

The easy way is to rush in for a cheap profit, but then you have to deal with feelings of regret and conscience.

The reality is that you cannot reverse the situation once it has happened, despite the fact that you may later regret your earlier decision.

My simple advice is this: Don't give the devil a foothold.

Ripping Off Social Welfare Programs

Countries such as Australia often have generous welfare programs, but anecdotal evidence suggests (and media agencies regularly confirm) that there are many people "ripping off" the system.

Some prime examples of this include claiming benefits for unemployment, sickness, sole parent status, or workers compensation when there's no genuine entitlement.

This behavior is then covered up in various ways:

- working incognito and accepting cash jobs;
- making false declarations about individual circumstances;
- making false claims about workplace injuries;
- ripping off the public housing authorities (by sub-letting rooms for extra money without authorization), or by an undeclared partner living on the premises so that maximum funds can be extorted from social welfare.

Such instances highlight that the love of money (greed) is more important to many than obeying God's Word. Anyone who professes Christianity should think seriously before engaging in this sort of behavior for the reasons outlined above. This whole scenario is based on lies and fabrication of evidence in order to commit fraud.

Many people think, "It's just a few dollars; what will it matter?"

Regrettably, some families now have up to three generations living on Social Security, which places an unsustainable financial burden on our government.

God has declared in His Word that He's our Provider, and we should trust Him at all times to meet our needs. Among other things, this means using Social Security only when genuine needful circumstances arise.

Respectful Interpersonal Relationships

We need to ask ourselves, "How can we possibly maintain a Christian witness in the market place or workplace and think that disrespectful or sexualized behavior is acceptable to God?"

Moreover, I've noticed over the years that the standard of dress and personal conduct of employees in some workplaces has diminished significantly.

If we want to be a lighthouse for the Lord in our workplace, we need to be conscious of how we present ourselves in our dress and in our conduct.

If someone attracts sexual attention mainly because of their clothing, their inappropriate speech, or their unwanted touch, then I would suggest that they're sending the wrong message.

We should always seek to follow a godly example. We need to be like Joseph in our workplaces, remembering that God gave him an ability to interpret dreams and wisdom above his peers—as a means of showing His favor upon Joseph's life.

One day an executive secretary named Helen came into my office. A conversation soon developed, and it wasn't long before God started to reveal to me things about Helen's past through a word of knowledge.

I began to speak to Helen about her being on a journey and having tried a number of different religions (including Jehovah's Witnesses) and alternative lifestyles. She was absolutely blown away and asked me how I could have possibly known. I replied, "God just told me as you came into my office."

It emerged that Helen was in difficult personal circumstances, and as God wonderfully touched this young lady's life, I found myself reaching for the tissue box I kept in my office as a permanent reminder of just how fragile people can be. Helen had just experienced a God encounter that was about to throw some new perspective into her life.

When it became apparent that Helen had been wearing many masks to cover the hurts of her past, the significance of this God encounter takes on a much greater dimension. Helen was often made fun of around the office, and she was called "crazy Helen" because of her colorful language and her alternative lifestyle. Although Helen had never spoken about this to me personally, others in the office had commented about her sometimes inappropriate language and sexualized conversations.

Helen had no idea that unknown aspects of her past were about to be revealed and that God was even giving me an understanding of her thoughts as I shared the things He was revealing to me. This was a confronting discussion to say the least.

However, what happened soon after this God encounter revealed the significant impact it had had on Helen's life. A week or two later, I was relieving a senior executive position on another level of the building where Helen happened to be working. On a particular day, Helen was asked to relieve my executive secretary at a time when I'd scheduled meetings with clients. The meeting involved two people, a man and a woman.

I cannot remember what the meeting was about, but I do remember that the young lady's dress was so short, and her top so low cut, that I didn't know where to look. It was one of those meetings where I couldn't wait for it to finish.

Although I was somewhat shocked, I was more taken back by what Helen had to say when she came into my office afterward. Helen expressed her absolute disgust at this young lady's dress and how she felt so embarrassed for me having to face this.

When you consider Helen's background and her past reputation about freely expressing her own sexuality, the nature of these comments told me that she had indeed been impacted by the Lord during her God encounter.

Scripture strongly encourages modesty in the dress of believers for a reason. The aim of modesty is not to curb any sense of fashion or dress style; it's all about a believer making sure that his or her testimony is credible in the market place.

> In like manner also, that the women adorn
> themselves in modest apparel, with propriety and
> moderation…which is proper for women professing
> godliness, with good works. (2 Timothy 2:9)

Here the apostle Paul is basically saying that if a women's attire doesn't reflect her profession of godliness, then she has missed the higher calling of God.

In today's society, modest clothing can often be a point of difference.

In terms of sexualized conversation, what may start as a friendly chat can lead to inappropriate, suggestive, or even lewd comments by one person to another. Sadly, too many women have been on the receiving end of unwanted suggestions or comments, often framed as a joke or carrying a double meaning. If they object, they may be subjected to further ridicule.

Believers who engage in such behavior, or who enable it by failing to speak out, can often be compromised, and their testimony can become totally ineffective. The remedy to this is quite simple:

- Let people know your values or beliefs up front when a contentious matter arises.
- Follow the example of how Jesus dealt with Satan. Rather than being intimidated, Jesus let Satan know that He was on a mission under the

Father's authority, and that no matter what temptation was put before Him, He would not deviate from obeying the Father.

- It doesn't have to be a sermon, but simply making a statement like any of the following would suffice (and don't apologize for it, because this is your point of difference):
  - ° I really don't feel comfortable with this type of discussion or behavior.
  - ° This doesn't sit well with my Christian values (sometimes this can lead to a serious witnessing opportunity).

A Starting Point

The thoughts presented in this chapter (and continuing in the next) are a good starting point for Christian believers to assess in a practical way the outworking of their faith in the market place.

Compromise is exactly what Satan wants every believer to do, because it means we're effectively bowing down to him. But never forget: Every time we say no to compromise, we become stronger in our faith and service to God.

14

More Market Place Concerns

Continuing from the previous chapter, let's look at further aspects of being above reproach in our actions and behavior in the market place.

Relationships Forbidden in Scripture

When you cross boundaries in relationships, your witness is seriously compromised before God, before the other person involved, and before everyone else who knows about it.

This is exactly the trap that Satan wants you to fall into. Satan wants us to give in to the lusts of the flesh because even if we back away before it gets out of hand, he'll try to torment us with the memory of violating God's law (written on our consciences) at every opportunity in years to come. It might not come to us packaged that way, but Satan doesn't want us to forget our failure.

The area of sexual sin is where the most damage is done to our character, our reputation, and ultimately our witness to others. Regrettably, it also greatly hurts our loved ones.

Regrettably, our society idolizes talent and sex appeal more than it respects integrity or honesty, and this is to our detriment. Just recall the spate of celebrity indiscretions appearing in the media in recent years. These people might be good at their professions (such as sports or entertaining), but seriously, any decent minded person would have to think twice before adopting their personal lifestyle. In every case, families and relationships suffered, often in silence, while someone went too far because they thought they could get away with it.

That's why our integrity and our testimony must be closely guarded at all times.

In the Sermon on the Mount, Jesus addressed the issue of lust (the next step beyond flirting) and likened it to the act of adultery: "You have heard that it was said, 'You shall not commit adultery.' But I tell you that anyone who looks at a woman lustfully has already committed adultery with her in his heart" (Matthew 5:27-28).

Jesus quoted from the seventh of the Ten Commandments (Exodus 20:14), which God gave through the law of Moses. Under this law, sex outside marriage was strictly forbidden, and if a man slept with an unmarried woman, there was an expectation of commitment and that the two would get married. For those already married, sex outside their marriage relationship was called adultery, and the consequences of this were extreme: "If a man commits adultery with another man's wife—with the wife of his neighbor—both the adulterer and the adulteress are to be put to death" (Leviticus 20:10).

So why did Jesus raise the issue of anyone who "looks lustfully"?

Jesus knew the truth that adultery starts in the heart, not in the act of committing adultery in the flesh.

- It starts with looking. A glance becomes a stare.

- Then comes flirting, as attraction builds and positive two-way responses occur.
- After this comes looking lustfully. This happens when evil thoughts are continually overriding the heart's guidance system (otherwise known as the conscience—a God-given part of every man and women).
- These evil thoughts become so intense that they can open the door to coveting your neighbor's wife (thereby breaking the tenth commandment), or coveting someone unmarried, and this finally becomes the act of adultery.

Although Jesus didn't mention whether the person doing the looking was married, He specifically declared the act of any man "looking lustfully" at a woman as being the same as having already committed adultery with her in his heart.

In the Gospel of Mark, Jesus says that evil thoughts originate in the human heart—a heart that is not in submission to the will and purposes of God:

> That which proceeds out of the man, that is what
> defiles the man. For from within, out of the heart
> of men, proceed the evil thoughts, fornications,
> thefts, murders, adulteries, deeds of coveting and
> wickedness, as well as deceit, sensuality, envy, slander,
> pride and foolishness. All these evil things proceed
> from within and defile the man. (Mark 7:20-23)

In the male-dominated Jewish society in which Jesus was raised, the Scriptures didn't even mention the prospect of a woman looking lustfully at a man. However, in today's liberally minded society, that behavior is common, and it would be both foolish and naïve to suggest otherwise.

Added to this, although what Jesus referred to in Matthew 5:28 would have originally meant looking lustfully at a woman in the flesh, today's society is awash with all forms of media (including the internet, television, movies, magazines) that seek to portray both the male and female form in a manner that encourages lustful looks by both men and women.

People should never underestimate the powerful delusion that lust can create in the heart of man when we choose to willfully disregard our God-given conscience as a believer.

One of the most well-known examples from Scripture of "looking lustfully" and "coveting" is the story of King David and Bathsheba in 2 Samuel 11. David's lustful desire for Bathsheba, the wife of Uriah the Hittite, was so strong that he eventually arranged to have Uriah killed in battle.

In essence, it doesn't matter who you are—from king to pauper, we're all subject to the same temptations on a daily basis, and we need to be aware that the enemy wants to entrap and compromise Christian believers at every opportunity.

One more comment on this topic: For anyone professing to be a Christian, failure to treat others with proper respect (including flirting) is an open door to trouble. Apart from sending the wrong message to workmates, people who engage in this behavior are doing extreme damage to their personal testimony and are seriously at risk of being labeled a hypocrite.

In practice, people need to be aware that an office romance or an extra-marital affair causes great emotional pain to the spouse and family, whether sexual intercourse is involved or not.

We need to understand that sexual attraction clouds people's judgment and often leads to sexual acts, even when that may not have been the original intent.

Our response to unwanted sexual advances needs to be one of exercising great care that we never go down that path.

Finally, it doesn't matter what form of sexual or lifestyle entrapment people may find themselves in—the only real danger is to believe the lie that Christ cannot redeem the situation. The testimonies of many who have escaped such ungodly bondage bears witness to this.

Partial Truths

It has become increasingly common in today's society for people to deal in partial truths.

When a person takes an oath in a courtroom, they're asked to swear that they will tell "the truth, the whole truth, and nothing but the truth, so help me God." If the person doesn't believe in a deity or its equivalent, they may make an affirmation and leave out "so help me God." Have you ever wondered why this oath is a requirement before the courts?

The original intention was for witnesses to give a commitment to the court, with their deity as witness, that their sworn testimony would be the whole truth. If the witness was later found to have lied while bound by their commitment, they were open to the charge of perjury before the court. Added to this, they were accountable to their deity, before whom they'd also lied.

From a Christian perspective, if a courtroom witness is a professing believer and they're found to have lied, then they'll need to face the consequences of the legal system as well as some deep soul-searching and repentance, in order to restore their relationship and conscience before God.

In the wider community, you only have to watch any of the crime shows on TV and you'll discover that they all have one thing in common: The story line is always based on partial truths that serve to frustrate the process of law enforcement. A serious crime is committed, and the crime fighters proceed to interview every possible lead they can find while getting only partial disclosure or partial truth at almost every turn. The level of drama appears to increase with the number of dead ends that occur, until finally there's a breakthrough, and the crime is solved about five minutes before the end of the show.

When the crime fighters finally piece together all the facts and confront the perpetrator of the crime with their findings, the climax to the story is usually accompanied by (a) a tearful or emotional confession; (b) a mysterious twist—such as the offender goes free because of some legal technicality or a left field outcome that no one saw coming; or (c) the judge's granting of a continuation, just to keep the suspense building and to maintain the show's ratings.

The underlying theme of these shows identifies a cry from within the heart of mankind to relate to each other in truth. Have you ever asked yourself why the viewers of these shows always find themselves wanting to be on the side of the crime-fighter good guys? They want the bad guys to get caught and held accountable for their deeds. Although there may be many reasons for this, here are some of my thoughts:

- The thought of innocence or trust being violated or abused by the unscrupulous is repulsive to the conscience of mankind.
- Although there's an intrinsic desire within the human heart to trust our fellow man, life experience generally teaches us about the perils of being too trusting.
- Every person who has experienced abuse (including emotional abuse, bullying, or harassment) can readily identify with the feeling of being violated.
- The good guys generally win, but we can all relate to the occasional situation where the bad guys go unpunished for their crime.

God has given every person a conscience that says "right" or "wrong" when we say or do things that impact our lives and the lives of those around us.

Have you ever wondered why you feel good when you do something good, and you feel bad when you do something bad? Why don't we feel bad when we do something good?

The reason is simple: God has deposited a little bit of Himself in every one of us in a place called our conscience.

Many unbelievers attempt to follow God in their own way by trying to keep a clear conscience and being prepared to ask for forgiveness and to forgive others when wrongs are done. I've helped many people reconnect with Jesus Christ, and one of the most common testimonies I hear from people is this: "I've always tried to be a good person and to help people where I can and do the right thing by others." In itself this is a good thing, because regardless of their belief in God, people are still following the law of the conscience that God designed.

If you think about this more deeply, you'll discover that the law of the conscience is what our society depends upon to maintain law and order. The alternative to this is everyone doing what's right in their own eyes, which would effectively lead to anarchy.

However, beyond the law of the conscience (being true to oneself), there's only one thing missing: knowing the Savior, Jesus Christ, who is the embodiment of all truth, and who declared, "I am the way, and the truth, and the life; no one comes to the Father but through Me" (John 14:6).

Our society deals heavily in partial truths (or selective disclosure), which is why there's so much mistrust, especially in the business world. One only has to mention used car salesmen and real estate agents, and there's an automatic air of skepticism.

If you ask around, you'll get a swift answer from many people about scams and rip-offs in which people have been told only part of the story, and then felt misled after the transaction. The underlying problem is a violation of trust.

For Christian believers, it's simply unacceptable to declare, "Well, I didn't tell a lie," while knowing all along that you didn't tell the whole truth.

The thing that needs to distinguish a Christian believer above all other things is honesty, especially when things go bad.

It may not be solely our fault, but we need to be prepared to admit to our contribution to the problem, and God will honor us through to its resolution.

One of the most transparent examples of this in Scripture was when Nathan the prophet confronted King David about his sin of adultery and of having Uriah the Hittite killed (2 Samuel 12). David immediately confessed his guilt with no attempt to hide the truth. As a result of this, God called David "a man after My own heart" (1 Samuel 13:14; Acts 13:22), even though he'd been seriously compromised and deceived in his decision-making.

Although tragic and long-term consequences resulted from David's actions, there's little doubt that David's restoration came as a result of his immediate admission of guilt when confronted by the prophet.

To see the genuineness of David's repentance, one has only to read the first verse of Psalm 51: "Have mercy on me, O God, according to your unfailing love." David further declares, "Surely you desire truth in the inner parts" (51:6 NIV; "innermost being" NASB; "inward parts" KJV), and in the same verse he acknowledges before God, "You teach me wisdom in the inmost place." David sets an example for us in both restoring and maintaining our relationship with God.

This is a source of hope and inspiration to me, especially when I realize that I could have handled things better on many occasions during my own life.

If we simply tell the whole truth, God will honor our decision, and restoration is only a prayer away.

Avoiding Responsibility for One's Actions

Blame-shifting began in the garden of Eden.

If this is part of a professing Christian's character, blame-shifting needs to be repented of, and the person needs to get things right with God, because the sinful nature still prevails in their life.

We are the redeemed of the Lord because we've made a choice to get things right with God. This also means sorting things out with our fellow man and taking responsibility for our actions. Shifting blame to others is a common worldly trait, but it isn't part of the culture in God's kingdom.

In business, I've had dealings with some hard-nosed government bureaucrats over the years, and although I may not always agree with their decisions, I generally respect them for their toughness and fairness.

However, I once worked with a bureaucrat known as "Teflon Man" because he made sure that nothing would ever stick to him, despite his atrocious record of misleading and deceptive conduct. Teflon Man would orchestrate service changes to government contracts at the expense of private sector businesses and make verbal promises of financial assistance to get things done. Once the changes were introduced, he had a habit of walking away from a considerable portion of his promises as soon as the question of payment arose. While this may have pleased his peers, among bus industry operators his reputation soon spread as someone not to trust.

To make matters worse, if operators complained to senior executive management, he would ensure that briefing papers were conveniently drafted to protect his decision-making and to paint anyone who challenged his authority as a whiner.

This type of situation is one of the clearest examples I've ever personally encountered of someone not wanting to take responsibility for their actions. From an industry perspective, the reputation of this person clearly suffered in terms of honesty and integrity. But it needs to be understood that no one is beyond the reach of the arm of the Lord, despite their past dealings.

Many people in this life are under the influence of deceptive spirits. The god of this world has blinded their minds to the things of God. Our encouragement from Scripture is to not give up on such people, but to pray until we see a breakthrough in the situation, and hopefully in the person's life as well.

We should never forget that Jesus came to set captives free (Isaiah 61:1) from bondage, lies, deception, trickery, and the like. When faced with situations like this, Scripture encourages us to pray and stay close to the Lord.

I generally encourage people to read Philippians 4:6-7 and to trust God for peace in the midst of the storm.

Integrity and Honesty in Dealings

In my experience, the business world is open to some of the worst forms of corrupt behavior, especially in situations that involve an explosive mixture of greed coupled with an abuse of power, authority, and control. Add to this excessive pride and sexual exploitation, and you have the potential for things to go from bad to worse when it all falls apart.

I'm also aware of situations involving teams of professionals from a number of business sectors, and at times the lack of integrity and confidentiality has been appalling.

I've struggled at times to come to grips with the deception existing in business when the same firm deals with multiple competing clients on the same project, and the key people aren't supposed to speak to each other—but the outcomes suggest otherwise. This is what can happen when profit and market power become more important than principles and ethics.

A similar pattern emerges in politics where a vote-winning policy is put forward favoring policy over principles. The end result generally involves spiraling unfunded expenditure, leaving an increasing national debt burden as an inheritance for the next generation. The political landscape in places is dotted with these types of decisions from all sides in politics. Regardless of the political configuration, the end result is a legacy of crippling debt for future generations through an ever increasing deficit.

This is no different from trade union officials supporting bogus wage claims or extorting money from developers by imposing overtime or other disruptive works practices on a building site, simply to increase the yield to their members.

I've personally interacted with trade union representatives at commission hearings when we've been on opposing sides of a wage claim, and I've been told privately that although the case had no merit, the claimants were members and had to be represented. While I can understand the sentiment, the absence of truth and any form of credibility is another matter.

I'm equally aware of quite a number of high profile business people and organizations who have been found guilty of ripping off their employees through underpayment of wages and not honoring the terms and conditions of agreements. This has even included unsafe work practices that can endanger people's lives, but which are in place simply to gain a higher level of financial return.

This situation is exacerbated by political lobbyists who are often engaged by big business to support their behavior, and who use their ideological and political alignments to gain an advantage in the market place.

All the above examples serve to highlight that the use of policy over principle is not uncommon across the various aspects of business and government, and where there are opportunities for personal gain, temptation takes on a more prominent role.

Having said this, the news media consistently demonstrates some of the worst ethics imaginable and constantly lives up to the old adage, "Don't let the facts get in the way of a good story." While this doesn't apply to all media, I've been appalled at the lack of integrity and honesty which has vested itself in one-sided reporting when it comes to politics and the many aspects of social policy.

The media is fully aware that it has incredible power to influence the populace one way or another. It should also be aware that with such power comes great responsibility to accurately and fairly present and report on any given situation.

Most people have no issue with honest, well-researched reporting which shows both sides of any debate, yet often this is stifled. The reporting becoming highly dependent upon the personal biases or agenda of the reporter, or of the people he or she represents.

At the end of the day, this is really a matter of integrity, which in my view most of our media outlets are seriously lacking. I once heard integrity defined as the person you are when there's no one around. I think that's an apt description. But I believe that true, heartfelt integrity goes a step further—by seeking to honor God through unbridled truth and a clear conscience, whether people are watching or not.

Integrity is being aware of the situational ethics that so often prevails in the world today, while choosing to take the pathway of principle based decision making instead.

This is one of the key reasons King Jehoshaphat instructed his appointed judges with these words:

> Now then let the fear of the LORD be upon you; be
> very careful what you do, for the LORD our God
> will have no part in unrighteousness or partiality
> or the taking of a bribe. (2 Chronicles 19:7)

The concept of doing business with integrity may be followed by some people, but to many the concept is totally foreign to their way of thinking. Indeed, many measure success by how much money, power, authority, and control a person possesses. Regrettably, this is part of the deceitfulness of riches that Jesus spoke about in the parable of the sower and the soils.

A final word on honesty and integrity: My encouragement is to be careful of the deceitfulness that comes with riches and power, which includes the type of bias mentioned above. As Lord Acton is quoted as saying, "Power tends to corrupt, and absolute power corrupts absolutely."

And while the news media are often the first to accuse politicians of hypocrisy, they need to take the log out of their own eye before they attempt to take the speck out of the eyes of others who may hold a different view, especially when it comes to matters like those outlined above.

Offensive Language

Such behaviors as swearing, coarse language, double-meaning jokes, and loud and aggressive speech will effectively render a Christian's witness as powerless. Identifying with this kind of worldly behavior effectively extinguishes our light before men.

I'll be the first to admit that some of these things can be funny, and at times it's incredibly hard not to laugh, especially when it happens unexpectedly. However, these things shouldn't be originated by believers, and shouldn't become a feature of our behavior in order to fit in with the crowd around us.

If you're known for these behaviors, you would be better off not presenting yourself as a Christian, since such behaviors brings reproach to the name of Jesus Christ. If you want to be a witness for Jesus in the workplace, then you need to repent and change your behavior before you open your mouth. Otherwise you can appear like the Christian who has a bumper sticker on their car that reads "One-Way, Jesus" and then proceeds to terrorize the street with reckless driving.

Put simply, if you want to terrorize the street—don't pretend that you're a disciple of Jesus Christ.

Addictions

If life-controlling problems such as compulsive gambling, habitual drinking, drug dependence, or addictions to pornography and sex are part of your lifestyle—you're already seriously compromised, and immediate intervention is needed.

If you genuinely want to deal with any of these problems, make an appointment with a pastor or counselor for appropriate professional help or referral, and follow through with fellowship and prayer support. Make sure that whoever seeks to assist you is appropriately qualified with professional skills in the area of addiction.

Accountability to a mature Christian believer and a fellowship group is also critical, because this will allow an individual to refocus on the things of God without coming under a continual cloud of guilt for an area of vulnerability in his or her character.

What is controlling my life? This is probably the most honest question every person needs to ask. If any of the behaviors above are controlling you, you need to get help—today.

For True Abundant Living

The list of items presented in these last few chapters are by no means exhaustive, but they come from life experience in the market place and workplace.

We need to seek an understanding of God's perspective on these matters and how they could be hindering our potential as effective carriers of the gospel message.

God's Word is rich with specific instructions and principles to live by, which can set us free from being enslaved to any of these things. Jesus came that we might have life—and life more abundantly—by being led by the Holy Spirit and not by our own selfish desires.

Do you have life? Or does life have you? In other words, are you in control of your life, or is your life being controlled by something or someone else?

If your answer is not what it should be and you want to change, I encourage you to say the following prayer with as much honesty of heart and faith as you can muster:

Father, I come to You in the name of Your Son, Jesus Christ.
As I've been reading this book, I've become aware
that I have issues with _____ [add the appropriate
words], and I'm sorry for my past behavior.

Today, I repent of these things, and I ask for Your forgiveness.

I ask You, Lord, to guide me and show me the
best way forward, because I don't want my
future to be determined by my past.

Here and now, I'm choosing to be different. I desire to be used
by You, Lord, as the light of the world, both in the market
place, my workplace, and wherever else You call me to be.

Father God, I want to follow You with all my heart,
and I believe that You have heard my prayer, for I'm
asking this in the name of Your Son, Jesus Christ.

15

My Personal Encounter with God

I came out of a totally unchurched family background, and although from an early age I held to the belief that God existed, I also concluded that He hadn't revealed Himself to me.

Through a series of tragic events—in my mid-teens, death claimed a close friend of mine named Austin as well as my beloved grandfather, and when I was twenty-one a cousin (by marriage) named Vernon passed away—I began to think more seriously about life and why we're here on earth.

Not long after Vernon died, the local Baptist church heard about the plight of his widow, Narelle, being left with three young children. Through this time of grief, the church gathered around and loved her and the extended family, providing practical support, food, counseling, and prayer. From these acts of kindness, Narelle and several members of her family—including her mother, Thelma—committed their lives to Jesus Christ.

I was close to Auntie Thelma, and after she shared her newfound faith with me, she gave me a *Good News Bible* to read. Although I was far from a believer at the time, I'd also learned never to knock something until you'd given it a fair hearing.

As I began to read the Bible over the coming months, I discovered that Jesus was an incredible person who traveled around the countryside doing all sorts of miraculous signs and wonders. He frequently got into trouble with the religious leaders, but they appeared to be jealous more than anything else.

I saw that Jesus also claimed to be the Son of God, and He'd come to earth with a mission to save a lost and dying world that had lost touch with God.

When I read about Jesus calming the storm or walking on water, feeding five thousand men and their families, or healing a man who was blind, mute, and demon possessed, there was a supernatural element I simply couldn't ignore. I saw how Jesus defended the women caught in the act of adultery and then declared to her, "Then neither do I condemn you; go now and leave your life of sin" (John 8:11).

I began to see the nail-scarred hands of Jesus Christ outstretched toward a lost and dying world, having already paid the ultimate price by dying in our place: "For God so loved the world, that He gave His only begotten Son, that whoever believes in Him shall not perish, but have eternal life" (John 3:16).

I went on to read heart-wrenching stories—like that of Jesus raising Lazarus from the dead, with His words to Martha, the dead man's sister: "I am the resurrection and the life. The one who believes in me will live, even though they die; and whoever lives by believing in me will never die. Do you believe this?" (John 11:25-26).

These verses were dealing with questions of life and death, and in reality I didn't have answers, because I was still trying to work out what I actually believed. I was on a faith journey, though I didn't realize it at the time. And although I didn't become a believer straightaway, God was beginning to reveal Himself to me, and I was starting to get a glimpse of what faith and belief really meant.

In my heart, I began looking at my life and at what the Scriptures had to say. I realized there were some things to which I could readily identify (such as wanting to help others wherever I could by following the law of my conscience). There were many other things that I didn't understand. But there was a ring of truth about what I was reading that went far beyond my present circumstances.

A Prayer from the Depths

About four months after Vernon passed away, I had an amazing encounter with God. Our family lived in an old two-story house (known as a Queenslander), and I had a bedroom on the ground floor where I slept and did my university studies. Around two A.M. one morning, I was wakened suddenly by a presence in my room. It wasn't a scary presence, but a holy presence. Although I couldn't see anything (it was pitch-black), I was totally aware of this presence all around me.

I immediately sat up on my bed, got on my knees, and prayed for the first time in my life. I still remember my prayer, word for word: "God, I know that I'm not living right. I want to change, I want to be the way You want me to be." This prayer came from the depths of my heart and soul.

Although this happened about forty years ago, it's still etched in my memory. I can honestly say that from that moment forward, God had my attention in a way that caused me to think about my life's purpose far more deeply than ever before.

Looking back, I can also confess an absolute belief that an angel of the Lord was in my bedroom that night, for Scripture declares, "Are not all angels ministering spirits sent to serve those who will inherit salvation?" (Hebrews 1:14).

It was all very real to me at the time, for I was on my faith journey. Little did I know that my own Damascus road experience was about to happen.

Surrender

Carmel and I were married in late December 1979. The following April, I was invited to a concert by our friend Lalita, who was attending a Bible college at the time. She was the sister of one of my best friends, Amrat, who like me was also on a faith journey. Leon Patillo was the singer and main speaker at the concert. He told the audience about his life as lead guitar in Carlos Santana's big band, and how they would get on a plane after a gig and begin to pass the alcohol and drugs. The band regularly experienced parties, fame, fortune, and women.

Leon said he had everything this life had to offer, but he would wake up the next morning sleeping next to some woman he didn't know and feel totally empty. He said he didn't realize at the time that man is a spiritual being, and that even if you have every material thing this world has to offer, it doesn't satisfy your real spiritual needs

He explained that a friend introduced him one day to the Lord Jesus Christ, and he found what he'd been looking for. Leon told of his surrender to God, and how he'd left the band, and how they'd offered him hundreds of thousands of dollars to return—but there was no turning back.

Then Leon challenged the audience: "You may not have done the things that I've done, but if you can identify with any of the things I've spoken about and you know something is missing, then have the courage of your convictions and come down the front and surrender your life to the Lord Jesus Christ."

That night, my friend Amrat and I, along with about five hundred other people, went forward and committed our lives to Jesus Christ. It was an amazing experience, and I had this incredible feeling of warmth as though my heart was going to burst with the love of God.

The following night I attended Northside Christian Family Church (now called Nexus Church) located at Everton Park in Brisbane. (I had heard about this church through another friend who was also on a faith journey.) I planned to just sit up the back and pretend to be invisible for the time being while I checked this place out. (I was coming from a totally unchurched background, and this was a Pentecostal church.)

To my dismay, I was greeted at the door by a steward and led down to a seat in the second row. I nearly died from fright, because this was quite a large church.

In the lead-up to the start of the service, people were talking with each other and genuinely engaged with each other. When the music started, there was an entire band. People actually looked like they were enjoying church and wanted to be there.

This was in stark contrast to the few times I'd attended a local Roman Catholic church with Carmel before we were married. There, no one really talked or engaged too much, apart from saying "Peace be with you" at some point during the service. And when it ended, just about everyone was gone within five minutes.

That night at Northside, a lady preacher spoke about the Holy Spirit. Most of it went way above my head. When the service was over, there seemed to be an air of excitement, and most people were still milling around talking and enjoying the presence of God.

As I sat there, I spoke to the gentleman next to me and told him I'd committed my life to Jesus Christ the night before. He seemed to get excited and began to say words like "Hallelujah" and "Glory to God," which freaked me out a little.

He then said to me, "Have you ever heard about a thing called the baptism in the Holy Spirit?"

"No," I replied. "What is that?"

He didn't try to explain it, but simply said, "Do you want to get closer to Jesus?"

After my experience the previous night, he had my full attention. "Yes," I replied.

"Come with me." He led me to the altar, where two men were praying for people. They laid hands on me and began to pray, and within a minute or so, I began to speak in a strange language. I felt once again that my heart was about to burst with the warmth and the love of God.

Although I soon joined a class for new Christians, it wasn't until several weeks later, when I was reading Acts 19:6, that I realized what had actually happened to me. This verse recalls how the apostle Paul visited Ephesus and encountered a group of twelve disciples of Jesus Christ who knew nothing about the Holy Spirit. When the apostle laid his hands on them, the Holy Spirit came upon them, and they spoke in tongues.

These two events were effectively my Damascus road experience (committing my life to Jesus) and my meeting with Ananias (prayer to be filled with the Holy Spirit), both of which are spoken of in Acts 9:1-17. This was the start of my journey as a Christian believer and my life has never been the same ever since.

Encounter with the Supernatural

At the time, I was working at a Ford Motor Company assembly plant at Eagle Farm, Brisbane, while I was in the final year of finishing my degree in economics. Starting almost as soon as I returned to work the following Monday, I can still remember sharing my newfound faith with a number of co-workers I'd befriended over time, and they were simply amazed at the change in my life. I was sharing Jesus Christ with my workmates on every possible occasion, and before long I was having regular fellowship with a number of Christian believers who also worked on the assembly line.

There was an older gentleman named Zoli who worked close to my spot on the assembly line. He told me that he was a believer in God but wasn't open about sharing his faith.

My first real encounter with the supernatural happened right there where I was working on the assembly line at a place called Door Locks. I'll never forget using the pliers one day, and they slipped and grabbed the flesh at the base on the inside of the middle finger of my left hand. The pliers pinched so tight that it literally crimped the skin together. A feeling of immense pain thundered through my entire body. It was excruciating.

Suddenly there flashed into my mind the scripture which says, "By His stripes you were healed" (1 Peter 2:24). I immediately began to thank Jesus for my healing, and I received it instantly.

I was so blown away that I went straight up and showed Zoli and told him what had just happened. Although my skin was still crimped, every bit of pain had left my body in an instant. Zoli could only look on in amazement, because this was truly a miraculous occurrence.

God was very gracious to me in those early days and I received miraculous healings on more than one occasion. These became a strong point of personal testimony for me.

As I shared these experiences, I often prayed for people who were sick, and I saw some miraculous outcomes, although not everyone was healed.

The assembly line was a fairly rough place to work, and was a bit like the United Nations in terms of different races and cultures, but this offered some wonderful opportunities to share the gospel message, even if I was often ridiculed because of my newfound faith.

Working in Public Service

By the end of 1980, I'd finished my degree and was ready to apply for full-time employment using my professional qualifications. I applied to the personnel section of government-owned Queensland Rail (QR) and was called down to the chief accountant's office. During the interview I was offered a job as a graduate clerk. I accepted the position with great delight and started working with QR in early 1981.

God taught me some valuable lessons over the next few years about working with people (some of whom were hard work), and about stepping up into leadership and management roles, and about the importance of nurturing relationships among fellow workers.

As I began to share my faith with a few of my workmates, word soon spread, and I often found myself having God-ordained conversations about all sorts of topics—some genuine and others in order to mock me. I also made a point of showing absolute integrity in all my work and sought to excel at every task that was handed to me. I aspired to excellence and saw this as a way of honoring God in the workplace.

Not long after joining QR, I was meeting with fellow Christian believers regularly for lunchtime fellowship, and then I approached a local inner-city church and was given permission to set up a prayer meeting and fellowship group on the church premises.

Many of those lunchtime meetings were inspired of the Holy Ghost, and we would praise God in song (often without music), share a message from the Bible, share testimonies, pray for the needs of people in the group and their friends and loved ones, and also give thanks for the great things God was doing in our midst.

During these formative years of working in the public service I began to move into junior management roles, and I realized there was a total lack of any form of mentoring for staff. Nonetheless, as I began to move into the managerial ranks, the most important training manual I possessed was my Bible and some godly teaching about leadership that I'd learned at church and from a few mature Christian friends. Scriptures such as the Golden Rule— "Do unto others as you would have them do unto you" (Matthew 7:12)—took on great prominence. I acted on this scripture by treating others the way I wanted to be treated. It was up to me to set the standard, not leaving it to others.

In order to grow in my understanding about the things of God, I realized that I had to gain a solid knowledge of the Bible and also spend time in prayer and fellowship with other believers. This was the daily pattern of the early church believers during a time of rapid church growth and spiritual revival (Acts 2:42-47), and I considered it necessary to align myself with this pattern if I wanted to experience the supernatural workings of God in my life.

I gave myself to service and leadership roles within the church, including everything from stacking chairs to board membership and later elder-ship roles on multiple occasions over the next four decades, as our growing family moved further out into the suburbs.

After six years with QR, I took on a role in Queensland Transport for another seven years, and finally departed the public service in June 1994, when I was offered a "Golden Handshake" redundancy payout and decided to take it.

New Directions in Ministry

At the age of thirty-six, I was able to pay off our beautiful five-bedroom home, and I immediately set up my own business, Roscar Management Consulting. Roscar was a consultancy service to the bus and coach industry that I'd previously been involved in regulating, and I could foresee major problems on the horizon for the industry as a result of pending reforms around the time of my departure.

About eighteen months after leaving the public service, I enrolled in full-time ministry training and spent the next two years at Strikeforce Ministry Training Institute while continuing to work part time in my consulting business.

I was asked to become the assistant pastor at our local church and enjoyed this role for a season, but always felt called to the market place rather than the pulpit.

During my stay at Queensland Transport, I'd met Tony Wyman. I also made a lot of industry contacts, which assisted Roscar in becoming a successful consulting business, first in Queensland and later in Victoria.

However, it was also during this time that I began to step out in faith and personally witness some remarkable signs, wonder, and miracles take place. It was also a great time of learning how to exercise spiritual gifts in the market place.

This is the subject of the next chapter.

16

In the Market Place: The Spirit's Vocal Gifts

E ver since Adam and Eve were expelled from the garden in Eden, God has supernaturally orchestrated *kairos* moments to allow mankind to bear witness to the pieces of His eternal plan falling into place. In many instances, God would speak about these *kairos* moments through His prophets, who would make prophetic declarations and then carefully record for future generations what they'd spoken or were shown.

As part of His eternal plan, God also revealed aspects of His nature and character through what theologians refer to as special revelation. This includes such events as theophany (a manifestation of God, as in Genesis 12:7-9 or Exodus 3:2), Christophany (a temporary appearance of Christ in the Old Testament, as in Daniel 3:25), and angelic visitation (as in Luke 1:26 and 2:9-15).

God also speaks through visions and dreams which the apostle Peter spoke about on the day of Pentecost (Acts 2:17), as the Holy Spirit brought to fulfillment that which had been spoken some nine hundred years earlier by the prophet Joel (in Joel 2:28-32).

Although these elements occurred during the Old Testament era, they were specific signs of the last-days outpouring of the Holy Spirit that commenced at Pentecost.

Another means of revelation that God has given to believers in the New Testament era is the gifts of the Holy Spirit. Nine gifts are described in 1 Corinthians 12 and 14. Scripture is clear that these gifts were given to early church believers as a sign of the indwelling power of the Holy Spirit being present in their lives.

The doorway or entry point to these gifts is what is known as the baptism in the Holy Spirit (Matthew 3:11) with the outward evidence of speaking in tongues (Isaiah 28:11; Acts 2:4; 1 Corinthians 14:21).

Among other things, these gifts were given as distinctives for outsiders to witness the power of God in action in the lives of believers, as the Holy Spirit ministers both to the body of Christ (the church) and through the daily lives of Spirit-filled believers. Scripture reveals that God has given these gifts of the Holy Spirit to believers as a means to operate in the supernatural realm for the common good (John 14:12; 1 Corinthians 12:7; 12:11; 13:8-10; 14:25) until the time of Christ's return.

With this in mind, these next three chapters are given as testimony of the operation of the gifts of the Holy Spirit that I've personally experienced, with particular emphasis on the market place.

We'll begin with what are known as the vocal gifts—the gifts of prophecy, tongues, and interpretation.

The Gift of Prophecy

Only a year or so after I became a Christian believer, my friend Amrat told me about how some people in the home fellowship group he attended were beginning to exercise the gift of prophecy (1 Corinthians 12:10), and that it was an incredible experience to see the Lord working powerfully in the meetings. Amrat encouraged me to begin to seek the Lord for the gifts of the Holy Spirit, and I did so immediately. I'd become familiar with the verse which says that believers should earnestly desire spiritual gifts, especially the gift of prophecy (1 Corinthians 14:1).

I love to pray and talk to God about the things happening around me, including the people I meet. When the opportunity arises, I've never been slow in coming forward. From the early days of my faith journey, I've had a deep yearning to bring God into any given situation.

Well, it wasn't long before an opportunity arose, and what happened next was simply amazing, and one of the most exhilarating experiences I've ever had in my life.

We had some friends named Tom and Mary who'd previously attended church with us. One Saturday after my morning devotions, I felt led by God to visit Tom and Mary, who lived less than five minutes from our home. We were good friends, so when I arrived, I knocked on the door and entered the living room only to see Tom, Mary, and another man I'd never met sitting at their kitchen table, holding hands and praying.

As I mentioned earlier, I was never a slouch when it came to prayer, so I immediately went in and sat at the table and added an extra set of hands to the prayer group.

I'd been sitting there no more than thirty seconds before I felt an incredible anointing of the Holy Spirit come upon me, and the Word of the Lord welled up within my innermost being to the point that I was almost ready to burst.

Suddenly, for the first time, I began to prophesy. While I cannot recall every word, I distinctly remember saying, "Why is it that you've turned your back on the Lord your God and gone off and followed foreign gods?" I also somehow knew that these words were meant for the other man.

To be perfectly honest, I nearly choked on my words and could hardly wait to get out of that place, because the words were nothing like what I expected. They seemed highly judgmental. I even wondered if I might have grieved the Holy Spirit or stepped over some forbidden line. Yet I knew that what had come forth was not from my own understanding, and certainly not the kind of words I would normally have used, especially since I'd met this person only a few moments earlier.

My heart was racing, and I motioned to Tom that I was leaving. He followed me to the door, and we went outside. I told Tom that I was unsure about what was going on, but I believed the words had come from God.

Tom informed me that this fellow at the table had been a really strong Christian at one stage in his life, but had come under the influence of some seriously wrong teaching and doctrine. Tom said that this man recently had been having strange dreams and had begun putting his faith in his dreams rather than God. Tom indicated that both he and Mary had become really concerned for him, because they knew his actions and beliefs were not based on faith in God. Tom identified the prophetic word I'd spoken as being from God.

Although I'd been somewhat distressed in my spirit, I immediately had a sense of relief, but this experience had also brought a greater sense of awe and reverence for God into my life. I had no desire to step over the line or to speak anything other than what God was wanting me to say.

Although my first encounter with the gift of prophesy was somewhat of a baptism by fire, I also learned a valuable lesson that day. I came to understand the need to always "be ready in season and out of season" (2 Timothy 4:2) for whatever circumstances the Lord might bring my way. That verse is part of the apostle Paul's charge to Timothy to faithfully carry out the work of ministry, and if we seriously desire to walk in the footsteps of Jesus Christ and His disciples, it should also apply to our lives.

This "being ready" simply means preparing our heart before the Lord and spending time in His presence daily. This includes essentials such as prayer, reading and meditating on God's Word, and listening to the Holy Spirit speaking into our lives.

In my role as a project manager of major events, there's not a single day when I'm not before the Lord seeking His direction and blessing before I start work. It doesn't matter how late I've finished work the night before. And although at times this may mean as little as four hours of sleep, I simply don't want to face any day without having first spent time with my God—and it's my delight to do so.

The Gift of Tongues and Interpretation

The first time I experienced the gift of the interpretation of tongues was in 1983. I'd been seconded from Brisbane to Melbourne to work in a joint state-federal government task force for four months. Through my local church in Brisbane, I became aware of a church in Melbourne where I could fellowship.

I was at a church service there one Sunday evening, and a message was spoken out using the gift of tongues. Although I felt a deep welling up within my spirit to deliver the interpretation, I was overcome with fear and remained silent, mainly because I was new to the congregation and had never experienced anything quite like this before.

Despite the powerful message in tongues, no interpretation was forthcoming, and I felt a sense of having grieved the Holy Spirit.

At the end of the service, I went forward and spoke to the senior pastor and told him what had happened. I shared with him the words I believed God had given me.

He told me that the message I'd been given was from God and would have touched the congregation. He also encouraged me to speak out the next time it happened. I was truly thankful for his counsel.

I'd been unexpectedly put on the spot, but I knew that there would be a next time and that I had to exercise faith and trust the Holy Spirit's leading in future.

Believers are encouraged in 1 Corinthians 14:1 to "earnestly [or "eagerly"] desire spiritual gifts, especially the gift of prophecy." My experience and observation over four decades of ministry involvement is that few believers actually pray for or desire to be used in the vocal gifts. The reasons may be many and varied, and I must say that my first encounters with these vocal gifts was not what I would have expected. However, in hindsight, I must say that faith must overcome fear, and our motivation and desire must be to bless others and to build up the kingdom of God.

Since these events unfolded, I've witnessed some amazing God encounters that have been unlocked through the use of these vocal gifts within the market place, workplace, church, restaurants, coffee shops, homes, and other ministry settings.

If you're a Christian believer and haven't previously exercised these gifts, I want to encourage you to pray and to begin to earnestly desire to be used by the Holy Spirit to bless and to build up the kingdom of God in your midst.

When you do, there's a new edge of adventure waiting just around the corner!

A Glimpse of Pentecost

A number of years ago I was having dinner with a business executive I was working with at the time. I'd been sharing the gospel message with this lady for quite some time, and now she was expressing a desire to accept Jesus Christ as Lord and Savior.

After taking her through a prayer for salvation, the Holy Spirit suddenly gave me the gift of tongues, and then came the interpretation.

When I was given the message in tongues, I had no idea that I was actually speaking in her native Filipino dialect, and the interpretation confirmed the words. When she told me this, we both had a sense of awe and amazement. I received a fleeting glimpse that night of what it must have been like for those who were listening to the 120 believers in the upper room on the day of Pentecost (Acts 2:5-11).

However, in all this we should not lose sight of an underlying purpose of this gift. In 1 Corinthians 14:22, Paul says that "tongues are a sign for unbelievers." In other words, tongues are meant to be observed by unbelievers in order to gain their attention, for tongues come from the realm of the supernatural uttering of mysteries with one's spirit (1 Corinthians 14:2). When a sign of this kind is seen, the faith response is like that of the people in Acts 2:12— "What does this mean?" What these people had just witnessed on the day of Pentecost left them "amazed and perplexed." In contrast, the response of those without faith was to mock and accuse the believers of having too much wine (Acts 2:13).

Either way, the gift of tongues demands a response. There are, and always will be, two choices.

Notwithstanding this, the vocal gifts are amazing instruments the Holy Spirit uses to build up and strengthen the church, as a body of believers.

The purpose of this chapter is not to go through the theological and doctrinal aspects of the vocal gifts, since these have been well covered by some of the greatest church teachers of our time. Rather, the purpose here is to offer encouragement for all believers to step out in faith and to ask

God for the greater gifts, with the understanding that He wants to use all believers as instruments for His glory.

As you begin to exercise the vocal gifts, it paves the way for God to use you in the supernatural realm, to open prison doors, to mend broken hearts and to set the captives free (Isaiah 61:1).

Just One Word

We can share, minister, counsel, teach, mentor, and tutor as much as humanly possible. But sometimes all it takes is one word from the Master—then the message gets through, the deadlock is broken, and the past no longer has to dictate the future.

This is one of the primary reasons that vocal gifts were given to believers: so that the listener can readily identify that God is involved. It's then inevitable that some form of breakthrough will follow.

On many occasions when I pray for people, whether unbelievers or believers, God will give me a powerful gift of tongues and the interpretation or a word of prophecy. I've learned to have confidence in the Holy Spirit to bring forth the Word of God into any given situation and to see the power of God manifest in changing people's lives.

We never know just when or to whom God may want us to speak, but being prepared, willing, and dependent upon the Holy Spirit's leading are the beginning of God encounters that are open for all.

Scripture is simply loaded with such encounters, and I dare to say that it's up to believers to keep living by faith and to continue adding to the last-days journals of the unfinished book of Acts.

17

In the Market Place: The Spirit's Revelatory Gifts

s we continue exploring the gifts of the Holy Spirit, remember again, amongst other things, that these spiritual gifts are given so that outsiders may witness the power of God in action in the lives of believers, as the Holy Spirit ministers to the body of Christ (the church) and into the daily lives of Spirit-filled believers.

In this chapter we'll look at what are known as the revelatory gifts, which include the gifts of the word of knowledge, the word of wisdom, and the discerning of spirits.

The Gift of the Word of Knowledge

The gift of the word of knowledge involves a supernatural impartation of knowledge from God to a Christian believer.

The reason for this knowledge transfer is to reveal something about a person or a situation in the natural realm that the believer never could have known out of his or her own understanding.

Whether it's in the market place, workplace, a church, or elsewhere, the word of knowledge can result in amazing outcomes whose ultimate purpose is to bring glory to God—not to the receiver of the gift. I've included below a few instances where a word of knowledge has brought great glory to God by touching the lives of people around me in some of the most remarkable ways.

Up until 2012, our family lived on an acreage, and we had a large shed where our cars were parked at the rear of the property. There came a period of time when I was aware of a business situation experiencing some problems, and I was praying for a friend of mine named Chris who was a manager and part owner at the business.

As I was walking up to the garage one morning, my thoughts suddenly switched to Chris, and as I sat in the car and went to back out, I suddenly heard the voice of the Holy Spirit whisper the following word of knowledge to me: "Chris resigned as a company director last night."

I immediately called Chris and waited for quite some time for his phone to answer. It was finally answered by his wife, who took the phone to Chris. He was in the bathroom at the time, weeping and on his knees, crying out to God about an ordeal he'd just been through.

When Chris regained his composure, the first thing he told me was that he felt compelled to resign as a company director the night before.

When I told Chris that the Holy Spirit had just revealed this to me, and that I'd called him in order to pray for him, he was overcome with a sense of awe and wonder far more powerful than the negative feelings he had been experiencing from the ordeal. Chris told me that nothing like this had ever happened to him before—where God spoke to a friend in such a way to reveal something impossible to know otherwise, in order to show His great love and care.

I had a precious time of ministry with Chris that day, and in time he worked through the necessary legalities but without all the emotional and spiritual harm that might have otherwise resulted.

To God be the glory!

While I was recalling this story, the Lord began to show me count-less other instances where this gift had operated during my lifetime. Quite often it was operating with another gift at the same time.

When a Christian believer receives the gift of the word of knowledge, this can sometimes be manifest by a slight pain or sensation in the body of someone they're interacting with or ministering to. This can actually happen in an acute way.

A number of years ago, I was co-leading a house church that went through the closest thing to revival I'd ever experienced. The other co-leader and I used to meet several times each week to pray for our group of about nine people. We would both pray, "Lord, do what You want. Touch our lives, and never let us be the same."

God heard the sincerity of our prayer, and within two to three weeks, up to forty people were coming to our house church meeting, and we were seeing the miraculous happen on a weekly basis.

A little while before we started the house church meetings, a lady named Shirley was diagnosed with leukemia. Shirley was a wonderful soul and the wife and mother of the host family where we had our meetings. Although her leukemia appeared to be a setback, it was also a challenge for our group to believe God for Shirley's healing. Amazingly, Shirley was prayed into remission, and the consulting specialist said that in his years of medical practice, he'd never seen a blood count reverse in the manner in which it had for Shirley.

Shirley would often lie on a foldout lounge beside me during those meetings. Although she wasn't well at times, she loved it when the presence of God would come and touch His people.

One particular night after we'd just been through a wonderful time of praise and worship, we were waiting on the Lord for His leading. I suddenly felt tightness around my throat, and as I looked down, I saw that Shirley appeared to be struggling to get her breath. She was looking at me intently. I pointed to my throat and nodded in her direction as if to ask about her apparent distress, and she immediately nodded with a sense of urgency and despair.

This was a word of knowledge given by the Holy Spirit to reveal that a spiritual attack was happening against Shirley in her weakened state.

I immediately rebuked the attacking spirit and, in the name of Jesus I commanded it to leave. Shirley coughed violently several times and then became completely calm.

I was then led by the Holy Spirit to press in and pray for the joy of the Lord to touch Shirley, for the Word of God declares, "The joy of the Lord is your strength" (Nehemiah 8:10). And that is exactly what Shirley needed at the time.

Shirley began to laugh in the Spirit, and then the Spirit of joy fell on me as well; then one by one, the entire meeting was touched.

When I left the meeting at midnight, Shirley was still drunk in the Spirit.

Oh, the joy that fills my soul as I recall those meetings, and I could certainly relate just a little to the outpouring of the Holy Spirit on the day of Pentecost, for the witnesses also thought the 120 people in the upper room were drunk (Acts 2:15).

God certainly revealed His glory that night.

The word of knowledge is one of the most powerful gifts that God has chosen to give to believers, primarily because He wants to get the attention of someone and is prepared to operate in the supernatural realm in order for this to happen.

Quite apart from this and depending upon the circumstances, it can also be to demonstrate that the favor of God is upon a believer's life as a testimony to their fellow workers in the market place.

The word of knowledge is a gift from God for believers to help unbelievers open a door to the things of God. Because the truth is that many people wear masks, and they try to hide what's really happening inside them because they don't want people to know, and they think they can work it out by themselves, given time. However, many things that trouble us do not cure themselves, and it's not until we hit rock bottom that we actually open the door to others, or more importantly, to God Himself, for help.

I firmly believe that the market place is one of the most important places where this gift can be used as it can bring great glory to God. It demonstrates that God cares about a person so much that He's prepared to reveal something about them in a supernatural manner. In my experience, there's no better way to get someone's attention than to reveal something God has shown you about them in a loving and caring manner, and solely for their benefit.

When God has used me to speak to someone in this way, the response has often been accompanied by tears, followed by questions like, "How could you possibly know that?" Or, "I've never told anyone that; only God knew." Or, "How could you possibly know what I'm thinking?"

The truth is that I wouldn't have known anything unless God chose to reveal it to me for the benefit of the person He's trying to connect with.

The Gift of the Word of Wisdom

As with many things in the kingdom of God, timing is like the key that turns knowledge into wisdom. For when the Spirit of God is involved, knowledge and wisdom take on a heavenly dimension with the power to set captives free, to bind up the brokenhearted, and to bring release to those who feel totally bound by life's circumstances.

This gift involves a supernatural impartation of wisdom from God to a Christian believer. The word of wisdom applies God's (*kairos*) time-clock by adding a dimension of revelation to knowledge, and having the power to both unlock and break through whatever situation is being faced. This gift comes with clarity and application in the natural realm.

I've frequently found that this gift can unlock situations in a manner that can leave you with a sense of awe and amazement.

This gift, which is mentioned in 1 Corinthians 12 and 14, is by no means restricted in its application to workings within the church. In the business world, the word of wisdom can also provide an amazing and distinct edge for believers who operate in this gift.

In the Old Testament, both Joseph and Daniel were identified as servants of God because of the wisdom with which they administered the kingdoms set before them. Scripture clearly reveals that this wisdom came from seeking God.

In like manner, as we put our trust in God and ask in faith, the Word of God promises to generously grant wisdom to all who believe: "If any of you lacks wisdom, he should ask God, who gives generously to all without finding fault, and it will be given to him" (James 1:5).

This has been a frequent prayer of mine, because we need to seek the wisdom that comes from God, if we want to walk in the blessings of God.

I can recall countless boardroom and business situations over the years where God has given me a word of wisdom to break a business deadlock, to open a new venture, or to close off something from the past. One of those occasions is still fresh in my mind though it happened many years ago, while I was in the public service.

A significant dispute had developed between the then lord mayor of Brisbane and the transport minister. The two were not on talking terms. In the midst of this dispute, a new bus service needed to be urgently implemented, which required licensing and a funding agreement between senior executives from the Brisbane City Council and the Queensland Department of Transport.

Prior attempts by senior executives had failed to settle this matter, and a meeting between the parties was scheduled for a certain afternoon. Upon arrival at the venue, the attendees were told by the executive directors of both parties that no one was leaving the room until the matter was resolved. About fifteen people sat around the boardroom table and were briefed about the situation and the issues requiring resolution. We were told that a proposal needed to emerge from the meeting that was both workable and within budget.

Considerable discussion followed among the various stakeholders, but no real progress was being made.

In the lead-up to this event, I'd committed the situation to God and asked for His wisdom to be manifest in the meeting. What then took place was simply amazing as an answer to that prayer.

As I sat at the boardroom table, suddenly it was as though the Lord had given me a complete download of a proposal and the strategy needed to implement a new transport service, which I was able to explain to the meeting in detail. The strategy was immediately taken up for further discussion, and the meeting broke into several groups to check the all-important operational and financial aspects of the proposal.

After about an hour or so, everyone came together again and reported their findings to the executive directors. The proposal was found to be not only operationally sound but also within budget, and it could be implemented as soon as the parties were ready.

The meeting, which had started with such tension and uncertainty, ended up with the entire boardroom of people departing for a late dinner together. It had indeed been a marathon session, but this word of wisdom from the Holy Spirit had allowed all the outstanding matters to be resolved, and some much needed oil was poured on the troubled wounds of government that existed at the time.

Soon after, I received a personal commendation for the contribution I made to resolve the dispute that night—but the Holy Spirit is the one who really needed to be commended, not only for answering my prayer but also for going well beyond and gifting me with an amazing word of wisdom. To God be the glory!

In another amazing experience, I was once assisting in ministry at a church attended by a young married couple named James and Dianne. I began to develop a relationship with this couple, and one day James asked if I could visit him at home, because he was wanting to grow in the faith.

I'd become aware that there may have been some tensions in their marriage. On my first two visits, Dianne locked herself in the family room and appeared to be somewhat annoyed at my coming. I left it to James to open the discussion about anything that was on his mind, and as James asked about a topic, I would simply take him to the Scriptures and discuss what the Word of God had to say. Meanwhile I kept them both of them in prayer during this time, and asked God for His direction and leading.

As I arrived outside their house for my third visit, the Holy Spirit whispered to me a word of knowledge: "Dianne will be joining you tonight."

I simply smiled and said, "Thank you, Lord," and went into the house.

When the door opened, I was greeted by both James and Dianne, and then I was informed that Dianne was going to join us tonight.

I smiled graciously, knowing that God was paving the way for something special to happen that night.

Dianne was forthright in her approach, and I wasn't at all surprised when she came straight out with what was on her mind. She laid her issues with God on the table. Dianne was angry with God because she'd had a miscarriage some time earlier, and for more than eight months they'd been trying without success to conceive a second child.

She informed me that they'd both undergone tests, and there was no physical reason preventing them from having a child. Her frustration had brought her to the place of questioning her faith in God, and this had now turned into being angry with God. My being there that evening gave her the opportunity to vent and to pour out her heart to someone—and I guess I was as good as anyone else.

At this point, you wouldn't need to be Einstein to realize that without God's wisdom, things could have gone awfully bad in the ensuing time of ministry. Yet God had ordained this time, for He alone is the restorer of hope, and He was about to bind up someone whose heart had been broken by the circumstances of life.

Over the next hour or so, I asked Dianne to take me through the events that had led up to this moment, and I listened intently. During this time, the Holy Spirit clearly revealed to me that Dianne was harboring unforgiveness against a number of people regarding her miscarriage, and this had been hindering her prayers.

As I began to speak out this revelation, it took on the form of a word of wisdom to this couple. Dianne received it as personal revelation, and she began to weep and to ask God to forgive her.

I led Dianne in a prayer of repentance, and she was restored in her relationship not only with God but also with her husband, who'd been on receiving end of her anger and frustration for quite some time.

I finished the night by praying for them as husband and wife, and I asked God to bless them by granting them the desires of their heart.

Some time later, I was approached by James and Dianne after church one Sunday. Dianne was almost beside herself with excitement as she told me that not only was she pregnant, but they'd pinpointed the time of conception to be the very night I'd ministered and prayed for them both. That was when the breakthrough had come.

God's timing is always perfect, and on that evening His gift of the word of wisdom had delivered His blessings in the most wonderful manner to this couple.

> So will My word be which goes forth from My
> mouth; It will not return to Me empty, without
> accomplishing what I desire, and without succeeding
> in the matter for which I sent it. (Isaiah 55:11)

Once again, I stand in awe and worship God.

The Gift of Discerning of Spirits

One of the most wonderful things about Jesus is that He is able to restore hope when the circumstances scream, "It's hopeless!"

He doesn't look at our past or present circumstances. Instead He looks at our potential with a heavenly inspired mixture of faith, hope, and love.

This is God's wisdom and goodness in action.

When a believer desires to enter into the deeper things of God, it's often the case that unwanted baggage from the past may try to raise its ugly head in an attempt to hinder the work of God from progressing in their spiritual growth.

The gift of discerning of spirits involves the work of the Holy Spirit to reveal the operation of evil, unclean, or demonic spirits (these terms have the same meaning) in a person or a situation being encountered.

I'm fully aware that some view this topic (as well as deliverance from the "discerned spirit") as controversial. However, I've personally witnessed this gift in operation on many occasions over the years, and I've seen many captives set free in the name of Jesus Christ.

My first encounter with the gift of discerning spirits was a very personal one that happened the day I dared to pray, "Lord, I want to be totally clean before You." A word of caution: Please don't pray this prayer unless you really mean it, because it has the potential to change your life forever.

My first experience of deliverance taught me that we have an enemy who wants to keep us so bound up in earthly things that we won't seek to embrace the deeper things of God that reside in the realm of the Spirit.

This was my first but not my only encounter with personal deliverance. I simply wanted to walk in holiness before the Lord and to enter into the greater purposes of God for my life, and I didn't want the baggage from my past to interfere.

About six years after I'd committed my life to Jesus Christ, Carmel and I had a modest house, a mortgage, and three children under three years of age. I earned just enough to keep on top of the bills. Carmel wasn't in paid employment at the time because we had prayed and agreed that she wouldn't reenter the workforce until our youngest child started school. Although things were tight financially, we kept to a budget, and this helped us make the most of our lot in life for this season of our lives.

However, when the offering bag would come around at church each week, I would feel guilty about putting in my leftovers. Although this was all I had to give at the time, deep down I knew this was not honoring God.

I'd come from a relatively poor family with six children, and my parents lived from week to week, struggling to make ends meet.

As I began to seek God and pour out my heart to Him, it was revealed to me through the gift of discernment that a "spirit of poverty" existed over my family line which needed to be broken.

I can still picture the setting of the room, the day, and the hour in which I was delivered from this spirit that had been holding back the work of God in my life. I prayed, renounced the spirit of poverty, and commanded it to go from my life and never to return. I witnessed some amazing manifestations as it departed.

Until this point in time, logic and reason had screamed at me, "You can't afford to tithe (offering ten percent of my income to God); you won't have enough money to pay the bills." But God's Word kept saying,

> "Give, and it shall be given unto you; good measure,
> pressed down, and shaken together, and running
> over, shall men give into your lap. For with the
> same measure that you measure it shall be measured
> to you again." (Luke 6:38, *KJ 2000 Bible*)

Little did I know what God had planned for my family as a result of this deliverance and the step of faith and obedience that I took by commencing to pay tithes from that week onward:

- Within one week, my salary was increased by more than twenty percent.
- Over the next seven years I had a total of six promotions, and I went on to be one of the fastest promoted in the history of our department within the public service. My salary increased by more than three hundred percent, and I was given a car to drive to and from work.

- I'd been relieving in the State Executive Service not long before I elected to take a "golden handshake" redundancy package at age thirty-six, and in June 1994 I paid off our beautiful five-bedroom second home.
- I set up my consulting business the next day, and have never looked back.

Today, God has blessed me to the point that I have a track record that's right up with the very best in the Asia Pacific Region in the project management of major transport events.

Way beyond that, God has granted me extraordinary favor with senior executives in government, many CEOs in business, and senior political leaders and business people. I've actively and unashamedly shared Jesus Christ with many of them, and led a number of them into a personal relationship with Jesus Christ.

To me, these souls are the hidden treasures—the riches stored in secret places that God wants to give us (Isaiah 45:3), because no amount of money or wealth could ever be enough to redeem a precious soul (Psalm 49:7-8). There's only one way for this to happen, and it involves making a commitment to God through His Son, Jesus Christ.

Before I made the decision to honor God with my finances, we had always known lack. I knew what it was like to have one pair of good shoes to my name.

As I've continued honoring God with my finances and my life, He has continually revealed Himself as *Jehovah Jireh*—our Provider—and He has blessed our family beyond our wildest dreams.

All this began when God revealed that a spirit of poverty existed over my life that was hindering His greater work in my life. At the time of this encounter, God took me through a season of learning, and then He began to lead me into situations where I needed to exercise the gift of discerning spirits, and then to pray for people to be set free—commonly known as deliverance.

I'm fully aware that there have been excesses with this gift, as also with many other spiritual gifts over the years. But I'm also aware that God gave this gift to the body of Christ so that people could be set free from spiritual bondage.

Just think about how many times the gospel messages of the New Testament contain ministry encounters where Jesus and His followers set people free from evil or demonic spirits. These God encounters included everything from a Jewish believer sitting in a synagogue and being set free from a spirit of infirmity (Luke 13:10-12), right through to a demon-possessed man who was totally out of control in the region of the Gerasenes (Luke 8:26-38).

Search the Scriptures for yourself and you'll find many such encounters of light and darkness. Here are some passages to examine: Luke 7:21; Luke 8:12; Mark 5:1-20; Mark 6:7; Mark 16:15-20; Acts 5:16; Acts 8:7; Acts 19:11-12.

With this in mind, and with the preponderance of evil that surrounds our society today, any thought that these demonic spirits (who are also eternal beings) have departed from earth can only be described as spiritual naivety in the extreme.

As the day of Christ's return draws near, believers should expect the tide of demonic activity to increase, because Jesus and the New Testament writers experienced it personally and foretold it would happen in the last days:

> Whoever believes and is baptized will be saved, but
> whoever does not believe will be condemned. And
> these signs will accompany those who believe: In My
> name they will drive out demons. (Mark 16:16-17)

For in the case of many who had unclean
spirits, they were coming out of them shouting
with a loud voice; and many who had been
paralyzed and lame were healed. (Acts 8:7)

God did extraordinary miracles through the hands
of Paul, so that even handkerchiefs and aprons that
had touched him were taken to the sick, and the
diseases and evil spirits left them. (Acts 19:11-12)

Now the Spirit expressly states that in later times
some will abandon the faith to follow deceitful spirits
and the teachings of demons. (1 Timothy 4:1)

The rest of mankind who were not killed by these plagues
still did not repent of the work of their hands; they
did not stop worshiping demons. (Revelation 9:20)

We need to consider these Scriptures and the circumstances they're depicting, and to realize that they're pointing to the very days in which we're living.

If you're open to the deeper things of God and have a courageous heart, ask the Lord to show you what is causing that area of difficulty in your life that you've continued to struggle with, despite prayer and submission to God.

Soulish Desires

You may have had some relief, but if deep down there's a continual soulish desire that you know is not what God would want for your life, I want to encourage you to ask Him to reveal the underlying cause, and trust Him for the outcome.

If this doesn't apply to you, then you're blessed. But be aware that many others face this kind of affliction and may need help in order to be set free.

You may well ask, "What is the source of these soulish desires and where do they come from?" Here are a few things the Lord has revealed to me:

When Adam and Eve were created, the picture we see is one of perfect harmony with God and each other. They wanted for nothing, and were one-hundred-percent provided for by God.

A fact of great significance is that they were both created as mature adults. And from the very beginning, God made His intention for their lives known to them:

> God blessed them and said to them, "Be fruitful and
> multiply, and fill the earth and subdue it; rule over
> the fish of the sea and the birds of the air and every
> creature that crawls upon the earth." (Genesis 1:28)

Adam and Eve and their offspring were born to rule and reign, to subdue the earth, and to have dominion over it. They'd been uniquely and wonderfully made, and they had God to thank for every possible provision and blessing upon their lives.

Despite this, God didn't want His creation to be robotic in worship or allegiance. He wanted Adam and Eve and their offspring to worship Him in spirit and in truth (John 4:23). So when God created Adam and Eve in

His own image and likeness, He also gave them the power of choice and the freedom to make their own decisions.

While this was incredibly liberating, God put one boundary in place for Adam and Eve to obey during their decision-making:

> And the LORD God commanded him, "You may eat freely
> from every tree of the garden, but you must not eat from
> the tree of the knowledge of good and evil; for in the day
> that you eat of it, you will surely die." (Genesis 2:16-17)

This boundary was put in place to allow the obedience of Adam and Eve to be tested. God made it clear what fruit they could eat and what fruit was forbidden. He also warned them of the consequences of crossing the line and eating the forbidden fruit. It should be noted that Scripture is silent about the thoughts that may have gone through the minds of Adam and Eve when they received this command from God, including what the concept of death might have meant to them.

Then came Eve's encounter with the serpent. Here are the critical elements of their exchange:

> Now the serpent was more subtle and crafty
> than any living creature of the field which the
> Lord God had made. And he [Satan] said to the
> woman, Can it really be that God has said, You
> shall not eat from every tree of the garden?

> And the woman said to the serpent, We may eat the fruit
> from the trees of the garden, except the fruit from the tree
> which is in the middle of the garden. God has said, You
> shall not eat of it, neither shall you touch it, lest you die.

But the serpent said to the woman, You shall not surely die. For God knows that on the day you eat from it your eyes will be opened [that is, you will have greater awareness], and you will be like God, knowing [the difference between] good and evil.

And when the woman saw that the tree was good for food, and that it was delightful to look at, and a tree to be *desired in order to make one wise and insightful*, she took some of its fruit and ate it; and she also gave some to her husband with her, and he ate. Then the eyes of the two of them were opened [that is, their awareness increased], and they knew that they were naked; and they fastened fig leaves together and made themselves coverings. (Genesis 3:1-7 AMP)

The picture we see here is of the serpent subtly questioning the command of God and suggesting to Eve that God was holding something back.

It was only when Eve entertained this thought that things went horribly wrong. Eve began to see this tree as something to be desired to make one wise and insightful. To the natural mind, a tree having these qualities seems almost nonsensical.

Yet God was indeed holding something back. He'd kept Adam and Eve free from sin and its consequences—such as grief, tragedy, devastation, separation, and death—which would ultimately result from gaining the knowledge of evil. Up until this point in time, Adam and Eve had only the knowledge of good, since they were born into the very presence of God. It was only after the serpent suggested, "You will be like God" (Genesis 3:5) that Eve's attention began to focus on the tree and its forbidden fruit.

It's not at all surprising that the serpent's own desire to be like God was the reason Lucifer was cast out of heaven (Isaiah 14:12-14; Luke 10:18). Yet this was the same desire that the serpent projected onto Eve, and which led to the fall from grace for both her and Adam.

Thousands of years later, when Jesus the Son of God sent out His twelve disciples, there's little doubt that His commissioning came with a warning for them to avoid the serpent's deception. Jesus saw fruitfulness from this ministry being dependent at least in part upon a mix of shrewdness and innocence: "Behold, I send you forth as sheep in the midst of wolves; therefore be shrewd as serpents and innocent as doves" (Matthew 10:16).

In like manner, listening to the Holy Spirit rather than the suggestions of the serpent is essential for both avoiding sin and having the favor of God upon our lives.

The first picture of mankind's fall from grace came as a result of Eve entertaining the serpent's suggestions and coming under deception. However, it was Adam's disobedience to the command of God that allowed sin to enter the world. This resulted in separation from God and banishment from the garden in Eden.

Ever since their fall from grace, every subsequent generation has inherited the bloodline of Adam, and every person born into this world is born in a state of inherited sin and separation from God.

Immediately following Adam and Eve's expulsion from the garden, the next mention of sin throws light on the question of identifying the source of these soulish desires. Scripture reveals that Adam and Eve's first children were Cain, the firstborn, and then Abel. Cain was a farmer, and Abel a shepherd.

Let's pick up the narrative in Genesis 4 (taken from the *Berean Study Bible*).

So in the course of time, Cain brought some of the
fruit of the soil as an offering to the LORD, while Abel
brought the best portions of the firstborn of his flock.

And the LORD looked with favor on Abel and his offering,
but He had no regard for Cain and his offering. So
Cain became very angry, and his countenance fell.

"Why are you angry," said the LORD to Cain, "and
why has your countenance fallen? If you do what is
right, will you not be accepted? But if you refuse to do
what is right, sin is crouching at your door; it desires
you, but you must master it." (Genesis 4:3-6 BSB)

Some things are obvious when you read a few verses like these. However, other things that aren't so obvious can hold the key to better understanding the obvious. What is very obvious in God's words to Cain is that this young man was clearly facing a point of decision.

Every time we have opportunity to do right or wrong, we need to realize that the power of choice is a God-given gift. However, the power of choice also brings consequences. *The Amplified Bible* provides further clarity of both our choices and the consequences, in the words spoken to Cain by God:

If you do well [believing Me and doing what is acceptable
and pleasing to Me], will you not be accepted? And if
you do not do well [but ignore My instruction], sin
crouches at your door; its desire is for you [to overpower
you], but you must master it. (Genesis 4:7 AMP)

When we make right decisions (accompanied by actions), we bring the favor of God upon our lives. But wrong decisions (and actions) open the door for sin to consume us. The serpent is still crouching at our door looking for an opportunity to overpower and take advantage of us.

What is not so obvious in these verses is that Cain actually *wanted* God's favor upon his life. His troubles started with anger, because God spoke favorably of his brother's sacrifice and not his. Anger soon gave way to jealousy, and rather than addressing his own character flaws, he took a shortcut and simply eliminated the opposition.

While it's a good thing to want God's favor upon our lives, we must do things God's way for this to occur. There are no shortcuts with God, because He wants us to be able to stand the test of time and have the strength of character to carry the anointing upon our lives that will bring the greatest glory to Him—as we become co-laborers in building the kingdom of God.

The overwhelming message coming through the Bible narrative is that our decisions matter, and they have consequences. This applies to every person on earth—past, present, and future. If we want the favor of God on our lives, we must learn to make right decisions and to follow them up with actions that display mastery of our own desires.

Although this is a complex subject, I would like to suggest that soulish desires come from our mind, our will, and our emotions when we choose to leave God out of our decision-making process.

God has made known His will for our lives in His Word. In fact, the Bible goes to great lengths to make us aware of the things that are acceptable to God and the things that are not.

Eve knew what God had spoken about the tree of the knowledge of good and evil, yet she still chose to eat the forbidden fruit. Up until that point, the Spirit of God had been guiding Eve's decision-making, and she'd experienced only the knowledge of good. When Eve allowed the serpent's suggestion to prevail in her decision-making, it also influenced Adam, and ultimately their relationship with God was irreparably damaged.

The eyes of Adam and Eve were opened—their awareness increased—and they became aware of their nakedness and made fig leaves to cover themselves (Genesis 3:6-7). Ironically, it was the knowledge of evil that made them aware of the need to cloth themselves before a holy God.

Although the serpent had exploited their innocence and naivety and caused sin to enter the world, God immediately initiated a plan for mankind's redemption (Genesis 3:15), which came to pass thousands of years later when God sent His one and only Son to become the Savior of the world (John 3:16). Because mankind had proven totally incapable of saving itself, God sent His Son who was conceived of the Holy Spirit and carried a precious bloodline that could never be corrupted by sin.

The prophet Isaiah foretold the gospel message in this way: "We all like sheep have gone astray, each one has turned to his own way; and the LORD has laid on Him the iniquity of us all" (Isaiah 53:6). In His suffering on the cross, Christ took upon His own body the punishment you and I deserved for every sin we've ever committed, and for our every failure to do the good we ought to have done but chose not to do. Christ took on our sin so that we can take on His righteousness. He died our death so that we can live the abundant life He has planned for us. Jesus bore the wrath of God that we deserved for our sin, so that we could receive grace from God that none of us deserved.

When we believe in Jesus Christ as our Savior, we're freed from our sins and we experience salvation. When we make this decision, our spirit is reborn into a relationship with God. As Scripture declares, we're born again (John 3:3).

In God's upside-down world, the following observations are worth noting:

- The eyes of Adam and Eve were opened to the knowledge of evil (Genesis 3:6-7) when they relied on their soulish desires and left God out of their decision-making.
- When we make the decision to believe in God through His Son, Jesus Christ, we suddenly have our spiritual eyes opened and gain an immediate awareness that aspects of our past life are unacceptable to a holy God.

From this point onward, bringing the soul realm into subjection to the spirit realm is one of the greatest challenges to all Christian believers. In the same way that faith and fear are always at work in our lives, we must learn to starve our fear and feed our faith through God's Word (Romans 10:17), prayer, and fellowship, if we're to be an overcomer in this life.

We also need to see temptation as an opportunity to make God-honoring choices and to remember that every time we experience a victory, we're strengthening our spiritual authority and are mastering our desires.

Finally, if we're seeking the favor of God on our lives, we must walk by faith and in obedience to God. These are the primary keys to a fruitful and blessed life.

A Timely *Kairos* Moment

As I was writing this chapter, I had a phone call from a young man I've been mentoring for some time. Ernie confessed to me that he had a real problem with lust and it was driving him crazy, because he knew it was not what God would want for his life.

He asked me if it was possible for him to have a spirit of lust, and I said yes. Then he asked how this could be, since he was a Christian. I explained to him that when Jesus died on the cross and rose again, He made incredible provision for all believers to call upon His name and witness miraculous signs: "And these signs will accompany those who believe: In My name they will drive out demons…" (Mark 16:17).

I explained to Ernie that many of these evil spirits *afflict* believers rather than possess them. In other words, the situation is not out of control. It has more to do with influence, and with the believer having a fierce internal battle between the spirit (which wants to please God) and the soul (which wants to please self).

The apostle Paul wrote about his own personal dilemma concerning this matter:

> So I find this law at work: Although I want to do good,
> evil is right there with me. For in my inner being I delight
> in God's law; but I see another law at work in me, waging
> war against the law of my mind and making me a prisoner
> of the law of sin at work within me. (Romans 7:21-23)

Ernie was identifying with the same sort of problem that all people who want to live a righteous life will encounter. Temptation is always crouching at the door, and Satan is always trying to sift us like wheat (Luke 22:31). But never forget that we have an Advocate who sits at the right hand of the Father, and who "ever lives to make intercession for the people of God" (Hebrews 7:25). Our Advocate is the Lord Jesus Christ.

I prayed that night with Ernie and led him in a prayer of confession. After he renounced the spirit of lust, I commanded the spirit to leave, and Ernie had his first experience with deliverance.

Ironically, like many other Christians, Ernie didn't believe that deliverance was necessary if someone believes in Jesus Christ as Lord. But I explained to Ernie that Jesus made provision at the cross for every believer to be set free from everything that afflicts us. However, for mankind to receive this provision in full, believers must be prepared to surrender their lives and let God thoroughly cleanse them and hold nothing back.

I can speak from experience when I say that the influence and level of activity of demonic spirits in our lives is often directly related to our submission (or lack thereof) to God. Our bodies are meant to be a temple of the Holy Spirit, and deliverance comes when we get serious about evicting the enemy from our lives.

For Ernie, this happened during a telephone conversation, and he was simply blown away by what happened in the moments that followed during his deliverance. The promise in Scripture that Jesus "came to set the captives free" (Luke 4:18) became a reality that night for Ernie.

Having said that, not everything that afflicts us is caused by demonic spirits; sometimes it can simply be our own desires getting in the way of fully surrendering to God.

Jesus gave the Great Commission as His parting words to next generation believers before He left this earth. He also told His followers to wait for the promise of the Holy Spirit, which we know was fulfilled on the day of Pentecost and accompanied by signs and wonders in fulfillment of words spoken by the prophet Joel.

The Holy Spirit was responsible for this dramatic shift in ministry focus and the birth of Christianity. Most importantly, this shift was going to be absolutely essential for the Christians to seriously impact their (and our) world with the gospel message.

With the outpouring of the Holy Spirit came also the ability to distinguish between spirits as one of the gifts of the Holy Spirit. In the same manner as the other eight gifts of the Holy Spirit, let there be no doubt that this gift was specifically given to assist Christian believers in carrying out the Great Commission.

In essence, going into all our world involves meeting people from walks of life, and while we need to be as gentle as doves, we also need to be as shrewd as serpents (Matthew 10:16).

The Gift of Discernment in the Business World

In the business world, companies can present themselves using all sorts of professional management and marketing teams—gifted people with incredible skills, talents, and abilities, often accompanied by a strong dose of pride and ego, and last but not least, a strong balance sheet.

The representatives from these companies will never tell you about the people they've scammed, or the half-truths they've told to climb the corporate ladder, or the people they've compromised along the way.

One reason the Holy Spirit gives the ability to distinguish between spirits is specifically to protect Christian believers who put their trust in God. By operating this gift, along with the leading of the Holy Spirit, Christian believers can avoid the deception and entrapment of the enemy and the consequences that might follow.

Remember that when Jesus sent out His disciples, He also told them they would be "like sheep among wolves" (Matthew 10:16).

When we do business with others in a joint venture, in a partnership, or even in a joint bid, we're actually yoking ourselves in spirit to others. If they don't share our core values (such as honesty, integrity, truthfulness), the scene is already set for major conflict down the track.

Scripture says, "Do not be unequally yoked with unbelievers" (2 Corinthians 6:14). Many Christians think this verse is simply for marriage. I can assure you that it means any type of relationship, and it definitely relates to business. When we enter into these types of joint business relationships, we're actually inviting the other party's spirit into the business. Let me explain this further.

I've worked in many organizations as a management consultant and previously as a senior manager in government, and I've personally observed major conflicts that regrettably often spilled over into the family lives of executive managers.

If you've ever had to work with someone who has a competitive spirit, a coveting spirit, a boastful or proud spirit, a controlling or manipulative spirit, a vindictive spirit, a resentful spirit, or a spirit of negativity, you should know why this particular gift of discerning spirits is so important to believers.

(People might not recognize this immediately, but remove the word "spirit" and replace it with "personality" or "character" as you reread the last paragraph, and you'll see what I mean.)

At the end of the day, the choice about who we bind ourselves to from a business perspective rests solely with us. But just like marriage, the consequences of a poor choice can be devastating.

In my earlier years, I made some poor business alignment decisions which cost me dearly from a financial perspective, but it also taught me some valuable lessons about how the love of money can change the nature of people whom I thought I could trust.

The school of hard-earned experience and a journey with the Holy Spirit—who brought me through it all—taught me to be careful about future business alignments and about those whom I should trust moving forward.

This is why the gift of discernment is so important to the body of Christ.

Always More

The three revelatory gifts all involve supernatural revelation as disclosed by the Holy Spirit to Christian believers. Although this disclosure can involve the person themselves, more often than not, the revelatory gifts relate to other people whom the Holy Spirit wants to minister to.

These gifts involve supernatural revelation in the spiritual realm, and when used under the leading of the Holy Spirit, will ultimately bring incredible glory to God.

One final word concerning these gifts is that there's always more in store as we hunger and thirst for God. God's Word reveals that secrets and hidden treasures are available to those who diligently seek the Lord.

Here are a few of these Scriptures worth pondering:

> It is the glory of God to conceal a matter, but the glory
> of kings is to search out a matter. (Proverbs 25:2)

> I will give you the treasures of darkness and
> hidden wealth of secret places, so that you may
> know that it is I, the Lord, the God of Israel,
> who calls you by your name. (Isaiah 45:3)

> The secret things belong to the Lord our God,
> but the things revealed belong to us and to

our sons forever, that we may observe all the
words of this law. (Deuteronomy 29:29)

O, the depth of the riches of the wisdom and
knowledge of God! How unsearchable His judgments,
and untraceable His ways! (Romans 11:33)

If there's a longing in your heart for more of the things of God, these
Scriptures are a great starting point.

Remember that with God, there's always more.

18

In the Market Place: The Spirit's Power Gifts

W e're continuing to look at the gifts of the Holy Spirit, especially as they relate to market place ministry.

Remember again that God has given spiritual gifts to believers as a means of operating in the supernatural realm until Christ returns. They're given to help outsiders witness the power of God in action in the lives of believers, as the Holy Spirit ministers both to the body of Christ (the church) and through the daily lives of Spirit-filled believers

Introduction to the Power Gifts

In 1 Corinthians 12, we see the three remaining gifts of the Holy Spirit, which can be referred to as the power gifts. These gifts reveal the power of the Holy Spirit to move beyond the vocal and revelatory gifts toward a demonstration of the power of the Holy Spirit.

The apostle Paul frequently operated in the power gifts, as he made this clear in his letters:

> My message and my preaching were not with persuasive
> words of wisdom, but with a demonstration of the
> Spirit's power, so that your faith would not rest on
> men's wisdom, but on God's power. (1 Corinthians
> 2:4-5; see also 1 Thessalonians 1:5; Romans 15:18)

The power gifts bring a direct confrontation between light and darkness, good and evil, spirit and soul. Darkness often seems to prevail until the name, authority, and power of the Lord Jesus Christ are called upon.

Jesus regularly operated these power gifts when He felt compassion for an individual or was deeply moved by a particular situation. It was His way of demonstrating the Father's heart of mercy, love, and goodness to the people He met.

Jesus knew that anyone standing in a crowd of onlookers who had even the slightest glimmer of hope—or faith the size of a mustard seed—couldn't help but be touched when they witnessed miraculous signs impacting a person in great need.

Take a moment to imagine how you might have felt if you personally witnessed Jesus performing any of these miracles:

- raising people from the dead (such as Lazarus or Jairus's daughter);
- feeding five thousand hungry and exhausted men and their families in one sitting (Bible scholars say this crowd could have been up to twenty thousand people);
- walking on water and calling Simon Peter out of the boat to join Him;
- calming a wild storm on the Sea of Galilee by speaking to it and effectively telling it to be quiet;
- casting out demons from many who were seriously afflicted by satanic bondages, and then seeing them set free, healed, and delivered.

Many times these power gifts undoubtedly paved the way for the greatest miracle to occur, as listeners became believers and were called into their eternal destiny.

It may not appear immediately obvious, but there are a few common themes associated with these miraculous signs. In each situation, there was desperation, or something was totally out of control.

Jesus knew that the answer to these out-of-control situations was never going to be found in the natural realm, so He simply called forth the answer from the supernatural realm, and every situation was remedied within a few moments of time.

When we're faced with these desperate or out-of-control situations, we also have a choice. We can let the circumstances dictate what we accept and therefore believe, or we can let the Word of God determine our response. Satan is the master of counterfeit, and he'll gladly mask the situation as "too hard" or "impossible," appealing to our natural senses (or the circumstances) when in fact God wants to show forth His glory through a miracle.

The Word of God declares that we're to "walk by faith [our sixth sense], not by sight [outward circumstances]" (2 Corinthians 5:7). When we choose the pathway of faith, we make way for the supernatural, in exactly the same way that Jesus encouraged His disciples. As part of equipping His disciples, Jesus gave them the authority to do likewise, through a number of important Scriptures. Jesus also extended this authority to all believers.

He did it for the task of training His workers:

> The seventy-two returned with joy and said, "Lord, even
> the demons submit to us in Your name." And He said
> to them, "...See, I have given you authority to tread
> on snakes and scorpions, and over all the power of the
> enemy. Nothing will harm you." (Luke 10:17-20)

Jesus extended this authority to believers also for commissioning workers:

> Go into all the world and preach the gospel to every
> creature…. And these signs will accompany those who
> believe: In My name they will drive out demons; they
> will speak in new tongues; they will pick up snakes
> with their hands, and if they drink any deadly poison,
> it will not harm them; they will lay their hands on the
> sick, and they will be made well. (Mark 16:15-18)

He also extended this authority to future workers:

> Truly, truly, I say to you, he who believes in Me, the
> works that I do, he will do also; and greater works than
> these he will do; because I go to the Father." (John 14:12)

These are some of the Scriptures that bestow on us power and authority over Satan. One of the objectives of this book is to encourage believers to step out in faith and into their God-ordained destiny, particularly in the market place.

The Scriptures shown above are also foundational for recognizing our God-given authority and for stepping out in faith, particularly into the realm of the supernatural. I call this place the edge of adventure. There's simply nothing like going out into our world each day carrying the presence of God and seeing lives touched through the message of Jesus Christ and the ministry of the Holy Spirit.

I would like to share with you a few personal experiences associated with the power gifts operating in the market place, in the workplace, or in just doing life.

The Gift of Working Miracles

So many of the actions of Jesus can only be described as miraculous, because they show Him reaching into the supernatural realm to bring forth a miraculous outcome in the natural realm. Dr David Paul Yonggi Cho describes this phenomenon as the "fourth dimension."

With each situation mentioned, the natural realm would scream, "It cannot be done!"—while the supernatural realm beckons for someone to step out in faith to see the glory of God released.

When you experience a miracle, there's always a sense of awe and amazement because of the heavenly exchange that takes place. Whatever terminology you may care to use (such as *kairos,* God encounters, or simply God's will being done "on earth as it is in heaven"), there's a certain surrealness to the experience that not only bears witness to the greatness of God, but also begs every witness to stop and think about what has just happened before your very eyes.

I can say with certainty that once you've experienced a miracle, you can never be quite the same.

I was introduced to my first miracle as a very young believer when I received a phone call from my mother informing me that her oldest sister Lorraine was "on her last" at the Holy Spirit Hospital in Brisbane.

Mum came from a large family, being the second youngest of nine children. Most of the children were born in the 1920s and 1930s, and they spent their early years growing up through the Great Depression.

Lorraine was the eldest child. I'd met her only a couple of times in my early years, since they lived a long way from our family. Lorraine was also regarded as the black sheep of the family. So when I received a phone call from Mum, I immediately prayed and sensed the Holy Spirit telling me to go to see Auntie Lorraine.

When I reached the hospital, I discovered that she was in intensive care, so I went to the nurses' desk and asked if I could visit my auntie.

The duty nurse gave me the room number and said, "Good luck. She's in a coma."

As I entered the room and stood beside her bed, I looked at her lying silently and said, "Father, I believe that you brought me here, but I cannot speak to her while she's like that."

To my amazement and delight, she instantly rolled out of her coma, turned over, and looked directly at me.

"Auntie Lorraine, I'm not sure if you remember me, but I'm Cecilia's son, Ross. I believe God has sent me to speak to you, because your time for departing from this life is near."

I'll never forget how she nodded toward me and acknowledged my presence.

Over the next few minutes, I spoke to her about Jesus and about making sure she made her peace with God. I then prayed with her, kissed her, and showed my love to her as best I knew how.

I left her with a sense of God's peace. Soon after, she rolled back into a coma and departed from this life.

I can only describe this act of mercy and grace as a miracle from God.

In Matthew 20:1-16, Jesus told a parable about equal payment for workers in a vineyard. It depicts the mercy and grace God shows to people in their later years.

It goes without saying, but just think about the eternal consequences had I not been obedient to the voice of the Holy Spirit—think about it the next time you're prompted to visit someone in serious need.

This was my first encounter of this kind with the supernatural realm. If I'd allowed my natural senses to dictate my response, I would have agreed with the nurses and given in to the circumstances. But I chose the pathway of faith, and then saw a miracle take place. To God be the glory!

And also for His glory, I include here an entry from my personal journal about another experience of the miraculous:

* * *

From My Journal—20 November 2016

The last ten days have been an incredible time of ministry.

A young man named Damian has been staying in my apartment and undergoing an intensive time of learning and understanding Scripture, healing, deliverance, and encountering the supernatural.

When God laid Damian on my heart to care for and nurture for a season, he was a bit like Jonah—heading in the wrong direction—and we literally had to bring him back from living on the streets in Sydney.

Damian had been a loyal follower in a church youth group when things went horribly wrong some years prior. The youth leader had a serious fall from grace and a number of young people, including Damian, backslid badly as a result.

Damian had also been a victim of workplace bullying, and at one stage he'd been taken at gunpoint as a hostage in a workplace incident which left him with serious emotional and psychological scars.

Although I knew little of the details behind his situation, I was led by the Holy Spirit to help with Damian's restoration from brokenness as well as from some poor personal choices he'd made for his life.

God also wanted me to let Damian know that I believed in him, and that God would bring him to a better place.

Over the ten days, I was involved in an intense time of intercession and spiritual warfare, and I began to see incredible breakthrough happening in Damian's life and family.

On many occasions, I would share the Word of God followed by times of prayer, which were often accompanied by prophesy or the gift of tongues and interpretation. The ministry of the Holy Spirit during this time was awe inspiring.

Visions and dreams were also happening during these ten days, and God was giving me the interpretation or understanding in every instance.

I was particularly led to pray in the Spirit for Damian's family at the time, and the battle was intense.

The Holy Spirit had identified that Damian needed deliverance from many evil spirits that had entered him over many years. Damian was fully aware of this, but he was more than a little apprehensive.

Part of Damian's concern was that he could be hurt by these spirits, as he'd once had a bad experience with deliverance and was in fact physically injured.

As I was about to pray for Damian, the Holy Spirit brought to my attention the time Jesus met with the man who was possessed by the legion of evil spirits in the region of the Gadarenes (Luke 8:26-39).

The Holy Spirit said to me, "What did Jesus do to cast out the spirits?"

I answered, "He simply commanded the spirits to leave."

The following Scripture came to me is a flash: "I have given you authority to tread on snakes and scorpions and to overcome all of the power of the enemy, and nothing will harm you" (Luke 10:19-20).

The Holy Spirit then asked me "What happened to the man who was set free from these evil spirits?" I replied, "He was not harmed in any way, Lord."

I shared this revelation with Damian as it was unfolding, and as a result, Damian had the faith to believe that he would be delivered unharmed, and I knew that if the Lord had delivered someone with so many evil spirits with a single command, I could also do the same "in His Name."

We sat opposite each other. I prayed for Damian and commanded the spirits to leave. He suddenly rocked forward, coughing violently. spirits departed from him, and then he sat back up.

This happened four times, and he was completely set free from these evil spirits.

I was then led by the Holy Spirit to pray for peace and the joy of the Lord to be Damian's portion, and both of these things happened like a mighty rushing river that seemed to go on for hours.

The presence of God in my apartment was simply amazing during this season, and many things happened in the supernatural realm.

This season of deliverance was nothing short of a miracle in Damian's life, and everyone who previously knew Damian also knew that something special had happened to him. There'd been a definite shift in the spiritual realm over his life.

Damian also knew that something special had happened in relation to his family, as the intercessory prayers were intense, and some responses to our prayers came almost immediately.

Little did we know at the time that a tremendous breakthrough was on its way, and several of his siblings have since commenced an exciting journey with the Lord.

* * *

My experiences with Auntie Lorraine and Damian are two examples of God's supernatural intervention through the working of miracles. One miracle occurred during my days as a young believer, and the other more recently. In both instances, it was absolutely essential for me to listen to and follow the leading of the Holy Spirit.

In the first of these miracles, I had absolutely no control over the situation. Apart from the mercy and grace of God, I would have at best experienced a quiet vigil at my Auntie's bedside.

I've prayed for many people in the past and seen them set free from evil spirits, but Damian's complete deliverance from many evil spirits in such a controlled and miraculous manner was something I'd never experienced before.

At a personal level, I also gained a new level of understanding and authority in the spiritual realm. What a blessing it is to be used by the Lord for His glory.

It was as though the Holy Spirit not only gave me clear instructions regarding Damian's deliverance—and He not only went before me to set Damian free—but He also gave him such an uplift of peace and joy that one could easily believe a little bit of heaven had come and invaded earth.

The Gift of Faith

The gift of faith happens when we're given a special impartation of faith that allows the outworking of miraculous acts. Some of the faith-related miracles mentioned in Scripture include the fig tree withering, the calming of a violent storm, and Peter literally walking on water toward the Lord Jesus Christ.

In the market place, I've often operated the gift of faith in my role as a project manager.

Some of my past roles (such as being project manager of the Games Family Transport for the 2006 Melbourne Commonwealth Games, and the 2011–2015 Regional Rail Link Project) have seen me demonstrate abilities that go well beyond my natural capabilities. During both these events, I relied heavily upon the gift of faith to carry me through and to cause me to excel in all that I did on a daily basis.

It's one thing to seek the Lord in a general way for strategic direction, for assignment of work tasks to the right staff, and for building strong relationships. It's altogether something else to have absolute clarity about priorities, about how to recognize pitfalls, about devising effective large-scale training methods, and about understanding contractual obligations—and hearing the affirming voice of the Holy Spirit whisper, "I have anointed you for this very purpose."

I owe any success that the Roscar Group of Companies may have to my talented team of hard-working colleagues and to the leading and guidance of the Holy Spirit on a daily basis.

I would also like to give glory to God for the following examples of the gift of faith in operation in my market place, remembering that with God all things are possible.

* * *

From My Journal—29 February 2016

Yesterday was quite an extraordinary day for a lot of reasons.

During my early morning devotions I was reading from Matthew 21:18-22 about the fig tree that withered at the command of Jesus.

In particular, my attention was drawn to the following words of Jesus: "I tell you the truth, if you have faith and do not doubt, not only can you do what was done to the fig tree, but also you can say to this mountain, 'Go throw yourself into the sea,' and it will be done. If you believe, you will receive whatever you ask for in prayer" (Matthew 21:21-22).

As I read these words, they leaped off the page and I found myself deep in spiritual warfare almost simultaneously with my reading.

For a short time, there was an intense battle in the spirit realm, but I sensed victory and then moved on. After this time of prayer, a cry arose in my heart and I remember saying, "Lord, I so much want to live this Scripture out in my life today!"

A little while later, as I was walking down to work, I spoke to my mum about seven A.M., who informed me that my brother John's back was giving him serious trouble and threatening his ability to work. John was working as a supervisor for me at the time.

At about 8:30 A.M., I received a phone call from John who confirmed his back problem and asked permission to leave work for a short time to buy some ointment to ease the pain. John said his back was stiff, he was getting spasms frequently, and the pain was excruciating.

I told John that this would be fine, and to just to keep me in the loop.

In the time leading up to this moment, I'd occasionally spoken to John about the things of God, but never pressured him. Although he listened, he hadn't specifically asked for help in the past.

Little did I know that a *kairos* moment was just about to happen.

Then, for the first time ever, John asked me if I would say a prayer for his back.

The moment I heard this, I heard the voice of the Holy Spirit say to me, "Now is your opportunity."

So now it was time, and unbeknown to me, God had already prepared my heart to pray for my brother. I said a simple prayer and asked God to intervene and heal my brother "in the name of Jesus Christ."

I sensed an incredible release of the presence of God as I prayed over the phone, and then I told John to go and do some stretching exercises that he couldn't do before, and to let me know how it went.

He agreed, and I returned to my office, as I was very busy at the time.

About ten minutes later, I received a phone call from John, and he was beside himself as he described to me how after I prayed, he did some exercises like I told him, and then felt this incredible heat and a tingling sensation.

He told me that the heat started in his right hand, traveled up his arm, across his shoulder then right down the middle of his back to where the spasms had been happening—where it stopped, and now he was totally free from pain.

John told me that he'd never felt anything like this in his entire life, and that he'd had this sort of problem with his back since he was a teenager.

He knew from past experience that it generally took pain killers and anti-inflammatory medication for four days to get things back on track, but Jesus had brought healing to his body in just a few moments of time.

But the story didn't end there. He told me that he had called his wife, Gyanu (who is Nepalese, and from a Buddhist background), and he told her what had happened.

When Gyanu heard this, she said to him, "John, you're not going to believe this. I've never had a dream about angels in my entire life, but last night, I dreamt about angels, and they were all around you."

All John and Gyanu could do was marvel. They were both blown away by the healing and the revelation God gave through this dream, which confirmed what He was about to do.

I said to John, "Do you understand the significance of Gyanu's dream?" When he said no, I told him what Scripture says: "Are not all angels ministering spirits sent to serve those who will inherit salvation?" (Hebrews 1:14).

I explained to John that the same word is used for both salvation and healing in the Greek language, which means that the angels were actually ministering healing to him as he stood there.

John told me that he'd never felt anything like that in his entire life, and he was absolutely amazed at what God had done.

I rejoiced with John, then told him how I'd also prayed for his work colleague, Anna, two weeks prior—and she was totally and instantly healed of vertigo.

He was stunned, and I encouraged him to go and share with Anna what had just happened to him.

To God be the glory!

* * *

The Author and Perfecter of Our Faith

Scripture constantly encourages us to walk by faith and not by sight (2 Corinthians 5:7). This is a common and fundamental thread of all Judeo-Christian belief.

However, when our backs are against the wall and we're facing a near impossible situation, walking by faith can pose some of the scariest and most fearful times imaginable.

This is when the enemy tries to turn our mind into a battlefield.

When you encounter these times, think about the great crowd of witnesses (Hebrews 12:1-3) cheering us on, because they've walked that road and have gone on to become heroes in the hall of faith. The greatest of these is Jesus Himself, who's described in Hebrews 12:2 as "the author and perfecter of our faith."

When we realize that our trials are meant to perfect our faith, we can begin to see the things we encounter in a different light. God has purposed the trials as a means of discipline (Hebrews 12:4-18) and for our personal growth (John 15:1-11), so that we produce fruit that will last.

It's difficult to see the purpose of severe trials at the time; it's often only in hindsight that we look back and realize how the Lord was actually saving us from a much more serious situation if the trial hadn't come about.

In the midst of the most severe trial, we also need to recognize that some mountains need to be cast down, while others need to be crossed. Either way, faith holds the key to victory.

The Faith Gift in the Market Place

A number of years ago, I was involved at joint venture level with one of the largest sporting events Australia had hosted in recent years. The build-up to this event took twelve months of hard work and involved a number of people working as part of my project management team to deliver the coach transport.

Our team encountered many difficulties along the way, primarily as a result of the inexperience and ineptitude of the event organizers. With only a few months to go, things were in a perilous state, to put it mildly. It got to the point that I became troubled in spirit, despite being before the Lord for hours each day, seeking a breakthrough.

I'd long forgiven the parties involved and sought to keep a right spirit, but the spiritual battle remained intense. I knew that a serious crunch time was coming, and the enemy was unrelenting in trying to bring us down.

For a few nights before my encounter with God, I actually wore an ear-piece to bed and played praise music while I was attempting to go to sleep. I was so exhausted from the workload and the spiritual battle that I would simply fall asleep with the music still playing. It was more important for me to listen to the Lord's praises than to the enemy of souls trying to whisper lies into my ear.

Despite the battle, I knew that God had been at the forefront of our winning bid for this major event, and it was also God's intention that we excel in its delivery.

The breakthrough that was about to happen was at a critical point of the faith journey I was on at the time. (One thing we all need to be aware of is that although the battle is often outworked in the natural realm, there can be a far more intense battle happening in the spiritual realm.) It was about two A.M., and I was awakened by the Lord. As had been the pattern for several days, I began to pray and seek the Lord through His Word (the Bible) and this went on for several hours.

Little did I know that a supernatural breakthrough was about to happen—the time of my deliverance was at hand.

As I was praying, I distinctly heard the voice of the Holy Spirit say to me, "Go and get a pad and a pen," and I had in my mind the picture in Psalm 45:1— "My tongue is the pen of a ready writer."

As I sat on the end of my bed, the Lord gave me a massive download of instructions, strategies, and messages that were needed to overcome the current impasse. I didn't have to think about anything, as the words I was receiving were crystal clear. When I'd finished writing, the notes covered many pages of paper.

After I finished writing, I heard the word of the Lord: "If you will follow these words of mine and carefully carry them out, I will give you success at every point along the way to victory."

I went directly to my computer and began preparing emails, letters, and instructions according to the words I'd been given, and from that day forward our team never looked back.

God had indeed come through in one of the most incredible ways I could have ever imagined. From that moment forward, a deep peace came upon my heart, because I knew that God had broken through.

Some might call this a word of wisdom, and I would agree with that, but I also believe that it was the gift of faith that opened the way for the word of wisdom to operate.

The thing to remember about this encounter is that the delivery of the event was not without its challenges, but at every juncture, God came through.

Following the event, we received a commendation from the CEO recognizing our outstanding contribution to the success of the event. As for me, I attribute any success we may have had to God. His ways are perfect, and all His ways are just. I happen to believe that it was faith in Him that unleashed His Word that never fails to breakthrough. This is of utmost importance.

So will My word be which goes forth from My
mouth; it will not return to Me empty, without
accomplishing what I desire, and without succeeding
in the matter for which I sent it. (Isaiah 55:11)

The Gift of Healing

The gift of healing is a manifestation of the Holy Spirit to undertake supernatural healing of a person. Healing can be directed to the whole person (body, soul, and spirit) as the Holy Spirit leads.

Although the gift of healing is most likely regarded as "the children's bread" by religious people, God will often direct the gift of healing toward nonbelievers as a means of showing forth His grace and mercy.

Whether those who have been healed are believers or unbelievers is of little importance to God. However, the response of the individual to God for His supernatural intervention is of utmost importance.

We must always remember that when Jesus was touched by people's infirmities and brokenness, compassion was released, and the gift of healing flowed to whoever was afflicted.

I'll now share a few specific examples of the outworking of this gift.

A number of years ago, I was working in conjunction with a specialist public relations firm. Soon after I commenced working with the business, the CEO told me about an ordeal he'd been through several years prior when he was awakened suddenly on an operating table by medics using electric paddles, after he'd suffered a massive heart attack.

David was a very likeable fellow, and he had a deep concern for his family, which included small children by his second wife.

In his earlier years, David had worked as press secretary to a prominent politician, and he certainly knew his way around the political landscape.

I caught up with David on several occasions for lunch and enjoyed sharing my testimony and having fellowship with him. David was quite receptive to the discussion and was very open to the things of God.

I always felt there was something special about David, and the conversations we had were similar to those I'd had with Tony Wyman in earlier years.

How we came to meet, and the conversations that took place, did not seem to be by chance. After we concluded our business dealings, we still used to catch up every now and then over the phone.

Retrospect is often a wonderful way of reviewing our decision-making, but it also provides an ability to fully appreciate the wisdom and power of God.

As I was preparing to include this testimony, I was reminded of the faithfulness of God, for it was He who laid it on David's heart to call me one Friday, many years ago, just after lunch.

I was just about to go into a business meeting when I received the phone call from a very distressed David. Over the next few minutes, David told me he was in a very bad way with severe chest pains. He said the way he was feeling had all the tell-tale signs of a heart attack coming on, just like the previous time it had happened. David told me he'd felt the onset of chest pain from early that morning, and that he was scared.

When times of serious trouble like this occur, God needs to be the One we turn to. We also need to realize that when the situation is totally beyond our control, it paves the way for the God of the supernatural to show forth His glory.

I was standing out on a driveway at the time, next to my parked car. As I began to pray for David, the Holy Spirit immediately took me to a place of deep intercessory prayer.

I knew David was in trouble and that there was little I could do to help him in the natural realm. But deep compassion began welling up within me for my friend, and I knew that my Father in heaven was listening intently.

From the depths of my soul I cried out to the Lord. After I finished praying, and had done everything I could possibly do, I knew it was in my Father's hands.

When times like this occur, we need to realize that we're simply an instrument of the Lord's grace and mercy. Prayer is our greatest weapon against the enemy of souls, and we need to pray with faith in our hearts until the breakthrough happens.

We also need to understand that healing happens because Christ is in us and working through us as we speak the name of Jesus Christ over any given situation. There is power in His name!

I stood firm in the belief that God was intimately involved with this moment in David's life as I committed him to God.

Although it was difficult to simply finish praying and then go off to a business meeting, I've come to understand the grace of God in such situations. I also know that God understands, and He works with us in whatever situation that may arise. As a matter of fact, I've come to know that God understands time very well—since He is the One who created it.

I had another phone call from David the following Monday, and the conversation went like this: "I don't know exactly what you prayed the other day, but I know that it worked, and for the first time in a long time I was in church with all of the family on Sunday."

Once again—when God shows up, His amazing grace and mercy abound.

These events happened around fifteen years ago, and I want you to know that I had a conversation with David only a few weeks ago, and he is still alive and well.

* * *

From My Journal—13 March 2016

What an incredible night!

A few weeks ago, Mike and Lindy—who both work with me—came into a personal relationship with the Savior, Jesus Christ.

Tonight was the first time Mike and Lindy brought their daughter and granddaughter with them to church.

The church service at Planetshakers, Melbourne was excellent, and the message from Pastor Russell Evans was inspiring.

After church we went to Lygon Street, Carlton for a meal and a time of sharing.

I shared my testimony with the family and answered many questions about Christianity. Lindy shared about her Jewish heritage and her newfound belief that Jesus was the promised Messiah.

What happened next was simply amazing. All I can say is that when God shows up, you need to expect the unexpected.

Lindy had been suffering from panic attacks for more than twenty-five years and had been taking strong medication to maintain any sense of normality.

Although this was unbeknown to me at the time, I did remember Lindy asking her daughter for a Panadol as we sat on tables outside the restaurant.

Lindy hadn't complained or even mentioned that she had a headache, but soon after this, Lindy went to the rest room, and I thought nothing more about it.

After dinner had finished, Mike walked his daughter and granddaughter to their car and Lindy returned to the table and told me what had just happened.

Lindy had experienced a panic attack when she arrived at Lygon Street, while they were walking to the restaurant.

When she asked for the Panadol and went to the rest room, she was experiencing not only a headache but another panic attack, and she needed to escape to get through this episode, which generally took around twenty-five minutes to bring under control.

Lindy had listened intently to Pastor Russell's message that night about faith, as well as my personal testimony and many stories that I shared about God's healing power and stepping out in faith to believe God for His supernatural intervention.

Lindy had certainly taken this message to heart, for she went into the rest room and prayed to God for the pain of the headache and the panic attack to go, and as she prayed, to her amazement, the panic attack simply left her in an instant.

What normally took twenty-five minutes to bring under control— in the face of much pain and anguish from a human perspective— was accomplished within a moment of Lindy's prayer being offered.

Lindy had experienced the Lord's healing touch, and was beside herself.

She needed to tell someone, and I was so blessed to hear her words as she gave glory to God.

God is indeed doing some amazing things among my staff and closest friends, and I'm looking forward to the next episode.

* * *

A Miraculous Healing on My Way to Work

In bringing this chapter to a close, I would like the share another word of personal testimony about a God encounter I experienced.

I was at home getting ready for work one morning, and in the midst of having a shave I distinctly heard the voice of the Holy Spirit say to me, "Auntie Mary."

I'd visited my Auntie Mary when she was in the Repatriation Hospital some six weeks earlier, after she'd been through some issues with her health.

My "grand" Auntie Mary had nursed my great-grandmother until she was ninety-eight years of age. In doing so, Auntie Mary opted not to marry but rather to look after her mother. Her mother passed away when Auntie Mary was forty-eight years of age.

Auntie Mary was a very dear person. She was of the Presbyterian faith, and although she'd never openly shared her faith with me before I became a believer, she later confided that she'd been praying for our family for many years.

After her mother died, Auntie Mary married a World War II veteran. They were together for about eight years, after which he also passed away.

After this, Auntie Mary was devoted to all kinds of charities to help returned soldiers readjust to civilian life after World War II. I can always remember as a young boy visiting Auntie Mary's house, and you couldn't get a seat in her lounge room. Auntie Mary made things like aprons, embroidered handkerchiefs, covered coat hangers, tissue box covers, stuffed toys, and many other works for charity, and they were stacked up all over her house.

During my visit to the Repatriation Hospital, I prayed for Auntie Mary, and she later told me that the woman in the bed beside her said that she'd never heard anyone pray like that in all her life. I mention this because we should never underestimate the value of our testimony (including our prayers) before others, because it has the power to change lives.

My mother let me know that Auntie Mary had returned home from hospital a few weeks later, and that she was well.

As I was driving to work, I heard the words "Auntie Mary" once again. As I approached the turn-off for the road leading to her house, I heard the Holy Spirit speak a third time. So I decided to follow His promptings and to go to her house.

Auntie Mary lived in a low-set house with closed-in verandas all round. I knocked on the front door for quite some time, and when I received no response, I became concerned. I knew that Auntie Mary would have to be at home with her sister Alice, who was also my grand-aunt. Both were in their eighties at the time.

I continued to knock—a bit louder this time—and eventually I heard a noise from inside the house. Then I heard footsteps approaching.

Auntie Mary opened the front window and said, "Hello, Ross."

I responded, "How are you, Auntie Mary?"

"I'm fine in myself," Auntie Mary said, "but ever since I left hospital, this dreadful sciatica has driven me mad with the pain."

Without my even thinking, it was as though the words gushed from my mouth: "Praise God! Now I know why He has sent me here—to pray for your healing."

I excused myself for a moment and told Auntie Mary I was going to the car to get my Bible (which I always carried with me). As I walked to the car, the Holy Spirit whispered in my ear the word "Dorcas." I was familiar with the ministry of the apostle Peter to Dorcas, and I had reread this passage only recently before this encounter.

The Holy Spirit then confirmed to me that Auntie Mary had the ministry of Dorcas to those around her, which was easy to see from her works of charity.

When I went into the lounge room, I told Auntie Mary what the Holy Spirit had just said to me. I then read from Acts 9:36-41, the passage that spoke about God raising Dorcas from the dead. I understood then from the Holy Spirit that I was to lay hands on Auntie Mary and pray for her, using these Scriptures as the basis for my prayer.

As I started to pray, the Spirit of the Lord came upon me in power, and I burst out in the gift of tongues, and then came the interpretation with the following words: "Even as that which was dead came to life for Dorcas, so this sciatic nerve, which is as dead, shall come to life for you. Receive my healing, saith the Lord."

At the time of my prayer, I had one hand raised to heaven and the other on her forehead, having just anointed her with oil as she sat in her lounge chair.

In an instant, I felt the power of the Holy Spirit go through my uplifted hand like electricity, and it ran through my entire body and then went through my hand into Auntie Mary's forehead. I could feel the power of God tangibly touching her.

As I felt the power of the Holy Spirit run through me, I also experienced first hand a sign and wonder of God's grace: Auntie Mary literally jumped to her feet and yelled, "I'm healed!"

She then almost begged me to walk around the house with her, which I did numerous times. The result was that she was instantly and totally healed.

Auntie Mary never experienced sciatica again, and she went on to live to the ripe old age of ninety-four before she went to be with the Lord.

Friends, God is faithful—and I believe that He earnestly desires us to engage in these kinds of God encounters so that His glory might be manifest to those we meet in our daily walk.

The interesting thing is that this miraculous healing did not stop there. The testimony associated with this miracle flowed through to a number of people:

- After her miracle healing took place, Auntie Mary could not wait to tell my mother about it.

- Some years later my brother Jeff and I were talking over the phone one day, and he mentioned that he was suffering terribly from sciatica. I immediately felt a prompting from the Holy Spirit to tell him the story about Auntie Mary. I was then prompted to pray for Jeff over the phone, and he too was instantly healed as I prayed.

- As part of a sermon at my church, I told the story about Auntie Mary one Sunday, and a lady came forward at the end of the service and informed me that she was instantly healed of a problem with her leg as I was speaking, while she was sitting in her seat. This healing was not a result of my prayer—it was simply her faith in God at hearing this testimony.

- The Presbyterian minister who officiated at Auntie Mary's funeral service was quite taken back when I told him the story, and it no doubt served as a testimony to him and to anyone else who might be reluctant to believe that God still performs miracles for those who are prepared to ask.

Our testimonies are a bit like unwritten sequels to the book of Acts which are recorded in heaven's diaries, and we should never discount their ability to impact lives as we share them with believers and unbelievers alike.

One day I was sharing this story in a workplace with a lady named Denise. Denise was a hairdresser by trade. She'd had a sea change and was working in the office of a company where I was a consultant.

Denise used to give free haircuts to the staff, and one day as she was cutting my hair, I told her the story about my Auntie Mary.

Denise was amazed. She then told me her story, and how the other staff called her a Nurofen junkie because she took up to eight tablets per day just to settle her stomach. Denise also confessed to practicing white magic, and that she was seeking inner healing through crystals and such.

In reality, I could see that Denise was spiritually hungry and searching for the answers to life—only she was looking in all the wrong places.

After hearing the story of Auntie Mary, she immediately asked, "Do you think you could pray for me, for my stomach?" to which I said "Yes."

I had her lay her hand on her stomach where it was unsettled, and I lay my hand on top of her hand and then I began to pray.

Immediately, she said, "I can feel something like bubbles happening in my stomach." She was actually laughing (with the joy of the Lord) while she experienced the power of God touching her life, and then she confessed, "It's gone."

Denise was absolutely amazed.

Once again, this miraculous healing came about because I took the time to share a testimony about a God encounter with Denise in her workplace.

> And they overcame him [the accuser of the
> brethren] by the blood of the Lamb and *by the*
> *word of their testimony*, and they did not love
> their lives to the death. (Revelation 12:11)

The Great Commission given to believers is simply to find the lost and to share the good news with them about the Lord Jesus Christ. As we do this, God has promised that signs and wonders will follow our prayers and actions, as our faith is outworked.

In the same way that Jesus told the expert in the law to follow the example of the good Samaritan by showing mercy to his neighbor, I believe the Lord has never stopped saying, "Open your eyes, the fields are ripe, ready for harvest!" There has never been a truer statement for the market places in our world.

As the above words from Revelation 12 indicate, we should never forget that the word of our testimony is one of the greatest weapons we can ever use against the enemy of souls.

My encouragement to all believers is simply this: Be brave, and prepare to do exploits for the Lord our God.

The power gifts are often considered to be the greater gifts, because they go beyond the vocal and revelatory gifts (which typically deal with the spiritual realm) by taking from the spiritual (heavenly) realm and bringing it into being on earth.

The distinctiveness of the power gifts is simple yet profound:

- People are miraculously healed of physical afflictions.
- Undeniable miracles take place.

- Something miraculous and unexplained takes place as the gift of faith is in operation.

The accompanying prayer that gives effect to the supernatural or the manifestation itself (such as a person's healing) cannot help but leave a lasting impression upon every person present. When God evidences Himself in this way, the miracle itself demands a response from every individual present.

Christian believers attribute the three power gifts mentioned above to the power of God. Others do not.

If you're not a Christian believer but are open to exploring the things of God (including His existence), I would like to pose this question: Where would you stand if you saw such a miracle happen right before you after a friend of yours was facing a terminal health issue?

I've personally witnessed such miracles take place after prayer, and I want to give all the glory to God. In fact, this book is full of such testimonies about the goodness of God. He's only a prayer away from being your Helper in times of trouble and your Comforter in times of distress.

When you experience the touch of God upon your life, you can draw only one conclusion: He is simply amazing! Yes, there is always more with our God—and the next chapter of your faith journey is up to you.

On to Visions and Dreams

The next step in my own personal journey relates to visions and dreams that were promised, among other things, to accompany the outpouring of the Holy Spirit in the last days (Acts 2:17-21). These are another part of God's way of revealing both Himself and His plans to mankind. They're a tremendously powerful means of communication, because they speak from the spirit realm a message that gives life to the listener by revealing aspects of people's lives or of future events.

These are incredibly powerful methods that God uses to reveal the gospel message to outsiders, either directly to the person or through someone communicating the gospel message to them. I can speak from personal experience when I say that they set the scene for incredibly powerful God encounters.

God, in His great mercy, will sometimes speak to believers using visions and dreams. These gifts are often given to increase revelation and to provide greater understanding of unfolding or future events, and to direct our footsteps as we walk by faith through this life. They're also a means to sound warnings when we're facing difficult times.

My experience has been that most believers don't experience the visions and dreams spoken of in Joel 2:28, a passage quoted by the apostle Peter on the day of Pentecost. However, if you have a desire for more of the things of God, then all you need to do is ask and begin to hunger and thirst after righteousness until a breakthrough comes.

There's no special formula to this. But unless the people of God step out in faith to become the heavenly conduit to the lost, the lonely, and the needy, the greater things of God simply won't be experienced. And the greater someone's need, the greater the opportunity for God to reveal His greatness and mercy in their situation.

All we need to do is introduce Jesus Christ to that person, and begin to speak words of life.

19

The Gospel Panorama

When I first planned to write this chapter, I was hoping to write a concise systematic theology of salvation accompanied by a chronology of the Old and New Testaments. After all, this would have put things nicely into perspective, not unlike a panoramic photo that I'm able to capture on my smartphone.

However, as time went by, I became more and more aware that such an approach best belongs to theologians and academics who would indeed provide a far more concise outcome than I could deliver.

It also became apparent that as a sower of the Word, I need to keep things simple—otherwise the listener might not be able to understand what I'm saying.

Interestingly, after hearing the message of the kingdom, it was the inability of the listener to understand the sown word that gave Satan the ability to steal that word from their heart:

> Consider, then, the parable of the sower: When anyone hears the message of the kingdom *but does not understand it*, the evil one comes and snatches away what was sown in his heart. This is the seed sown along the path. (Matthew 13:18-19)

I wonder: Is it possible that people's perceptions about the gospel message have become so fragmented over time because the church (universal) hasn't presented or communicated the gospel in a manner that people could readily understand?

To answer that question for yourself, I suggest that you ask a number of outsiders what message they see the church sending into the local community. I think most believers would be horrified to learn the response to that question.

When I present the gospel message, I'm frequently informed by the listener that they've never heard anything like what I just shared, and that it actually makes sense.

In order to communicate the gospel, we need to realize that while the messages of Jesus Christ were never complex, the underlying meaning was often quite profound to the listener.

For example:

- It's the humility and trust that comes through childlike faith (which Jesus spoke about in Mark 10:15) that lead to salvation. People can easily visualize a child having absolute trust in their parents.

- Jesus said that it only takes faith the size of a mustard seed to release a miracle (Luke 17:6). No matter what the circumstance, people can generally visualize (and believe) that they have the smallest amount of seed-like faith.

- If we truly believe, we can see the glory of God in our hour of greatest need or most severe trial (John 11:40). Desperate and out-of-control situations can lead to a miracle when people catch hold of this hope.

- The core message of the gospel is revealed in this verse that we return to again: "For God so loved the world that he gave his one and only Son, that whoever believes in him shall not perish but have eternal life" (John 3:16). Jesus spoke these words to His disciples in the early part of

His three-year ministry to reveal the purpose of His life and mission on earth. Through these words, He foretold the gospel message of salvation and the promise of eternal life that was going to be available to whoever would believe in Him.

The above examples are not complex, but they all have one common theme: having faith and trust in God.

Paul's Gospel Message to the Gentiles

What really is the gospel? The word *gospel* simply means "good news." The spiritual power of this good news is what was so alive and compelling to the apostles.

The apostle Paul was widely known as the apostle to the Gentiles (that is, to those who weren't Jews). Paul's miraculous encounter with Jesus Christ on the road to Damascus (Acts 9:1-19) became the turning point in his life. We learn in Acts 13:9 that he soon changed his name from Saul (his Hebrew name) to Paul (his Roman name), most likely to more closely identify with the Gentiles he'd been commissioned to reach.

The gospel message that came as part of the apostle Paul's revelation from the Lord Jesus Christ was passed on to the fledgling churches he planted, and to anyone who would listen to his testimony. So powerful was his encounter with Jesus Christ that he could confidently make such statements as these:

> Dear brothers and sisters, I want you to understand
> that the gospel message I preach is not based on mere
> human reasoning. I received my message from no human
> source, and no one taught me. Instead, I received it by
> *direct revelation* from Jesus Christ. (Galatians 1:11-12)

Then after fourteen years, I went up again to Jerusalem…meeting privately with those esteemed as leaders, I presented to them the gospel that I preach among the Gentiles…. As for those who were held in high esteem [that is, church leaders]… *they added nothing to my message.* (Galatians 2:16)

Here's a typical and shortened gospel message from Paul:

For what I received I passed on to you as of first importance: that Christ died for our sins according to the Scriptures, that He was buried, that He was raised on the third day according to the Scriptures, and that He appeared to Cephas [Peter's Aramaic name] and then to the Twelve. After that, He appeared to more than five hundred brothers at once…then to James [a brother of Jesus] then to all the apostles, then finally… He appeared to me also. (1 Corinthians 15:3-7)

In a nutshell, the gospel presented by the apostle Paul encompasses…

- the sacrificial death of Jesus Christ (the Messiah) to pay the ultimate price for the sins of mankind for all time and eternity.
- the burial of Christ and His resurrection on the third day (as had been foretold in the Old Testament).
- the gospel account being supported by eyewitness testimony of more than five hundred people after his resurrection, in addition to personal visitation with the apostles, and lastly to Paul himself.

It should also be noted that the apostle Paul would always give an opportunity for his listeners to believe in the Lord Jesus Christ when he presented the gospel message.

When the apostle Paul went into Gentile territory, his first point of contact was generally the local synagogue, where for several weeks he would share his testimony of being transformed from a persecutor of the Way into becoming one of its staunchest followers after his encounter with the resurrected Christ (Acts 13:13-52).

Paul's preaching of the gospel message was often accompanied by signs, wonders, and miracles, followed by an invitation for his listeners to become believers in Jesus Christ.

In addition to the local synagogue, Paul would go into market places and shape the gospel message to impact his listeners by appealing to cultural or historical evidence of God having visited their city. To the Epicurean and Stoic philosophers on Mars Hill in Athens, Paul presented the good news about Jesus and the resurrection as a further revelation of the unknown God (Acts 17:16-32) who had visited Athens some six hundred years before.

Paul stayed a year and a half in Corinth teaching the Word of God after many were saved—putting their faith in Christ—after hearing the gospel message. At the time of Paul's visit, Corinth was a cesspit of iniquity, yet the Lord led him to plant a church in the midst of this satanic stronghold.

The apostle Paul's faith journey, especially his ministry at Corinth, should serve as an example to believers that God can save the lost no matter how difficult their circumstances may appear.

Why would God do this?

I believe the answer is quite simple. God had purposed to be merciful to this city in the same way He had for Nineveh (Jonah 4:11) more than seven hundred years earlier, when one hundred and twenty thousand people were spared divine judgment after they heard the prophetic warning from the prophet Jonah and repented of their wickedness.

Little did Paul realize that his subsequent letters to the Corinthian church leaders would form the basis of the most concise books in the New Testament in dealing with problems within the church. In retrospect, we can easily see that Paul's planting and nurturing of this church was the wisdom of God in action.

Peter's Gospel Message to the Jews

On the day of Pentecost, the Holy Spirit empowered the apostle Peter to prophesy (Acts 2:17-21) from the book of Joel (Joel 2:28-32) after he addressed the "amazed and perplexed" crowd outside the upper room. Peter explained that what they'd just witnessed was the promised outpouring of the Holy Spirit (Luke 3:16).

These signs and wonders were orchestrated by God to fan the flames of the gospel message through God-fearing Jews who were in Jerusalem from every nation under heaven. This was all part of God's *kairos* timing and plan to commence the spread of the gospel message to the uttermost ends of the earth (Acts 1:8).

So powerful was the outpouring of the Holy Spirit that Peter, who'd recently denied his Lord, now stood before a crowd of thousands preaching an incredibly anointed sermon that included the gift of prophecy.

This was the beginnings of the early church. It was birthed and baptized in the Holy Spirit from its conception, with signs, wonders, and miracles following all believers who chose to step out in faith, under the leadership of the apostles.

Here is what happened on the day of Pentecost:

> When the day of Pentecost came, the believers
> were all together in one place. Suddenly a sound
> like a mighty rushing wind came from heaven and
> filled the whole house where they were sitting.
> They saw tongues like flames of a fire that separated
> and came to rest on each of them. And they were
> all filled with the Holy Spirit and began to speak
> in other tongues as the Spirit enabled them.
>
> Now there were dwelling in Jerusalem God-fearing
> Jews from every nation under heaven. And when this
> sound rang out, a crowd came together in bewilderment,
> because each one heard them speaking his own language.
>
> In wonder and amazement, they asked, "Are not
> all these men who are speaking Galileans? How is
> it then that each of us hears them in his own native
> language? Parthians, Medes, and Elamites; residents
> of Mesopotamia, Judea, and Cappadocia, Pontus and
> Asia, Phrygia and Pamphylia, Egypt and the parts of
> Libya near Cyrene; visitors from Rome, both Jews and
> converts to Judaism; Cretans and Arabs—we hear them
> declaring the mighty works of God in our own tongues!"
>
> Amazed and perplexed, they asked one another,
> "What does this mean?" But others mocked them and
> said, "They are drunk on new wine!" (Acts 2:1-13)

How did the apostle Peter respond to these questions from his listeners? Bearing in mind that he was speaking to an audience made up of pious Jews from every nation under heaven, he addressed the crowd by heavily referencing Old Testament Scriptures:

Men of Judea and all who dwell in Jerusalem, let this be known to you, and listen carefully to my words. These men are not drunk as you suppose. It is only the third hour [nine A.M.] of the day! No, this is what was spoken by the prophet Joel:

"In the last days, God says,
I will pour out My Spirit on all people;
Your sons and daughters will prophesy,
your young men will see visions,
your old men will dream dreams.
Even on my servants, both men and women,
I will pour out My Spirit in those
days, and they will prophesy.
I will show wonders in the heavens above
and signs on the earth below,
blood and fire and clouds of smoke.
The sun will be turned to darkness,
and the moon to blood,
before the coming of the great and
glorious day of the Lord.
And everyone who calls on the name of the
Lord will be saved." (Acts 2:14-21)

In delivering this prophetic word, the apostle Peter was declaring that the promised last-days outpouring of the Holy Spirit had been fulfilled on the day of Pentecost, as those listening could testify.

The crowd he was addressing contained thousands of Jewish residents, including at least fourteen different ethnic groups and languages, all of whom heard these Galileans declaring the mighty works of God in their own native tongues. This was clearly a supernatural act that required an explanation, which the apostle Peter was quick to provide. The message was clear. God had commenced pouring out His Spirit on "all people," as Joel had prophesied.

When reading the above Scriptures, notice the types of people upon whom the Holy Spirit was to be outpoured. Peter spoke of "all people" and "everyone." That has always been God's plan for His church.

God wants His church to be full of prophetic people who are prepared to move in the realm of signs and wonders, leading others into relationship with the Lord Jesus in order that they might be saved.

After bringing this prophetic word, the apostle Peter goes into considerable detail to explain the gospel message to his Jewish listeners using many Old Testament Scriptures to confirm the day's events.

The apostle Peter then addressed the crowd:

> Men of Israel, listen to this message: Jesus of Nazareth was a man certified by God to you by miracles, wonders, and signs, which God did among you through Him, as you yourselves know. He was handed over by God's set plan and foreknowledge, and you, by the hands of the lawless, put Him to death by nailing Him to the cross.

But God raised Him from the dead, releasing Him from the agony of death, because it was impossible for Him to be held in its clutches. David said about him:

> "I saw the Lord always before me.
> Because he is at my right hand, I will not be shaken.
> Therefore my heart is glad and my tongue rejoices;
> my body also will rest in hope,
> because you will not abandon me
> to the realm of the dead,
> you will not let your holy one see decay.
> You have made known to me the paths of life;
> you will fill me with joy in your presence."

Fellow Israelites, I can tell you confidently that the patriarch David died and was buried, and his tomb is here to this day. But he was a prophet and knew that God had promised him on oath that he would place one of his descendants on his throne. Foreseeing this, David spoke about the resurrection of the Christ, that He was not abandoned to Hades, nor did His body see decay.

God has raised this Jesus to life, to which we are all witnesses. Exalted, then, to the right hand of God, He has received from the Father the promised Holy Spirit and has poured out what you now see and hear. For David did not ascend to heaven, and yet he said,

> "The Lord said to my Lord: 'Sit at my right hand until
> I make your enemies a footstool for your feet.'"

> Therefore let all Israel know with certainty
> that God has made this Jesus, whom you
> crucified, both Lord and Christ!"

Peter's listeners responded immediately:

> When the people heard this, they were cut
> to the heart and asked Peter and the other
> apostles, "Brothers, what shall we do?"
>
> Peter replied, "Repent and be baptized, every
> one of you, in the name of Jesus Christ for the
> forgiveness of your sins, and you will receive the
> gift of the Holy Spirit. This promise belongs to you
> and to your children and to all who are far off, to
> all whom the Lord our God will call to Himself."
>
> With many other words he testified, and
> he urged them, "Be saved from this corrupt
> generation." Those who embraced his message
> were baptized, and about three thousand were
> added to the believers that day. (Acts 2:22-41)

The apostle Peter's address to the crowd was the first sermon preached after the promised outpouring of the Holy Spirit. As such, from a biblical perspective it's significant in establishing foundational doctrine for preaching and teaching about salvation in the name of Jesus Christ, who is the cornerstone of the gospel message.

In a nutshell, the gospel presented by the apostle Peter encompasses:

• Jesus was crucified for our sins.

- God raised Him from the dead, making Him both Lord and Christ (the promised Messiah).
- The apostles were eyewitnesses of the resurrection.

By way of response, outsiders need to repent and be baptized in the name of Jesus Christ for the forgiveness of sins, and they'll receive the gift of the Holy Spirit, since the promised outpouring of the Holy Spirit belongs to all future generations of believers.

The Gospel Message of Jesus

So what did Jesus say about the gospel message? Here is the instruction He gave His disciples just before His ascension into heaven:

> He said to them, "This is what I told you while I was with you: Everything must be fulfilled that is written about me in the Law of Moses, the Prophets, and the Psalms." Then he opened their minds so they could understand the Scriptures. He told them, "This is what is written: The Christ will suffer and rise from the dead on the third day, and repentance and forgiveness of sins will be preached in his name to all nations, beginning in Jerusalem. You are witnesses of these things. I am going to send you what my Father has promised; but stay in the city until you are clothed with power from on high." (Luke 24:44-49)

When reading these verses, it's important to realize that before this point in time, the apostles simply weren't able to make a connection between their Lord and the suffering servant spoken about in Isaiah 53, even though Jesus told them on at least three specific occasions (Mark 8:31-33; Luke

9:43-45; Luke 18:31-34) that His death and resurrection had been foretold by the prophets.

Not only were their minds incapable of comprehending what the prophets had spoken concerning their Lord, but Peter was so incensed when Jesus first predicted His death and resurrection that he challenged Jesus about it, and was summarily rebuked with the infamous words, "Get behind me, Satan!" (Mark 8:33).

Prior to their final meeting on the mountain of Christ's ascension, the apostles' minds were veiled. Yet God in His wisdom had purposed this to happen, to ensure that human motives didn't interfere with the words of the prophets (Mark 8:33).

However, as soon as the above Scriptures were fulfilled through the resurrection, Jesus was able to open their minds to look back with understanding on all that had been spoken in Scripture about the Christ. This is the significance of those words spoken to His disciples after He had opened their minds: "*This is what is written…*" (Luke 24:46).

Of first importance, Jesus spoke about three things:
- the gospel message (including the death and resurrection of the Christ; repentance and forgiveness of sins to be preached 'in His name');
- the Great Commission (to all nations);
- the promised outpouring of the Holy Spirit, which was about to happen in Jerusalem.

The purpose of the promised outpouring or baptism of the Holy Spirit (Acts 1:5,8) was to empower the apostles and all believers to preach the gospel message accompanied by signs, wonders, and miracles in the name of Jesus.

The apostles and disciples of Jesus were able to give powerful eyewitness testimony of these things (particularly the resurrection) to all peoples and nations, starting in Jerusalem, Judea, and Samaria, and then to the uttermost ends of the earth.

The reason I've focused on the foretelling by Jesus and then the ongoing teaching of the apostles Peter and Paul is that they collectively set the pattern for the early church to grow and prosper among both the Jewish and Gentile worlds—among all nations.

Let's look next at how *we* take this message to our world.

20

How Am I to Share the Gospel?

So how are we to share the gospel message in this day and age? The answer to this is simple yet profound: Bring Christianity (or even basic beliefs about God) into a conversation with someone (this is "sowing the Word")—and see what response you receive. Then shape the message according to the parable of the sower and soils that we explored earlier (in chapter 6).

Our goal is for the listener to hear and understand the good news about Jesus Christ and to bring their life to the point of decision, either immediately or over time.

Although the gospel message may be shaped in many different ways, one thing that distinguishes Christianity from all other world religions is that the death and resurrection of Jesus Christ the Messiah was foretold by Old Testament prophets as well as by Jesus Himself—and it came to pass as predicted. Jesus also foretold that the outpouring or baptism of the Holy Spirit would start in Jerusalem and then spread to all nations and that also came to pass.

To share the gospel message in the most effective manner, our lives need to embrace all three things that Jesus spoke about as matters of first importance:

- the *gospel message* (most particularly the resurrection)

- the *Great Commission* (to reach all nations)
- being empowered by the *baptism in the Holy Spirit*

When the apostle Paul entered a city, these central planks of Christianity would always shine through his ministry, and the results could range anywhere from a riot to revival.

It really didn't bother the apostle Paul, because whenever the light of the gospel shines into darkness, there can only ever be a struggle or agreement.

For the early years of his life, Paul (formerly known as Saul) struggled and fought against the light. But after his encounter with the resurrected Christ, his life was totally transformed.

Moreover, from that time forth, the most important thing in his life was to share the light he received, by testifying about his encounter with the risen Lord and to encourage others to believe in the same manner.

Some of the most incredible God encounters in the Scriptures followed the times when the apostle Paul stepped out in faith, by choosing to believe God no matter what his eyes could see or his circumstances were dictating.

Being able to see through the eyes of faith changed everything for Paul. For this same reason, Jesus told His disciples to open their eyes and to see the harvest.

The only thing missing at the time was the workers.

When God's people begin to look through the eyes of faith, they can experience people asking them the same question the Philippian jailer asked of the apostle Paul in the midst of a hopeless situation: "What must I do to be saved?" (Acts 16:10). If you've never had this question asked of you, I can assure you it's one of the most incredible experiences you'll ever have in this life. It's when your time of sowing turns to reaping, and the harvest of a precious soul into God's kingdom is at hand.

A Gospel Message in Prison

Paul and Silas had some extraordinary distinctives about their lives on the night that statement was made, which brightly reflected their faith in the Savior, Jesus Christ.

After being stripped, beaten, and severely flogged, they were locked in a dark inner prison cell with their feet in chains. In view of their circumstances, who would have thought Paul and Silas would be praying and singing hymns to God at midnight, with all the other prisoners listening?

Paul and Silas had no thought or notion of being victims, for they saw themselves as being victorious in Christ Jesus, since they knew God was ordering their footsteps.

As they prayed and sang, they not only got the attention of the other prisoners, but their God was also listening intently.

Their ability to pray and praise God in the middle of desperate circumstances paved the way for one of the most incredible miracles and God encounters mentioned in Scripture. That same night, God decided to inhabit their praises in a special way—by sending a violent earthquake that shook the very foundations of the prison (which happened to be the jailer's workplace).

Can you imagine the jailer's reaction when he suddenly awoke to the news that every prison door had just flown open?

It gets better, because he soon discovered that the prisoners' chains were all loose as well.

Just as the jailer was about to commit suicide, he heard Paul shouting, "Don't harm yourself! We are all here!" (Acts 16:28). Imagine how the jailer might have felt.

This emotional rollercoaster took place within a few moments of time. Suddenly the roles were reversed, with a miracle that saw captivity itself being taken captive. God had fulfilled literally what was spoken by the prophet Isaiah: "The Spirit of the Sovereign LORD is on me, because the LORD has anointed me…to proclaim freedom for the captives and release from darkness for the prisoners" (Isaiah 61:1).

God, in his perfect *kairos* timing, intervened in a life and death moment, and the jailer's life was spared.

The jailer immediately knew, and with absolute certainty, that God had ordered these circumstances, and his own moment of truth was at hand.

When confronted with the miracle of an earthquake, cell doors flying open, and unshackled prisoners staying in their cells, the jailer had the choice either to use logic and reason to try explaining away these events, or to embrace the grace of God and realize that his life had been spared for a reason. Fortunately, the jailer chose the pathway of faith, and he'll forever be remembered as the one who cried out, "Sirs, what must I do to be saved?"

In contrast, it's interesting to note that so many of the "wise and learned" of today's society take the pathway of logic and reason by default when they can't explain something that happens in the supernatural realm. Words such as random, freakish, chance, coincidental, or even spontaneous remission (when it comes to some health professionals) are often used to describe a miraculous healing or event when traditional treatment methods have failed, or there's no apparent reason for the healing.

How ironic it is that we can connect with God—the Creator of all wisdom and knowledge—only through humility and faith in His Son, Jesus Christ. This can only be by divine design. Logic and reason will never get anyone into heaven, but logic and reason are the norm for today's society, which operates in the natural realm. On the other hand, faith is the conduit to heaven, and it's available only in the supernatural realm.

When the jailer asked the above question about being saved, the apostle Paul and Silas responded, "Believe in the Lord Jesus and you will be saved, you and your household."

> Then Paul and Silas spoke the word of the Lord to him
> and to everyone in his house. At that hour of the night,
> the jailer took them and washed their wounds. And
> without delay, he and all his household were baptized.
> Then he brought them into his home and set a meal
> before them. So he and all his household rejoiced that
> they had come to believe in God. (Acts 16:31-34)

Although it's obvious that this supernatural chain of events played a great part in the conversion of the jailer and his family, his response to this physical life and death situation saw his faith conquer his fears. The jailer also knew with absolute certainty that God had not only spared his life, but had also called him into His greater purposes.

In the same way, our own personal salvation experience needs to be recognized and valued as a divine exchange without equal.

For those who choose to believe, Jesus Christ is the Lamb of God who was born to die for the sins of the world. His life was sacrificed to pay a ransom that no man could ever pay. The ransom price to redeem and restore relationship between a fallen race and its Creator required the shedding of sinless blood. This could happen only through a divine exchange initiated by God.

Because man was totally incapable of saving himself, God sent His Son to offer up His own blood to provide the perfect sacrifice for our sins.

A Personal Encounter

Not long ago I started visiting a local gym, as I needed to get my physical body into better shape.

The first day I went to the gym, I met a young man about thirty years of age named BJ, who was to become my personal trainer. When we sat down, the first thing he said to me was, "Tell me about your life."

Well, for the next twenty minutes, BJ heard my testimony and the gospel of the Lord Jesus Christ in no uncertain terms.

I had recently been in Papua New Guinea (in August 2017) for a missions trip with Planetshakers, and it was life changing. God did some incredible things, and amazing miracles happened. I shared some of these with BJ, and he was quite taken back by them.

BJ had gone to a Catholic school and had some basic Bible understanding and teaching, which was good. But he saw something in my faith that seemed strikingly unusual to him.

At one stage while we were talking, I broke open my smartphone to a Planetshakers music video on YouTube and said, "Here, have a look at my church, man. It rocks." He viewed the video and said, "Wow, that's different."

I said to him, "Imagine the God who created the universe, so incredible—just look outside—and this God wants us to have fellowship with Him and to worship Him as the Creator. Could you imagine that He would want that worship to be dull and boring?"

I said, "Man, there's a party going on in heaven, and we need to be part of that. And I love Planetshakers because we party when we praise and worship. We enjoy the presence of God, we encounter God. It's the most incredible church I've attended in my life."

Over the next few weeks, BJ and I had many discussions. I was praying that God would open his heart.

Then one day something very special happened.

BJ was working me out pretty heavy, but between a few of the exercise sets we came to a pause and had a time of sharing.

He said to me, "You know, as I was standing at the tram station on the way in this morning, I had a pretty deep thought. I thought to myself, if I was to die right now, how would I feel about my life? And you know, I just stepped back for a minute and thought about it." BJ went on to mention how he loved his job, and how he got to travel a lot. I knew also that he had a fiancée. And he said, "If I was to die tomorrow, I would feel pretty happy."

I said, "BJ, I can understand where you're coming from, but have you thought about the big picture?"

He looked at me rather inquisitively.

I continued, "It's one thing to be happy here, but where would you spend eternity?" I told him, "The Bible is black and white on this. There is a heaven, and there is a hell."

Then I said to him, "About two weeks ago, I went and visited a bus driver friend of mine by the name of Bernie." I told him Bernie's story (which I shared here in chapter 8). Then I said, "I want you to know that Bernie died last Saturday, and we're burying him next Monday. Bernie is now in the presence of Jesus Christ. He surrendered his life to Jesus. He took that step."

I said to BJ, "You know the story—Adam and Eve were in the garden of Eden, and God spoke to them and said, 'You can eat the fruit of any of these trees, but don't touch that one—the tree of the knowledge of good and evil. For the day you eat the fruit thereof you will surely die.'"

I said, "We know through history that they ate the fruit, yet they didn't die physically, but they were spiritually cut off from God. As a result of their sin and disobedience they were put out of the garden in Eden. Fast-forward thousands of years, and one of the greatest teachers in the history of Israel—a man named Nicodemus—came to Jesus. He said, 'Lord, no one can do the things that you do unless God is with him (John 3:2b).' Now Nicodemus made a right call on this, for Jesus was doing things that had never been seen before, like healing the sick, raising the dead, cleansing lepers, blind people seeing, the deaf hearing for the first time. He walked on water, He raised all sorts of situations out of the ashes and made them into a thing of beauty. God was doing amazing things through His Son, Jesus Christ. And after Nicodemus made this statement, Jesus turned to him and said, 'Unless a man is born again, he will not see the kingdom of heaven. (John 3:3)'"

I said, "BJ, what was lost in the garden in Eden, which resulted in mankind becoming spiritually dead, could now be found by believing in Jesus Christ, the Savior of the world."

I quoted for him Romans 10:9-10: "If you believe in your heart that Jesus is Lord and confess with your mouth that God raised Him from the dead, you shall be saved." And I said, "BJ, this was the decision that Bernie made—to believe in his heart, not his head. To believe with all your heart, all of your being, so that's who you are—then you'll be saved. When we're born into this world, our default is that we're spiritually dead to God. We have to activate our relationship with God during this life through faith and believing in His Son, Jesus Christ."

BJ said, "I get it." Then he asked, "What happens if you wait until you're seventy years of age? Can you still do it then?"

I said, "You sure can. But you never know the day or the hour when your time might be up, and you've left it until it's too late. Jesus also said,

'I have come to give you life and life more abundantly' (John 10:10)—meaning right now. Ever since I made the decision to follow Jesus when I was twenty-two years of age, I've never looked back. I've never had regrets. These days, yes, I've done very well in life in terms of worldly acquisitions and wealth. Yet, I would give all of that away tomorrow if it meant losing my salvation. I live one of the most happy and fulfilled lives I could ever imagine. I love people, and I love God."

BJ said, "I see that in you. You're incredibly content and joyful."

"Well, that's God."

We talked a bit more, and I'm confident that BJ could see the truth of what I was saying. I believe he's being challenged to the core. This is BJ's journey, and he's listening and counting the cost (Luke 14:28), like any wise person would do before making any life-changing decision.

Look for the Common Thread

If you want to share the gospel message, you need to find that point of crossover. I believe that when we pray God will open hearts enough for at least a glimpse into people's lives, so a moment of encounter may follow.

I found it with BJ when he told me about his moment of deep reflection.

I find the point of crossover with many people by just taking an interest in what they say and do—being interested in them as a person, in the same way Jesus did when He met Zacchaeus (Luke 19:1-10). Jesus spent time with Zacchaeus because He knew he was ready for a God encounter, and Jesus wanted to see his life transformed.

When Zacchaeus exchanged his money for the true riches of salvation, Jesus affirmed him as a son of the Abrahamic covenant. Zacchaeus was now walking as a son in the faith of his father, Abraham. For Zacchaeus, his confession of faith came as a result of the love and acceptance Jesus showed to him as a person.

In the same way, we must love and show genuine care for people, and want to see good things happen in their lives, if we're to reflect the love of God that's working within our own hearts.

Our goal is to find that crossover point and then to find a way to shape our message to convey the truth that Jesus Christ is the good news.

Jesus is our greatest example of a faith-filled person, and He was absolutely bomb-proof and unshakeable in His beliefs.

The irony of all this is that despite having infinite wisdom and knowledge about all aspects of life and creation, Jesus never preached a deep theological message to the people He met on life's journey. He simply encountered people and conveyed a message of hope, love, faith, mercy, compassion—and the list goes on.

Although He challenged religious leaders about their lack of understanding of theology when they should have known better, at no time did He present legalistic arguments to His followers, because He knew that such an approach would only alienate people from His primary purpose of establishing the kingdom of God on earth as it is in heaven.

Focus on the Market Place

I've also found through personal experience that legalistic arguments about doctrinal preferences do not hold up well in the market place. For most outsiders, legalistic arguments are simply fuel for the fire, while for most earnest believers, they should be seen as a sign of disunity.

In the market place, outsiders want to see your life. They want to see that you're real, that your faith can stand the test of time and pressure, no matter what comes your way, and that you truly speak as an ambassador for Jesus Christ and live a life consistent with your faith.

This is the starting point of building credibility with those around us. The extent to which our lives are shining brightly will be the extent to which our message is received.

Sunday Christians simply don't cut the mustard with a world that's already skeptical about Christianity.

As Jesus talked to religious leaders and their staunch supporters, He called them hypocrites (Matthew 23:2-3) because they professed one thing while their lives told a different story. Our lives as Christian believers will make a difference only if we consistently live out our faith and become the salt of the earth—people that others seek out, especially when all else fails. People are attracted by the stability of our life when it reflects our faith in Jesus Christ.

When others see this stability, and trouble arises in their own lives, they'll often want to find out whether Christian believers really have answers from God—through His Word (Matthew 7:24-25) as the primary point of reference. My counsel is frequently sought in such situations, and I consider it an honor and a privilege to speak into people's lives when they're seeking direction and godly counsel.

If there has ever been a time in world history when people are wanting something solid to believe in, it's now. The world around us is falling apart. People have generally lost faith in governments and other institutions of society, so full of corruption and disunity. Meanwhile the revelations about rampant sexual harassment and abuse coming out of the entertainment and news media—as well as the corporate world and religious institutions—have left people quite disillusioned.

As for our culture's celebrities—how many of them have stood the test of time and remained a shining light to the next generation? History reveals that very few pass the test without being consumed by such things as alcohol or substance abuse, affairs, scandals, family breakdown, domestic violence, or ugly divorce and/or separation.

So many people can learn only the hard way that fame and fortune mean very little when you end up alone in a rehabilitation center, sitting on the rubbish pile that your life has become, and you're wondering, "How could this have happened to me?" When a person's life takes on the persona of excess as the new norm, they're prone to go astray because they'll always be looking for something more rather than finding contentment with what they have. At this point, sin and temptation will always be crouching at the door waiting to consume whoever comes their way.

In the same way, many of our sports stars are incredibly talented on the field but their off-the-field behavior lets them down dismally. More often than not, they haven't had time to develop their character before worldly success arrives along with the promise of big pay packets, luring them into a false sense of security.

In the absence of a strong moral and ethical compass and good mentors, many stars come unstuck as a result of serious character flaws a few years down the track. This is a tragedy for the sport as well as for fans—especially the young, who often idolize these stars.

Much of our media has been corrupted by self-interest, pushing their own agendas by highlighting pet causes rather than exhibiting any conscience as to what's actually good for the people or the nation. Undoubtedly, the sensationalist approach makes for better ratings and financial returns than presenting an unbiased report, but in terms of integrity and self-respect, the media sector needs to take a good look at itself before it casts the stone at others.

History shows mankind consistently tends to cast off all forms of restraint, including morality, virtue, discipline, self-control, and many other biblical values. The only real difference today is that the decline has been more apparent, due to the increased availability of telecommunications, especially the internet, which has placed social media right at people's fingertips.

In contrast to the patterns of this world, Christian believers need to recognize that God's Word is the truth about every aspect of this life. God's Word has withstood the test of time. In fact, it's one of the few absolutes that still exist in our society, despite being constantly under attack by people having different values from the Creator.

Christian believers need to open their eyes and see themselves as workers in the end-time harvest by taking this precious gospel message into their market places. They need to be determined to make a difference in their world—a world constantly bombarded with ungodly values pushing the agendas of atheism, agnosticism, hedonism, secularism, and political correctness to the extreme.

Jesus openly declared His disciples to be the salt of the earth and the light of the world to their generation. He also gave this promise: "And I, when I am lifted up from the earth, will draw all people to myself" (John 12:32). As we lift up the name of Jesus in our daily lives, He'll cause people to come across our paths for *kairos* moments, presenting personal situations that are at times almost beyond belief.

The most incredible miracles I've witnessed always involve my stepping out in faith and just letting God be God.

When Jesus told His followers to "ask the Lord of the harvest to send out workers into His harvest field" (Luke 10:2), He was speaking into the lives of twelve largely unlearned men from all walks of life. The one distinguishing thing that His disciples possessed was their willingness to take a step out of their comfort zone when Jesus said, "Follow Me," and their lives were forever changed.

All these men gave their lives for the sake of the gospel. They turned their worlds upside down, because they had their eyes and their minds opened by Jesus the Messiah.

Step Out

Until our Lord returns, this is the Great Commission given to all believers: We've been commanded to go into all the world, to preach good news to all creation, to make disciples of all nations, to baptize believers in the name of the Father and of the Son and of the Holy Spirit, to teach believers to obey the teachings of Christ, and to expect those who believe to perform miraculous signs and wonders in the name of Jesus Christ (Matthew 28:16-20; Mark 16:15-20).

Many professing believers are probably unaware of this, but at the present time heaven is being populated by the faith of the current workers in covenant relationship with God. However, many more workers are needed to bring in the end-time harvest that will hasten the Lord's coming.

If you're not an active participant in any part of the Great Commission, then I encourage you to step out of the valley of decision and into the purposes and plans that God has for your life.

The Father has already invested heavily into our lives by sending His Son to take away our sins. When we believe in Jesus Christ and are born again, our newfound faith is meant to be accompanied by good deeds that glorify our Father in heaven (Matthew 5:16; 1 Peter 2:12; James 2:18; 2 John 1:8). These good deeds are also our means of storing up rewards for when we go to heaven.

With certainty, it's important for believers to know and understand that our future rewards in heaven will be directly related to our acts of service to others while we're here on earth (Matthew 6:19-20; Luke 12:13-34; Matthew 25:31-46).

Commitment is always a choice—but so are consequences.

Never forget the words of our Lord:

> From everyone who has been given much, much will be required; and from him who has been entrusted with much, even more will be demanded. (Luke 12:48)

21

How to Connect in the Market Place

T he world is so full of broken people that there's no shortage of opportunity to meet and connect with people searching for answers to the questions of life.

Christianity holds the keys to life's answers, and as disciples of Jesus we should always be ready to give an account of our faith and the reasons for our belief in the Savior. In this chapter we'll explore a number of different ways to pursue this connection with others in the market place.

Starting a Fellowship Group

I've often found it inspiring to set up fellowship groups where Christians can connect with others and reach out to others who want to inquire about the Lord. Below are some of the principles I've used for helping these groups succeed:

Start Small

Connect with a few believers who are people of faith and well regarded in their market place.

It's important to spend time building relationship with this group. Get to know them at a personal level, including their family situation, their passion, and their gifting.

Start meeting at lunchtime in a local coffee shop or restaurant, and make it your goal to be a blessing to others in the group.

Find a Venue

As the group begins to grow, you'll need to find a venue that can accommodate a small group of around eight to ten people. I've found this size to be most effective.

In my experience, I've usually approached inner-city churches, which are mostly unoccupied during the week, and asked if they could assist with providing a venue for a prayer and fellowship group meeting during the week.

Inevitably, the answer was yes, and then it was simply a matter of setting a day and time for the group to start. Usually the group ran each week for an hour or so around lunchtime.

Set the Format

The format for the meetings can be flexible and doesn't need to be programmed or heavily time-sensitive.

If someone can bring an instrument and lead a worship song or two, that's fine, but I've personally run these groups with no instruments, and a few well-known songs can be sung with great effect when they come from the heart.

Another option is to play a few recorded songs. This sets the atmosphere for God's presence to be released as the Holy Spirit is invited into the meeting.

As an icebreaker, someone would generally bring Scripture and a few words of encouragement to the meeting.

It's important to ensure that some of the material being related is of relevance to the market place, especially as an outreach to fellow workers.

Provide an opportunity to encourage attendees to share something good concerning their relationship with God or their faith journey. Encourage testimonies, and when specific prayers are answered a praise note is welcomed, since this raises the faith of the group.

If a member of the group has specific prayer needs, these should become a focus of the meeting.

Attendees should also feel free to invite people to the meeting who are genuinely inquiring about the gospel or asking questions about the journey of life, in general.

Finally, the group should pray for each other and any situations they're facing that need the Lord's specific intervention.

It's also important that we have faith to see the miraculous happen. I firmly believe in the ministry of the Holy Spirit in these meetings, because He searches the hearts and minds of those present, and He knows our real needs well before we even think to ask for help.

Expect the Unexpected

When the Holy Spirit shows up—expect the unexpected.

Back in chapter 5, I mentioned a divorced woman named Jessica who responded with tears when I shared with her the words of promise from Isaiah 1:8— "Though your sins be as scarlet, they shall be white as snow." Following this encounter I had with Jessica at her work desk, I had several discussions with her about the Lord Jesus, and it was encouraging to see

Jessica beginning to pray. She was so excited to share with me when her prayers were answered.

At this stage, Jessica hadn't yet made a decision to follow the Lord, but she was openly asking questions about God.

Jessica readily accepted when I invited her to attend one of our fellowship meetings. However, I'm quite sure that neither she nor anyone else at the meeting expected the encounter that was about to happen. The fellowship meeting was progressing well until one of the men asked us to pray for a particular situation. This brother stood in the middle as a proxy for the situation being prayed for, and we all laid hands on him.

Jessica wanted to join in, so she stretched forth her hand and also touched the person being prayed for.

A few seconds later I looked up and Jessica's face revealed that she was in serious trouble. Jessica was motioning with her hands to her throat. She pointed to her mouth, because she couldn't breathe. She was literally being choked by an evil spirit and was in a state of despair.

Looking back, I think that most of the group had never witnessed anything like this and were also in a mild state of shock.

Jessica was looking to me as the leader, and I immediately rebuked the spirit that was attacking her in the name of Jesus Christ. In an instant of time, the spiritual attack stopped, and she was immediately released.

After that day, Jessica never had any second thoughts about whether God was real. All around Jessica's neck were red marks, and it was highly visible to all that she was being choked.

Jessica experienced the presence of God that day, and as we were walking back to work, she said to me, "I always wondered why you come back to work after lunch with a smile on your face and so happy. Now I know why!"

This type of situation was definitely an exception to the regular flow of meetings, but God calls us to be ready at all times with our spiritual armor in place so we can take our stand against the devil's schemes (Ephesians 6:11-18).

In any Christian meeting, we must never forget: "God is our refuge and strength, an ever present help in times of trouble" (Psalm 46:1 GW). We must learn to expect the unexpected when the Holy Spirit shows up.

Developing an Evangelistic Culture

Have you ever considered how many times Jesus went out of his way to meet up with that one person who was facing a hopeless situation?

Jesus showed mercy to everyone He had opportunity to help, because He knew the human race was hopelessly lost and in need of a Savior. If we're to follow in His steps, we also need to adopt a redemptive approach to the lost by showing the love and mercy of God at every opportunity.

One of the primary purposes for writing this book is to alert all Christian believers to our great responsibility to see our market places and workplaces as fields of people that are ripe for harvest and in need of a Savior.

In the remainder of this chapter, we'll explore more door openers for market place ministry—including practical suggestions of how to connect with outsiders through market place evangelism.

Showing Hospitality

Invite people around to your home or meet with them outside of the regular market place environment.

Make sure you say grace and give thanks to God.

Always seek to have a rich time when you're together, and always remember that we're blessed so that we can be a blessing to others.

During your time together, always leave open the opportunity to discuss values, beliefs, and perspectives that pave the way for a Christian worldview to be presented and discussed. Society has become so fragmented that many people are genuinely searching for answers. When an important topic is raised, you can always refer to what the "Good Book" says, and share why you hold to this belief.

Hospitality is an investment in time, energy, resources, friendship, and finances. Most importantly, it's an investment in the people we meet who are also on life's journey. Jesus referred to these people as our neighbors, and He regularly went out of His way to spend time with the one who was lost. He didn't devote all His time to the ninety-nine righteous, as was the practice of the religious leaders. Most importantly, what He gave to that one was able to change the person's life for eternity.

The questions we need to consider are these:

- Do we show mercy like the good Samaritan?
- Do we get our hands dirty and actually provide help? Or do we make excuses and bypass any form of trouble when it beckons? (Luke 10:25-37)

From a scriptural perspective, it's when we make time to help a lost soul find the Savior that the kingdom of God is being established here on earth—and God's will is being done as it is in heaven.

Visiting People Who Are Unwell

Going out of our way to visit people who are sick or infirm is one of the most rewarding and merciful ministries a believer can undertake.

We often read in the Scriptures about Jesus being moved by a deep sense of compassion when He saw the multitudes "like sheep without a shepherd" (Mark 6:34). It was compassion that ultimately released the power of the Lord to heal (Luke 5:17). When we're touched by the infirmities of others and have a deep sense of compassion, we too are walking in the steps of Jesus, which can open the door to the supernatural.

As a market place minister, I've regularly visited extended family of business owners and their staff in hospitals or their homes to pray for their loved ones. In many cases, this will extend to the people nearby who hear me praying and also ask for ministry.

People need encouragement and hope, especially those reaching out for help. By following the "new" commandment of Jesus to "love one another as I have loved you" (John 13:34), we create a bridge of friendship that has the potential to open the door for people to reconnect with God.

Although our love comes from a place of compassion and seeking to provide comfort and relief, it's also important for our motivation to come from an expression of God's love and mercy. People we minister to can sense when this is genuine.

I've personally helped put people into ambulances, and sometimes even traveled in the ambulance with them. This is an act of love and mercy. But I also have learned that just being there, even during periods of silence, makes all the difference. Your very presence is a testimony to the one you're trying to help.

In the same way that Jesus said, "I will never leave you," we can also stand beside someone in need whether they believe in God or not, because this act of friendship reflects the nature and heart of the God in whom we believe. God desires mercy, justice, truth, and faithfulness in our inner being (Psalm 51:6) far more than He desires any act of sacrifice (Matthew 23:23).

I've also learned that when we're weak and feeling inadequate for the task, God turns up and shows Himself mighty to heal, mighty to deliver, mighty to restore hope, and mighty to defend. Just like the apostle Paul, I will gladly boast about my own inadequacy if it shows forth the strength and greatness of the One in whom I believe. Paul asked the Lord three times to remove a thorn in his flesh, but Jesus told him, "My grace is sufficient for you, for My power is perfected in weakness" (2 Corinthians 12:9). In other words, it's only in our absolute dependence on the Lord that His power is perfected in us and released through us.

This same power is available to those we reach out to, when we realize that God's grace meets every person at the point of their greatest need.

Once the place of struggling is done away with and unconditional surrender takes place, the grace of God abounds, and this sets the scene to allow God to be God in every situation.

Helping Those in Need

As I've mentioned, I attend Planetshakers Church in City Road in Melbourne, Australia. This is a wonderful place to encounter God, and over the last two years, upwards of two hundred people each week have been making first-time decisions to commit their lives to Jesus Christ as Lord and Savior.

At Planetshakers, we have an outreach ministry called Empower that reaches out to the homeless, the helpless, and the needy of Melbourne with the love of God accompanied by the gospel message. As an extension of this ministry, I have on occasion taken people into my apartment for short periods and loved and cared for them. I've listened to their stories, their hopes, and their dreams. I've also seen their lives indelibly touched through wise counsel based on God's Word, and through praying with them and seeing them have an encounter with God, whether at church or in my home.

Many of these people are no different from the man lying on the side of the road to Jericho (Luke 10:30). They've often been beaten and robbed by life's circumstances, and they find themselves struggling for daily existence, grasping for hope of a better life.

When Jesus told the expert in the law to "go and do likewise," He was saying that being a neighbor (as God intended) required believers to show acts of mercy through practical aid and assistance to those in need (Luke 10:37).

For the church of Jesus Christ to impact our generation, we also need to go and do likewise and by ready to show mercy rather than excuse ourselves from offering help to those in need.

It's so easy to put a label on people and then excuse ourselves from helping them. But the only label I can ever recall Jesus using was the word "hypocrites," when He spoke of the religious leaders of His day. Of particular note, He said this: "Woe to you experts in the law! For you have taken away the key to knowledge. You yourselves have not entered, and you have hindered those who were entering" (Matthew 11:52).

The important thing to remember out of this parable is that Jesus correctly interpreted the law by defining "neighbor" as anyone we pass by, rub shoulders with, or meet on a daily basis.

Our task as an ambassador for Christ is to make a difference to their world by "going and doing likewise."

Keeping Informed of World Events

Although world events keep happening and are highly visible in our technology-driven world, it's equally insightful to know that Jesus Christ spoke prophetically about "the increase of wickedness" that would occur, to the point that "the love of most (believers) will grow cold" in the last days before His return at the end of the age (Matthew 24:12). Matthew 24 also records other signs of the times that Jesus said would happen before His second coming.

While we shouldn't be alarmed at unfolding world events, we need to be mindful that Jesus spoke clearly about the signs that would accompany His return.

As believers, we know that Jesus Christ holds the answers to the questions of life, and no matter what situation we may face, there's a right path to take if we're prepared to seek Him for guidance.

Although this counsel is primarily meant for believers, many people who are on the brink of losing hope because of tragedy, loss, or other adversities have found the Savior, because they've reached out to God for help at a time when the world offered no permanent or lasting solution.

Spending eternity in heaven is the ultimate answer to the questions of life, and Jesus Christ has already declared: "I am the way and the truth and the life. No one comes to the Father except through me" (John 14:6).

Bringing Hope at Funerals

There's nothing like a funeral to bring home the reality of our mortality.

Having the blessed assurance of eternal life beyond the grave is something we as Christians can speak about because of our relationship with God.

Where we spend eternity matters. However, many people who don't know God are often without hope and full of despair at the loss of a loved one. But there's always hope—if we will only believe.

A few years ago I went to the funeral of a good friend named Frank who had been the financial controller for one of my management consulting business clients. Frank had just lost his battle with cancer at age forty-nine, leaving behind a loving wife and two children.

The funeral was spoken almost entirely in Italian, which made it difficult to follow, but it appeared to mostly follow the format of a traditional Roman Catholic mass.

At a personal level, the most important part was about to unfold. The traditional mass is followed by a ceremony called "commiserations," in which the extended family of the deceased will stand in a receiving line so that funeral attendees can pay their respects. As I walked toward the commiserations line, Frank's father and mother stood there crying. Seeing this, I spoke to them directly from my heart, since I knew that nothing else would impact their obvious grief. I said, "I loved him too; he was my friend," as tears were streaming down my face.

Frank's dad said to me, "It's not right that children should go before their parents. Why not take us and leave him?"

I said to them, "You will see him again, if you believe."

They looked at me rather strangely. I said to them, "Don't you understand about the resurrection of Jesus Christ? Jesus said, 'I am the resurrection and the life. He who believes in me will live, even though he dies.'" Then I said to them, "You'll see your son again in heaven if you truly believe, and we'll all know each other in heaven as part of God's family."

When I said this, it was as though a light bulb had been turned on. Frank's parents cried even harder—but this time it was tears of joy, not despair. They had their hope restored, because they too believed in Jesus Christ.

As they were crying, Frank's dad began to thank me in a manner that I found truly humbling. Amid his tears, he put his arms around me and began shaking my hand and said, "Thank you, so much, we never understood this, but now we know."

These people, like so many, had been faithful in attending church all their life, but had never been taught about the reality of the resurrection and what it means for those who truly believe in Jesus Christ.

This was one of the most touching funerals I've ever attended. However, the lasting memory I have is not so much honoring the life of a friend who'd passed on from this life, but seeing new life spring into his parents, who gained renewed hope and faith in Jesus Christ.

Our God is truly amazing!

Finding Friends in the Market Place

I've found many friends among the small business owners in market places close to where I work in Melbourne's central business district. As a small business owner, I'm highly aware of the many challenges a business owner can face. With this in mind, I often ask the question, "How is business?" because I'm aware that cash flow issues can often lead to problems. This in turn can result in family problems, relationship issues, denial, depression—and the list goes on.

Apart from having a background in management and financial matters, the one thing I can always bring to a business owner is hope for a better future through the gospel message. However, while I'm passionate about winning people to Christ, I'm also seeking fruit that lasts (John 15:16), which is why I spend time loving people (and building relationship) before I attempt to lead them to Christ.

Earlier I went into considerable detail explaining how our life needs to *become* the message we're sharing, if we want to seriously impact our world for Jesus Christ. This is sometimes referred to as lifestyle evangelism. It's the primary method Jesus used to win the lost during His many one-on-one encounters with people mentioned in the Gospels.

In essence, lifestyle evangelism is modeling Christlike values (such as strength of character, integrity, honesty, loyalty, morality) and the biblical equivalents otherwise known as the fruit of the Spirit (Galatians 5:22)—modelling these on a daily basis before others.

Lifestyle evangelism is also the doorway to discipleship, which is fulfillment of the Great Commission to "go and make disciples."

In a nutshell, much of this book is a personal narrative of what the Lord has revealed to me about the need for church culture to embrace the understanding that lasting fruit is needed for the kingdom of God to grow. It's my firm belief that both Scripture and real-life experience confirms that this is best achieved by *loving* before *leading*—loving others according to the Great Commandment, before leading them to Christ in fulfillment of the Great Commission.

While there is and always will be a place for mass evangelism (and indeed I received Christ at one of these rallies), unless there's appropriate follow-up—one on one—many do not continue in the faith. In the aftermath of mass rallies, the often-quoted statistic of "souls saved" is retrospectively replaced with the wording "decisions made," simply because discipleship may not have happened. This observation is well known by church leaders.

For this reason, I believe the most fruitful pattern for growing the kingdom and reaping lasting fruit is the one-on-one ministry that Jesus mainly performed. It's not at all surprising to me that this one-on-one ministry model is what market place ministry is all about.

Church leaders have often viewed the market place or workplace as very hard to break into from a kingdom perspective. This is possibly because the predominant pattern of church renewal over the centuries has been traditionally viewed through the lens of mass evangelism.

In my experience, this would never work in the market place or workplace, because there are too many opposing interests to the gospel message, and there's no longer the freedom to hold mass rallies in workplaces as there was with the miners at the time of the Welsh revival.

I'm persuaded that Jesus's brief parable about leaven more accurately describes what the kingdom of God is like when it comes to sharing the gospel message in the market place or workplace:

> To what can I compare the kingdom of God? It is like
> yeast that a woman took and mixed into three measures
> of flour until all of it was leavened. (Luke 13:20-21)

Here Jesus likens the gospel to a little yeast working its way through the entire loaf. This speaks figuratively of the gospel message being sown by faith-filled workers into their field (or market place) using a one-on-one approach to make disciples in accordance with the Great Commission.

At the end of the day, there appears little doubt that the making of disciples is simply what Jesus referred to as lasting fruit.

Being Generous, Giving of Yourself

As a business person who's passionate about sharing the gospel message, I know that it's important to reflect the character of the God in whom we trust. Otherwise our kingdom influence will be limited.

God is generous in every way. He gives the seasons, the sunshine, and the necessary rain to sustain life throughout the earth. God also gave the most precious gift mankind could ever imagine through the sacrificial death of His Son, Jesus Christ. He did this because He chose to love His creation and its inhabitants.

In order to reflect the nature of the God in whom we trust, we also need to be generous to those around us. This can take on many forms:

- giving of ourselves to others, which can include sharing our business and life experience from a godly perspective;
- mentoring those who will come after us, and making a difference in their lives;
- showing generosity to our fellow workers and staff, and letting them know that we value their efforts;

- showing mercy and compassion to those in need and being prepared to donate time, resources, and finances to worthy causes.
- as our business grows, rewarding those who contributed to making it happen, which can take on many forms—including pay increases, bonuses, time off, and gifts. The important thing is not to be miserly with those around us, because this in itself makes a statement about how we view their worth.

When you read the story of Job's life, one thing that stands out is that he was the wealthiest man on earth at the time and yet he took the time to be generous with people from all walks of life. Consider Job's testimony:

> Because I delivered the poor who cried for help,
> And the orphan who had no helper.
> The blessing of the one ready to perish came upon me,
> And I made the widow's heart sing for joy.
> I put on righteousness, and it clothed me;
> My justice was like a robe and a turban.
> I was eyes to the blind
> And feet to the lame.
> I was a father to the needy,
> And I investigated the case which I did not know.
> I broke the jaws of the wicked
> And snatched the prey from his teeth....
> To me they listened and waited,
> And kept silent for my counsel....
> I smiled on them when they did not believe,
> And the light of my face they did not cast down.
> I chose a way for them and sat as chief,
> And dwelt as a king among the troops,
> As one who comforted the mourners. (Job 29:12-25)

I wonder what our fellow workers have to say about our own generosity? Think seriously about this question, because the answer will directly reflect your ability to bring influence for the kingdom of God (either positively or negatively) into your market place, your workplace, or your life.

Sharing Ministry Tools

If you're serious about reaching out to the lost, it's essential to have some ministry tools you can give away to genuine inquirers.

I've found some amazing books that I purchase in bulk and simply give away to the people God brings my way. Here are some of these resources:

- *Close Encounters of the Divine Kind* by Che Ann.
- *A Divine Revelation of Hell* (best to read this one first) and *A Divine Revelation of Heaven* by Mary Kay Baxter.

These books (plus others you might care to add) are for people asking life's biggest questions and who genuinely seek to encounter God. The books are evangelistic in nature and tell a story that needs to be heard.

Praying

Realize also that prayer is the key to opening an effective door to ministry.

Earlier in this book we looked at how laying a foundation of believing prayer effectively paves the way for God's kingdom to come and His will to be done in our lives. Every great victory in the Bible is either undergirded in prayer or came about as a sovereign act of God leading ultimately to spiritual renewal throughout the land.

- Jesus often spent the entire night in prayer on many occasions before He performed the greatest miracles.
- When Jesus came down from the mount of His transfiguration with Peter, James, and John, the other disciples had been unsuccessfully try-

ing to cast a demon out of a young boy. When they asked why they were unsuccessful at this, Jesus responded by saying this kind of demon comes out only with prayer.

- Jesus was comforted through prayer and angelic visitation in His moments of greatest anguish in the garden of Gethsemane before facing the cross.
- When the Holy Spirit was poured out on the day of Pentecost, 120 people had been in the upper room praying.
- Peter and John were on their way to the temple to pray when they encountered the crippled man outside at the city gate. As they began to pray using the authority of the name of Jesus Christ, not only was his crippled body healed, but his lost soul was redeemed as he was introduced to the Savior of the world.
- Peter and Cornelius were both praying at the time God spoke to them about meeting each other. This historic meeting resulted in the outpouring of the Holy Spirit upon Gentile believers and setting the early church on fire.
- God opened effective doors of ministry for the apostle Paul as a direct result of prayer.

I mention these Scriptures to highlight the truth that there's always a price to pay before a door can be opened to effective ministry. This door isn't opened by simply spending five or ten minutes in prayer whenever you feel like it, or whenever you hit the wall on something that's too big for you to handle and you then expect God to come to the rescue.

One lesson we need to learn from the children of Israel is that although they were a people of the covenant, they didn't pray unless something went awfully bad. They simply relied on their leaders to lead and direct them and to tell them what to do. They lived in the hope that this approach would keep them out of trouble, but inevitably—because their minds were not being transformed—they kept setting their hearts on evil things. Whenever they encountered difficulty, all they did was complain, murmur, grumble, and test the Lord. Because their hearts weren't surrendered to God's purpose and plan for their lives, they ended up committing idolatry and sexual immorality.

That's why Scripture declares that although the children of Israel saw "the acts of God," it was Moses who knew "the ways of God" (Psalm 103:7).

We see this especially in Numbers 13–14, in the story of the men sent on ahead by Moses to spy out the Promised Land that Israel would be entering. All twelve spies sent out by Moses knew that the land they were exploring had been promised by God under oath to Abraham and his descendants (Genesis 15:18-19) as their inheritance. Yet when the time came to lay hold of the Promised Land, only two of the twelve spies could actually see it as their inheritance, because they were looking at it through the eyes of faith. It was only through a faith response like Abraham's that God was going to allow any of the Israelites to step into their destiny.

There's so much irony in this story. It's hard to understand their lack of faith after they had witnessed so many miracles and encounters with God.

Consider the following:

- All these spies were leaders among their tribes.
- They were all circumcised on the eighth day, in accordance with the Abrahamic covenant.
- The Abrahamic covenant was initiated by God Himself in response to the faith of Abraham and his obedience to God's call upon his life.

What this generation failed to realize was that their patriarch, Abraham was regarded as the father of faith, and the father of all those who believe without seeing. For the Israelites to think the inhabitants would simply hand over the Promised Land without a fight was as foolish as thinking they wouldn't have to exercise faith (like Abraham's) to inherit it.

While the report of the other ten spies focused on the giants who ruled the land, the reports of Joshua and Caleb focused on the greatness of their God. Those other ten spies walked by sight—while Joshua and Caleb walked by faith.

Facing Our Giants

Consider also the well-known story of David and Goliath in 1 Samuel 17. How is this story relevant in our day?

- The truth is that we will always face giants like Goliath if we want to step out of the natural and into supernatural to do exploits for God.
- If David had been worried about the size of the Goliath he was facing, he would never have stepped forward from the battle line where all the other "faithless" soldiers stood frozen in fear and intimidation.
- David had been anointed by Samuel the prophet, and now was his time to step into the destiny God had planned for him.
- David had learned to protect the flock using a slingshot and his bare hands, and he had killed both the lion and the bear. At the age of about thirteen, this would have been impossible for him in the natural realm.
- David had come to know God by having a relationship built on prayer and worship.
- Phrases in David's psalms such as "Early will I seek Thee," "I love Your presence," and "Take not Thy Holy Spirit from me" do not come from a casual relationship with God. They're intimate expressions of devotion based on a life of prayer, worship, and intimacy with God. Meditate for a few moments on the words of Psalm 63, and I'm confident you'll draw the same conclusion about David's intimacy with God.

- David's intimacy with God constantly set him apart from his peers in terms of leadership and hearing God's voice, but it also sustained him through his darkest hours, which we all face.

In order to please God, we need to understand one fundamental thing about God's ways:

> Without faith it is impossible to please and be
> satisfactory to Him. For whoever would come near
> to God must [necessarily] believe that God exists and
> that He is the rewarder of those who earnestly and
> diligently seek Him [out]. (Hebrews 11:6 AMP)

Spending time in devotions and in prayer with God is the most precious time of my day. It's out of these daily interactions with God that our intimacy grows.

If you don't experience a sense of wonder and awe on a regular basis, I strongly suggest that you need a fresh encounter with God.

If I sugarcoated the message about the importance of prayer to achieving effective ministry, I would not be honoring the Scriptures or what God has shown me through personal revelation. For this reason, I want to encourage you to pray daily for God encounters to occur. Then be open and ready to encounter the people God brings your way. Be full of mercy and grace, just like the good Samaritan.

Pray for opportunities to reach the lost in your workplace or market place, and always remember that taking the enemy's territory (the kingdom of this world) requires all of us to walk by faith coupled with a genuine love for our fellow man.

Pray for the leading of the Holy Spirit and for spiritual gifts, especially the word of knowledge and the word of wisdom. These are invaluable when hearts need to be opened to receive the Word of God.

May we all have the courage to pick up our slingshot each day and catapult faith into the face of the enemy, until every doubt is slain and every Goliath subdued and defeated.

Embracing Servanthood

In conclusion, it's important to understand that there are no set formulas to winning the lost in our market places. I've simply attempted to provide an understanding of what has worked for me.

I adhere to the general principle of market place evangelism that the apostle Paul so eloquently spoke about: "I have become all things to all men, so that by all possible means I might save some of them" (1 Corinthians 9:22). Paul was determined to become the servant of all, thereby following the example and instruction set by his Lord and Savior, Jesus Christ: "Whoever wants to become great among you must become the servant of all" (Mark 10:44-45).

To embrace this role of servanthood, Paul needed to have a genuine love for his fellow man. In fact, you must have a love for people to become like them so as to win them to Christ.

Whether it was going to the Jews or Gentiles, or to the strong or the weak—it didn't matter to Paul. He learned to live and thrive in whatever situation he faced, in order to progress the gospel of Christ. He was prepared to identify with different cultures, races, and even classes of people, while never losing his freedom in Christ. Paul always looked for an opportunity to shape the gospel message to make it relevant to anyone's life journey, regardless of how this might impact upon his own personal circumstances.

When you read the following Scriptures, it's abundantly clear that Paul was a man ready for all seasons—and whose enabling to complete every task came from his reliance on the Lord:

> For I have learned to be content regardless of my
> circumstances. I know how to live humbly, and I know
> how to abound. I am accustomed to any and every
> situation—to being filled and being hungry, to having
> plenty and having need. I can do all things through
> Christ who gives me strength. (Philippians 4:11-13)

When we adopt a similar attitude toward winning the lost for Christ, we can learn the secret of praising God despite being battered and bruised by life's circumstances.

Like the Philippian jailer, perhaps those looking at our life might also be inspired enough to ask the question: "What must I do to be saved?" (Acts 16:10).

22

Warnings and Encouragement

As the time drew near for His life's purpose to be fulfilled, Jesus took His disciples to Jerusalem and spent time preparing them for their next phase of ministry.

In Matthew 21–26 we see a number of significant conversations between Jesus and His disciples that include a number of specific warnings and encouragements relating to end-time events before the return of Christ to earth.

In the lead-up to the Passover, Jesus continued speaking in parables as He addressed the crowds, but it was becoming increasingly obvious that many of these parables were now being directed toward the religious leaders (as with His parable about the tenants in Matthew 21:33-46, and the one about a wedding banquet in Matthew 22:1-14).

As the time was fast approaching for the fulfillment of all that the prophets had spoken, the language used by Jesus began to take on a prophetic edge, and He began to speak plainly about the hypocrisy of the religious leaders. Jesus used the word "woe" seven times in Matthew 23 as He denounced the religious leaders who trusted in their own righteousness rather than the righteousness of God. He also exposed a number of other indiscretions that had brought the ministry into disrepute and undermined the purposes and plans of God for their generation.

In Matthew 24, Jesus went on to describe the signs of the end of the age, including the gospel being preached to all nations prior to His return. The events expressed in the lead-up to His return include national upheaval, signs from the elements, false Christs and false prophets arising and performing great signs and miracles, betrayal, increased wickedness, the love of most growing cold, hatred of Christians, and particularly distressing times for Israelites, including the "abomination that causes desolation." All this would culminate with the Son of Man appearing in the sky—visible to all nations—and then finally the ingathering of the elect from the earth by the angels, following a loud trumpet call.

Jesus then sealed these words with this decree: "Heaven and earth will pass away, but My words will never pass away" (Matthew 24:35).

End-Time Parables

After Jesus had finished speaking about these events, He gave three parables that specifically speak into the lives of professing believers as the end times of our world approach, just prior to the time of His return.

These parables were given by Jesus as a warning to all who claim to be believers but whose lives may not reflect the faith they profess (James 2:26). This warning transcends religious denominations or belief systems in favor of each believer's personal devotion to Jesus Christ as their Lord and Savior (2 Peter 1:1).

Each parable describes a series of events with a central character, a central theme, and finally an outcome that's effectively a statement of judgment by God as to where the person will spend eternity

In each of these three parables, it's the faith of the individual being expressed through actions and deeds that determines the person's eternal destiny.

The Parable of the Ten Virgins

In Matthew 25:1-13 we read the parable of the ten virgins. Its context is God's declaration that having a personal relationship with the Bridegroom (Jesus Christ) is a mandatory requirement for entry into heaven. As Jesus said, to enter the kingdom of God we need to be born again (John 3:3).

In this parable, the five foolish virgins took along their lamps but no oil. Although they knew the Bridegroom (Jesus) could come at any moment, they were unprepared. But the five wise virgins took oil in jars along with their lamps—they were ready and prepared. Their faith and actions were in alignment.

The oil in jars speaks of devotion to their Lord, not unlike Mary's devotion expressed to Jesus through the alabaster jar of ointment (Mark 14:3-9).

Those who are ready at the time of Jesus's coming will have prepared their hearts with oil that cannot be purchased by silver or gold. Their lamps will never run dry because of their devotion to the Savior. They've found their precious pearl (Matthew 13:46), and they know the Savior personally.

Perhaps the greatest shock for professing but unprepared believers will come when they're turned away at the door of the wedding banquet (which speaks figuratively of the gates to heaven) by Jesus (the Bridegroom) with these words: "I tell you the truth, I don't know you." These words are spoken about people who call themselves Christians but who don't have a personal relationship with Jesus Christ.

Those who profess Christianity need to understand that our religious affiliation or church attendance will not get us into heaven. This was the mistaken belief of the five foolish virgins.

This parable is spoken specifically to the church—all Christian churches and denominations—and is a wake-up call to take the Word of God seriously, for our salvation is never something to take for granted.

When all else is stripped away, being ready means knowing with certainty where we'll spend eternity, based upon our personal relationship with Jesus Christ.

The central theme of this parable is being ready for the return of Christ.

In Luke 6:46-49, Jesus also spoke a brief parable about another group of wise and foolish people, but this time they were builders. The wise builders built their houses on a solid foundation of rock that could withstand the storms of life. As Jesus clearly states, the rock-solid foundation represents not only hearing His words but also *doing* them (Luke 6:47).

The foolish builders are described by Jesus as those whose actions didn't measure up to their profession of faith. As He said in introducing this parable of the builders in Luke 6:46, "Why do you call Me 'Lord, Lord,' but not do what I say?" The foolish builders hear the Word of God, but it doesn't impact their lives.

At the end of the day, Jesus uses the analogy of a house (our lives) without a solid foundation (not built on obeying God's Word) as being struck and completely destroyed by the torrent.

For Christians in the market place, the following questions must be asked of our lives:

6. What is our foundation?
7. On what evidence do we base this claim?
8. What are we building? Is it God's kingdom our primarily our own?
9. Are we building for now or are we also sowing into eternity?
10. What fruit is being produced from our life and our business that is adding to the kingdom of God—producing fruit in people's lives?

These questions are like a spiritual barometer for our faith.

In Jesus's day, the wealthy thought they could donate large sums of money, attend the synagogue whenever it was convenient, obey the commandments (more or less), and sacrifice an animal occasionally to square things up with God. They just took for granted (without really understanding) the commandments to love God with all their heart, soul, mind, and strength, and to love their neighbor as themselves (Luke 10:27).

The expert in the law would have had to do some serious soul-searching when he learned that the true meaning of loving his neighbor was to show mercy (Luke 10:37). It meant following up his faith with actions. The prevailing religious thought was that you're simply born into the faith, in the same way that many people today who are brought up in a certain church or denomination seem to think they have an automatic room reserved in heaven's mansions.

The Word of God declares that we cannot be born physically into the faith; we must be born again of the Spirit to enter the kingdom of God. There are no favorites when it comes to heaven, and no one can make a reservation.

The kingdom of God is not impressed by our worldly status or wealth or the religious denomination that we follow.

This especially applies to business people who often possess more power and influence from a worldly perspective, and who are maybe of the mistaken view that this provides leverage for opening the door to heaven.

We must never forget that we came into this world naked and will leave in the same manner.

We can be very wealthy, very poor, or anywhere in between in this life—but eternity begs the question: Have we been careful to store up treasures in heaven along the way? (Matthew 6:20)

The Parable of the Talents

In Matthew 25:14-30, Jesus spoke a parable about a master who was soon to depart for a long absence. Before leaving, the master entrusted his property to three servants. To each servant he gave a different but very substantial amount of wealth—measured in "talents." The amount each servant received was in accordance with the master's perception of their ability.

After his long absence, the master returned and asked his servants to give an account of their stewardship of the talents entrusted to them. The master then evaluated each servant's stewardship by assessing their faithfulness in making wise investments of their talents.

It's clear from the parable that the master had an expectation of profit (fruitfulness), since the two servants who gained more talents were recognized as "faithful." They were rewarded by being given "charge over many things" and being welcomed into the master's happiness.

The servant who produced no profit was described as "lazy and wicked" by the master. This servant had known that the master expected him to trade and make a profit, yet he chose to bury his talent in the ground.

What the servant didn't expect was that this decision would become a defining moment for his destiny.

The parable emphasizes that the master was willing to receive even the slightest trading effort on the servant's part, which would at least have gained interest. But by burying his talent and doing nothing with it, the servant was actually showing contempt for his master and despising his wishes.

To make matters worse, the servant then tried to justify his inaction by painting a picture that demonstrated a total lack of personal relationship with the master (not unlike the five foolish virgins in Matthew 25:12). Each aspect of the servant's excuse was based on his fearful and distant view of his master:

- "I knew that you are a hard man…
- "harvesting where you have not sown…
- "gathering where you have not scattered seed….
- "So I was afraid and went out and hid your talent in the ground."

Regrettably, many people who profess belief in God see Him in the same light—as a hard taskmaster, and so often their religious life is based on obeying a set of rules in order to be accepted.

Professing believers need to understand that God never intended for us to worship Him in this manner, nor is it the type of relationship He has ever sought with His children.

King David was one of the richest kings in Israel's history. He could easily have brought thousands of sacrifices and offerings to God, but he came to see that what meant so much more to God was a sense of brokenness and dependence upon Him, arising from a grateful heart—because this demonstrated intimacy of heart and personal devotion toward God.

David reflects these thoughts in Psalm 51 after going through one of the darkest times in his life. When David wanted to get things right with God, this was his revelation:

> For You do not delight in sacrifice, or I would bring it;
> You take no pleasure in burnt offerings. The sacrifices
> of God are a broken spirit; a broken and a contrite
> heart, O God, You will not despise. (Psalm 51:16-17)

When our hearts are devoted to God, we gladly offer our bodies as living sacrifices, which are holy and pleasing to Him, and this becomes our spiritual act of worship (Romans 12:1).

God doesn't want our sacrifices or the things we can do for Him out of a sense of religious duty, when our hearts are far away. It's the same as offering prayers of meaningless repetition and expecting to be heard. When we want to pray, Jesus said we should go into our inner room, shut the door (closing out distractions), and pray one-to-one with our Father in heaven, who knows our every need before we even speak a word (Matthew 6:6-8).

The expert in the law genuinely thought he was obeying the greatest commandments to love God and his neighbor. It was only when his faith was put under the spotlight that he realized (possibly for the first time) that he knew far more about religious activity and sacrifice than he did about showing mercy by helping someone in genuine need.

All the religious sacrifices and traditions mean little unless they're attached to faith being activated and outworked in our lives. To ignore this truth is to run the risk of becoming a modern-day version of the supposed expert in the law.

The last servant in the parable of the talents also failed to see something in the unseen realm—the blessings from God on his master's life. People who know their God also know that it's within the character and nature of God to bless His servants with a harvest in places where they haven't sown seed. This speaks of opportunities arising in our lives that we never contemplated, because God is ordering our footsteps.

This also speaks of provision happening when you least expect it. It speaks of the favor of God upon our lives as we continue to live in covenant relationship with Him.

The reality is that when God is on our side, we all have a Promised Land, a destiny, and a future.

During the time of Jeremiah the prophet, God's people were in exile and being held captive by the Babylonians. When the people needed their hope restored, God sent a word of hope through the following prophetic declaration:

> For I know the plans I have for you, declares the
> LORD, plans to prosper you and not to harm you,
> plans to give you hope and a future. Then you will
> call on me and come and pray to me, and I will listen

to you. You will seek me and find me when you
seek me with all your heart. (Jeremiah 29:11-13)

It doesn't matter what has kept us captive in the past; our deliverance is
at hand if we turn, seek, and follow the Lord with all our heart.

* * *

However, the market place is full of opportunists who look for a two-way bet (so to speak) with their profession of faith, and just hope for the best.

I've dealt with many people in the past who may give allegiance to God for a short time to see how it pans out, and if things fail to go according to their wishes, they return to their old ways. They're like the seed sown on the rocky soil. In effect, they were looking for success more than they were looking for the Savior.

This comes from a worldly paradigm that defines success as your bank balance or the value of your assets. The Word of God has a warning for those who choose to pursue this definition:

> Those who want to be rich, however, fall into
> temptation and become ensnared by many foolish
> and harmful desires that plunge them into ruin
> and destruction. For the love of money is the
> root of all kinds of evil. By craving it, some have
> wandered away from the faith and pierced themselves
> with many sorrows. (1 Timothy 6:9-10)

People who know their God also know that true riches cannot be purchased by our worldly wealth. True riches (Luke 16:11) are the souls of men and the value we place upon the people we meet in this life, remembering that Christ died to pay the ransom price for all mankind.

As we journey through this life, it's how we treat people and how we use the talents, gifting, and resources God has given us that allows us to store up treasures in heaven (1 Timothy 6:19).

From a Christian perspective, we also need to understand that it's obedience to the Word of the Lord that opens the door to abundance, as Jesus said: "I came that they may have life and have it abundantly." (John 10:10). This place of abundance comes through our personal relationship with Jesus Christ. And spending eternity in heaven will be the ultimate reward of those who seek first the kingdom of God and His righteousness (Matthew 6:33).

Choosing God to be our focus will in itself bring richness into our present lives, and that's often accompanied by worldly wealth—but this should always be a byproduct of our relationship with Him, and not the other way around.

Beyond that, the principle of sowing and reaping applies to business and every other area of our lives.

The type of supernatural increase that happened to the master in this parable is open to every believer who allows the Word of God to change and impact their heart so that it's devoted to God. This in turn opens the door of potential to bring forth a crop that is thirty, sixty, or a hundredfold.

At the end of the day, the first two servants honored their master by investing their talents and producing a hundredfold increase. Their stewardship followed the pattern of abundance that had been set by their master.

Not surprisingly, the central theme of this parable is stewardship. In the bigger picture of things, God has given every person talents, skills, gifts, and abilities, and He expects us to use them for His glory.

When we use our God-given gifts to build His kingdom, it makes a statement about our faith and allegiance to the King of kings and our honoring of the covenant relationship we enjoy with our God as His sons and daughters.

The finale to this parable is threefold:

1. The one talent is taken from the "wicked and lazy" servant and given to the "good and faithful" servant who has ten.
2. The servants who used their talents wisely were given more, and they have more than enough (supernatural increase).
3. The picture then immediately turns to the judgment seat of Christ where the servant who despised his talent receives the judgment of a "worthless slave" and is sentenced to hell—thrown into the outer darkness, where there will be weeping and gnashing of teeth.

How We Use Our Talents Matters to God

As I was pondering these things one night, I committed them to the Lord and prayed for greater revelation as I went to sleep.

As I awoke the next morning, the word of the Lord was on my lips and bubbling within. I immediately grabbed my voice recorder, and this is the prophetic word that came forth:

> From eternity to eternity, Thou art God. There
> are few constants in this world, but one of them
> is the love of God. It knows no end. God loved
> and He gave. He created, He spoke, and it came

into being. He restored, He healed, He did everything known, and He gave gifts to men.

Even the resurrection—the greatest gift He ever gave to man. When He ascended on high, He gave gifts to men, He left gifts in His train.

Our talents are a love gift from God. But as with everything, for a gift to be enjoyed, it has to be opened. You can never get the value out of a gift when it is closed. By hiding it the ground, it shows that we actually choose to despise the gift of God. But God, out of His great love, would always have us use our talents for His glory. For talents have within them the power to multiply, which is the very nature and character of God. They also have the power to bring supernatural increase, hidden away.

If we find the Master's code, which is the Word of God, and program our lives according to the pattern that He sets, with obedience being the key—then even as the love of God knows no bounds, the Word of God has within it the potential to bring supernatural increase simply by us following the Master's code.

It doesn't matter how smart or talented or brilliant people are; the Master's code has the power to unlock supernatural increase, whether you have five, two, or one talent.

We are all on the same level, and it is all relative to the gifts and talents we have been given. We all have the same ability to have supernatural increase where thirty, sixty, and a hundredfold become possible—because we follow the Master's code, which is the Word of God.

Our lives can never be the same without it.

The Parable of the Sheep and the Goats

The third parable from Jesus in Matthew 25 is a picture of sheep and goats at the time "when the Son of Man comes in his glory" (Matthew 25:31). It shows the judgment of the nations following the return of Jesus Christ. The Good Shepherd, Jesus Christ, will then separate the sheep (representing the righteous) from the goats (the wicked).

The righteous will receive eternal life, and the wicked eternal punishment. Judgment will be based on how we treat our brothers and sisters who need help, just as in the story of the good Samaritan.

The type of help mentioned in the parable of the sheep and goats includes feeding the hungry and thirsty, showing hospitality to strangers, providing needed clothing, and visiting the sick and imprisoned. The parable explains that whatever we do along these lines to help those in need should be regarded as if we're ministering unto Jesus Christ Himself. This is the basis upon which we'll be judged.

In the big picture of things, we need to take a step back and realize that God is the Father of all creation, and His love is to all peoples, races, tribes, and nations. We've all sinned and fallen short of the glory of God (Romans 3:23), but God in His great mercy sent His Son to be the Savior of the world. By believing in Jesus Christ as our Lord and Savior, we can now experience spiritual rebirth, which opens the door to the kingdom of heaven.

Believers are encouraged to produce fruit in their lives—to live in such a way that we become the light of the world and the salt of the earth in our communities, so we can positively impact the people we meet for the kingdom of God. This means carrying the love of God wherever we go, to those we meet and rub shoulders with daily. The extent to which we show social conscience and care for our fellow man is in effect a reflection of how much we understand about the nature and character of God, who is the Father of all creation.

The parable of the sheep and goats speaks directly to our sense of responsibility by effectively holding up a mirror to our lives, allowing us to see how we treat the people we meet when they're lonely, hungry, thirsty, sick (and possibly hospitalized), or imprisoned. In today's society, you could probably add victims of abuse, the elderly, the infirm and those unable to care for themselves, the destitute, the depressed, and the distraught. I'm sure we all know people who fit these and many other categories of serious need.

Those who profess Christianity need to understand that the list goes way beyond our natural or church family and reaches out to those in need in our communities.

The world is full of people who are precious to God but need to be discovered, loved, and cared for by God's people as a reflection of the Father's love.

This parable is profound in its meaning. The question for those who claim to be disciples of the King is this: Is our faith accompanied by actions (good deeds) that make a difference to those around us?

Where do we stand when we meet someone in serious need? Do we actively show mercy by getting involved, or is it easier to pass by on the other side of the road?

I'm fully aware that we need to be guided by the Holy Spirit, and that we cannot get totally involved in every situation of need we become aware of. However, what I'm referring to is being open to the prospect of offering specific help and being prepared to make time available for it.

Our Use of Time Matters to God

Many business people are among the most time-poor people in our society. I'm one of those people myself, but God regularly brings people into my path who need to be shown mercy and to experience the love of God.

As the Good Shepherd, Jesus continually modeled what it meant to be looking out for the one who is lost, and to bring that one back into the flock. We should follow His example.

One day a bunch of outsiders—tax collectors and "sinners"—were gathering around Jesus to hear His teaching. Meanwhile some Pharisees and teachers of the law began muttering among themselves, "This man welcomes sinners and eats with them" (Luke 15:2).

When Jesus became aware that He was being stigmatized and labeled as a friend of sinners, He told the religious leaders the parables recorded for us in Luke 15—about the lost sheep, the lost coin, and the lost son. In these stories He painted a vivid picture of the Father heart of God always reaching out to the lost, the lonely, and the desperate who've lost their way on life's journey.

Rather than judge and label these people, God chose to forgive and restore them—and so should we, if we want to be a reflection of the God in whom we profess belief.

If we're to impact our world, our light needs to be seen in a manner that reflects the Father's heart to those who are lost and in desperate need of the Savior. This allows others to see our good works and to glorify our Father in heaven (Matthew 5:16). But our motivation should always be about serving the Lord as opposed to putting on a show to be noticed by others.

The End-Times Mirror

For all who profess Christianity, the three end-time parables in Matthew 25—about the ten virgins, the talents, and the sheep and the goats—provide a mirror to be able to look at ourselves and assess our standing in the kingdom of heaven. In the same way that a mirror reflects our physical image, these parables provide an opportunity to examine ourselves and our actions as they reveal our identity.

We need to make time to hear what the Lord has to say about our faith:

- Are we more like the wise virgins or the foolish ones? For people to enter heaven, they must be born again. This is shown figuratively in the five wise virgins who were ready and prepared with oil in jars as well as in their lamps.
- Which of those three servants entrusted with talents do we identify with? Upon entering heaven, our rewards will depend on how wisely we've used our God-given talents during our time on earth.
- Will the Lord see us as belonging to the sheep or the goats? At the final judgment, what will matter most to our Lord (the judge) is how we've treated our fellow man when they needed help.

Jesus regularly went out of His way to help people in need, showing them love and mercy when no one else seemed to care. And when He speaks to the righteous (the sheep) and gives them their inheritance in the kingdom of God, He acknowledges their every act in helping someone in need: "I was sick and you looked after me," "I was hungry and you gave me something to eat," and so forth. Jesus follows this up with these words: "Whatever you did for one of the least of these brothers of mine, you did it unto me."

The unrighteous (the goats) are assigned to eternal punishment in hell because they did nothing to help the sick, the hungry, and those in need. At the end of the day, judgment of this kind may seem harsh. However, if we call ourselves believers and then ignore those for whom Jesus died, we can easily be branded as hypocrites.

The new commandment given by Jesus is this: "Love one another, even as I have loved you" (John 15:12). We are to *act* upon this command, and not just merely hear it.

The apostle James went to great lengths to contrast the difference between what he described as hearing and doing:

> Be doers of the word, and not hearers only.
> Otherwise, you are deceiving yourselves. For anyone
> who hears the word but does not carry it out is
> like a man who looks at his face in a mirror, and
> after observing himself goes away and immediately
> forgets what he looks like. (James 1:22-24)

The apostle is saying that if we choose to hear and not obey the Word of God, we're deceiving ourselves. Here are inescapable truths:

- If we truly believe in something, it will change our heart.

- Whatever changes our heart will also impact our lifestyle.
- Whatever impacts our lifestyle will also change our world.

In short, our beliefs must translate into actions. Otherwise they're little more than intentions.

The end-time parables are intended to serve as a warning or safety checklist for all who call themselves believers.

Simply believing and not having actions brings the tragic reality that the apostle James speaks of in a later verse: "Faith without works [deeds] is *dead*" (James 2:26).

From a market place perspective, Christians are called to use their talents, skills, gifts, and abilities wisely and to be ready to help those in need.

God's heart was and always will be toward those without a voice, society's most vulnerable—the poor, the widow, the orphan, and the needy. God is the heavenly Father of us all and if we neglect or choose to ignore those whom the Lord loves and cares for, we can easily identify ourselves in this parable with the wicked rather than the righteous:

> They also will answer, "Lord, when did we see you
> hungry or thirsty or a stranger or needing clothes
> or sick or in prison, and did not help you?"
> He will reply, "Truly I tell you, whatever you did not do
> for one of the least of these, you did not do for me."
> Then they will go away to eternal punishment, but
> the righteous to eternal life. (Matthew 25:44-46)

This might be a sobering thought for many who profess belief in God, but it's the Word of God, and if it cost our Lord His very life, then it isn't something that we should take lightly.

Equally sobering are the parallel verses spoken by the Lord Jesus just after He gave the Sermon on the Mount. All those who profess Christ and call Him Lord need to be mindful of these verses:

> Not everyone who says to Me, Lord, Lord, will
> enter the kingdom of heaven, but he who does
> the will of My Father who is in heaven.
> Many will say to Me on that day, Lord, Lord, have we
> not prophesied in Your name and driven out demons in
> Your name and done many mighty works in Your name?
> And then I will say to them openly [publicly], I never
> knew you; depart from Me, you who act wickedly
> [disregarding My commands]. (Matthew 7:21-23 AMP)

The outcome of both the above passages are effectively the same. Those who disobey the Lord's commands and have no personal relationship with Him—despite their profession of religious belief—will be greeted with this public declaration from our Lord: "I never knew you."

Professing believers will not be able to hide behind their religious denomination, their church attendance or participation record, the rituals or ceremonies they've participated in, or the people they may know in high office in the church. The only thing that matters when it comes to seeking entry to the gates of heaven (Matthew 25:10) is knowing and being known by God at a personal level through His Son, Jesus Christ, as Lord and Savior.

An even further sobering thought from Matthew 7:21-23 is that the Lord's judgment of "I never knew you" is being directed toward those who disregard the Lord's commands yet still operate powerfully in ministry gifts of the Holy Spirit (prophesy, driving out demons, and doing miracles).

Matthew 24 records the words of Jesus about the prevailing world conditions in the days leading up to the return of Christ. The picture is painted of great upheaval among the nations and even the elements. Society will experience a level of turmoil that has never previously been experienced by mankind, and the church will experience the great apostasy—a falling away from the faith (Matthew 24:10; 2 Thessalonians 2:3; 1 Timothy 4:1). Twice in Matthew 24, Jesus specifically warns of false ministries arising that will lead many believers astray:

> For false Christs and false prophets will appear
> and perform great signs and wonders that would
> deceive even the elect, if that were possible. See, I
> have told you in advance. (Matthew 24:24-25)

We know that Christ will return at a time when no one will be expecting Him, just like the bridegroom at the midnight hour in the parable of the ten virgins (Matthew 25:1-13).

When Jesus was preparing for His crucifixion, He specifically warned His disciples on three occasions that it was about to happen. Despite His warnings, they were all taken by surprise when it actually came to pass.

The three end-time parables all speak about being ready and prepared for the return of Christ—which begs reiteration of the question: When we look into the mirror of God's Word (using these parables), where do we see ourselves?"

Being ready and prepared for Christ's return is a central theme of Matthew 25. If we take this teaching to heart, we'll order our lives accordingly, and we'll wisely use our God-given talents.

This also speaks of honoring our calling as disciples to be a light and a help to those whom God brings into our lives. We should never forget the words Jesus spoke about receiving the ones He sends into our lives: "Truly, truly, I tell you, whoever receives the one I send receives Me, and whoever receives Me receives the One who sent Me." (John 13:20).

In the great busyness of life, it's so easy to make excuses rather than making the things of God our priority.

When Amos the prophet spoke to the people of Israel who were putting their trust in their profession of religion rather than obeying the Word of God, He brought the following prophetic word: "Woe to them that are at ease in Zion" (Amos 6:1).

Amos delivered this prophetic declaration of woe to those who effectively saw Zion as a church state, and who put their trust in its structures and the fortified walls with a sense of pride and impregnability. They enjoyed Zion's privileges and saw themselves as secure, comfortable, and at ease. This especially applied to the rich, who trusted in the uncertainty of riches and showed no concern or social conscience for the needy, when the latter things reflect the heart of God to His people.

This is the same reason the foolish virgins were assigned a place with the hypocrites, as they too put their confidence in their profession of religion and in the submission to human traditions and rules taught by men (Isaiah 29:13, quoted by Jesus in Matthew 15:8-9).

The church at Laodicea is often regarded by theologians as a type and shadow of the end-times church, prior to the return of Christ. The following verses are from the revelation Jesus gave to the apostle John as a word for the church in Laodicea:

> I know your deeds; you are neither cold nor hot. How
> I wish you were one or the other! So because you are
> lukewarm—neither hot nor cold—I am about to vomit
> you out of My mouth! You say, "I am rich; I have grown

wealthy and need nothing." But you do not realize that
you are wretched, pitiful, poor, blind, and naked....
Those I love, I rebuke and discipline. Therefore be earnest
and repent.... Behold, I stand at the door and knock. If
anyone hears My voice and opens the door, I will come in
and dine with him, and he with Me. (Revelation 3:15-20)

This prophetic declaration undoubtedly contains a different message
from the way Laodicean church members viewed themselves. This church
saw itself as cruising the faith journey, and it had obviously gone down the
pathway of seeing worldly wealth as a yardstick for success. And yet our
Lord's description of them was "wretched, pitiful, poor, blind, and naked."
The church at Laodicea had no clue whatsoever that they were about to be
spat out of the Lord's mouth because of their lukewarm faith and lack of
good deeds.

Our Lord loves His church enough to warn each one of us about the
need to repent, because Jesus is knocking on the door of our hearts, wanting to come in and have fellowship with us. For those who obey and repent,
a rich reward is waiting both now and in heaven.

As a final sign to our generation, Jesus gave the following picture about
the things that will accompany the days of His return.

Just as it was in the days of Noah, so also will it be
in the days of the Son of Man: People were eating
and drinking, marrying and being given in marriage,
up to the day Noah entered the ark. Then the flood
came and destroyed them all. (Luke 17:26-27)

In Noah's day, everyone around him had adopted a business-as-usual approach and ignored the message of this preacher of righteousness. In the end, that generation was destroyed by their apathy.

The Word of God contains many more warnings to the people of God. However, for any benefit to arise, believers must first read and try to understand the Word of God, and then obey whatever revelation they receive.

Choosing Our Eternal Destiny

In my experience, the majority of people making their journey through life are totally oblivious to the need for salvation or the prospect of Christ's return to this earth.

Ironically the same people will often include "having an encounter with God before I die" as an item on their "bucket list." The reality is that God has already put eternity into the hearts of men (Ecclesiastes 3:11). It's not something people could or should deny, since there's evidence of the Creator all around us just waiting to be found.

While we all live with the realization that beyond the grave is the great unknown, those who have a personal relationship with Jesus Christ have no fear about one day meeting their Maker, for they've already had a taste of heaven on earth and know that there's nothing like it.

Always remember that our eternal destiny is determined by the choices we make this side of the grave. When we make the decision to follow Jesus Christ as Lord and Savior, we can know that we're saved and have eternal life—right now! This is the good news—the gospel—that Jesus Christ brought to earth, and it's bound up in the love of God for His creation.

23

Equipping Disciples

Over the years, I've shared many of the concepts and testimonies in this book with church people, including business people, board members, and church elders who are dispersed throughout the week in their market places across a variety of industries and occupations. Almost without exception, their response to this content has been, "Wow, we need to hear more about this sort of testimony as an encouragement to evangelize our own work places."

I'm aware that the ministry of equipping the saints to evangelize their market places is not a topic that's likely to be taught from pulpits across the nation during Sunday services. However, during the week when believers are in the market place, they often feel inadequate or unequipped to share their faith for a variety of reasons, many of which I've identified in this book.

One of the primary purposes of this book is to provide a resource to assist church leaders to equip their church in the market place, because Jesus has commanded His followers to go into all their world and preach the good news (Mark 16:15). My desire is to challenge professing believers to look outside the comfortable environment of church, family, and friends, looking instead to others around us who are lost and in need of the Savior.

Reflect upon the Scriptures and you'll find that Jesus always referred to the kingdom of God in His teachings, because He had His Father's DNA and perspective on life. When He told His disciples to open their eyes, Jesus wanted the religious and cultural veils to be lifted from their minds so they could see every person as a potential candidate for the kingdom of God, regardless of their race, culture, or creed.

With more than two thousand years of New Testament biblical history and teaching behind us, it's apparent that the church universal still struggles with seeing the harvest of people all around it, particularly in the market place where Jesus spent much of his time. While many profess to be disciples of Christ, the sign of true discipleship given by Jesus is the bearing of much fruit—fruit that will last beyond this age and into eternity (John 15:8,16).

As the time of the cross approached, Jesus spoke a word and performed an act that was parabolic in its application, specifically in relation to the bearing of fruit. Mark 11 records Jesus cursing and pronouncing judgment on a fig tree because it had a show of leaves, giving the promise of fruit, but it proved to be a hypocritical tree (Mark 11:12-14 and 11:20-21). The next day His disciples marveled when they saw the tree withered from the roots, but there was a much deeper meaning to this unusual miracle.

When Jesus came to "His own" (Israel), He did so expecting to find spiritual fruit such as godliness, righteousness, love, faith, and obedience to God's Word. Instead, he found hypocrisy, deadness, empty profession, forms of godliness without reality or power, and pride rather than penitence and faith.

Jesus despised hypocrisy and He constantly condemned profession without productivity (or fruit). The hypocritical fig tree afforded Jesus a splendid opportunity to portray the fallen state of the nation of Israel. His judgment upon the tree was indicative of the judgment of God that would soon fall on the nation of Israel, beginning in Jerusalem in A.D. 70.

All professing believers need to take seriously the lesson of the barren fig tree, because if our life isn't producing fruit for the kingdom of God, it's time to repent and to get serious about wholeheartedly following God.

From the earliest chapters, I've sought to use the words, parables, and stories that Jesus used to encourage His disciples to look differently upon their world. Jesus knew only too well that humanity had lost its way, but rather than speak words of judgment and condemnation, He choose to show mankind a better way by bringing the kingdom of heaven into their midst on earth. This allowed people to experience a taste of heaven on earth.

When Jesus took His disciples into Samaria for the first time, it was to meet a woman at a well (John 4:1-42). Little did she know—and little did the disciples know—that spiritual revival was about to break out in Sychar. Leading up to this, the disciples were at best indifferent about going into Samaria, yet Jesus was about to use this encounter to further enlarge their mindset about the kingdom of God.

Jewish history and tradition had failed to embrace an inclusive kingdom culture of the God of all nations, in fulfillment of His covenant promise to make Abraham (and his descendants, by implication) a father of many nations (Genesis 17:5-7).

Jesus, however, was ready to engage with anyone the Father would bring across His path, and this included a broad range of people, including Gentiles (not-Jewish), agnostics, atheists, pagans, and many others who appeared to have no time for the things of God. Jesus took the good news into market places, work places, houses, synagogues, lakesides, mountainsides, towns, villages, and anywhere people gathered. He knew the message of the kingdom had the power to bring life into every situation where the slightest glimmer of faith was evident, and He was encouraging His disciples to embrace this same type of kingdom culture. The day of the week, the location, and the makeup of the audience were irrelevant to Jesus, because the good news needed to be shared in order to fulfill His own commission (Luke 4:18-21).

As strange as it may seem to some, Jesus has also commissioned every believer to go into their world and to share the same gospel message of good news. If Christ is living in us, we have a message that needs to be shared, and our relationship with God should impact every area of our lives.

I don't see the secular as any different from the sacred, because the two were never compartmentalized in Scripture, certainly not by Jesus. In other words, I see my work as my ministry.

As God's people in the market place, we can reach people sitting around boardroom tables or in lunchrooms, or others who might be standing beside the photocopier or the water fountain. They're people who might never set foot inside a church. In fact, many people will never encounter Jesus Christ except by rubbing shoulders with God's people in their market place.

For this reason, we also need to see God's people being active in the market place as an essential arena of ministry within a vast field of people who need to be harvested for the Lord.

For Evangelistic Ministry in the Market Place

So how can we be equipped to pursue evangelistic ministry in the market place?

Often this is started by believers who are wanting to become harvest workers, pushing the boundaries of their own revelation and experiences with God.

Potential harvest workers look for teaching and equipping on how to evangelize, but what's available in many churches is often minimal, and if the primary giftings of the church leaders don't have an evangelistic focus, the matter is not given priority.

The irony of this is: If you don't sow seed, there's no crop to harvest.

Some church leaders struggle with diminishing and aging congregations, and they have difficulty trying to stir up interest in the things of God. Yet the same programs and methods are used year after year, while the church continues to flounder.

Something clearly needs to change. If our younger generation is to be attracted and impacted for Christ, the message and the presentation need to be modernized and birthed in prayer and vibrant worship.

I attend a rapidly growing church that has embraced these things, and I can assure you there's nothing that stirs the faith of a congregation more than seeing multiple services on a weekend with many people surrendering their lives to Jesus Christ.

My personal joy only increases when I see friends I've brought in from the market place who are now following Jesus and growing in their faith.

As someone who's passionate about ministry in the market place, I also see the necessity of having a home church where people will be nurtured and cared for. If churches don't have adequate support through prayer, fellowship, and discipleship, people who make decisions to follow Christ are easily lost—either back into the world or to another fellowship that offers these things.

Many church leaders are so tied up with administration that they can easily lose touch with the outsiders who their church in the market place encounter on a daily basis. Church leaders are well advised to keep themselves fresh by rubbing shoulders with outsiders, since this is the cutting edge of ministry, and there's always a tremendous need wherever you look. Even allowing small windows of time can have tremendous results not only for those being touched, but also for the power of the leader's testimony of personal encounters as they are shared with their churches as an encouragement to go and do likewise.

As the project manager of large transport events involving large numbers of staff and resources, I've often been reminded by the Lord that the greatest generals in history were known to spend time among the troops, and it has been my delight to do the same.

Jesus kept Himself fresh through prayer, and He relied heavily upon the Holy Spirit during His encounters with outsiders—and He taught His disciples to do the same.

While Jesus was training His disciples, He first spent time teaching them what the kingdom of God was really like using parables and principle-based teachings to challenge their thinking toward an inclusive, kingdom of God culture. He then added credence to His teaching by performing signs, wonders, and miracles that demonstrated with great power and authority what the Father's heart was really like toward the lost.

Jesus was actually modeling friendship-based evangelism to His disciples, and then He released them to do likewise. This had mixed results at times, but Jesus corrected them and then encouraged them to learn from their mistakes and to continue proclaiming the message of the coming kingdom wherever they went.

The Great Commission was a clear mandate for the church of Jesus Christ to go and do likewise, yet the typical model of church life is often devoid of any specific form of equipping the saints of God for evangelistic ministry and outreach. This results in many believers struggling to share their faith with confidence. The desire is there, but they don't feel empowered or enabled to go out and take action.

The body of Christ needs to pay attention to the task of equipping believers for market place ministry, if it seeks to reach one of the greatest bastions of unreached people groups in the world today.

If the market place is where most of the flock are scattered throughout the week, why isn't the church of Jesus Christ having a greater impact in terms of evangelism?

In my experience, if the people of God aren't confident to share their faith, they'll often remain silent—at a time in history when I believe the rocks and stones are wanting to cry out (Luke 19:40). There has rarely been such a time in history when the church has been under such attack from the secular media for its past indiscretions. This has severely undermined the authority of the church in many nations, especially when they need to take a stand for righteousness on social issues that tend to erode godly values and beliefs.

In spite of this, I believe that God is beginning to raise up His righteous standard as believers are being prepared to step out in faith and courage, refreshed with a new boldness from the Holy Spirit to be His witnesses to this generation (Acts 1:8).

It's also my belief that this will coincide with the promised latter rain (Zechariah 10:1) of the Holy Spirit. It's up to our generation to realize the time and season we're in, within God's *kairos* time-clock. If Pentecost represents the former rain on the early Jewish church, the latter rain is yet to come on the global church in the lead-up to the full harvest of the nations being in-gathered to God.

To be ready for this, it's of utmost importance for the church of Jesus Christ to arise and lift up the name of the Lord Jesus Christ across the nations, to see God's glory revealed. We must never forget that when Jesus told His disciples, "Open your eyes and see the harvest before you," He was referring to the harvest of people for whom He was about to lay down His life. These are the same people we daily rub shoulders with in our market places, and He wants us to see the harvest of peoples before us through the eyes of faith.

The gospel message is the greatest gift we can ever share with another person. In fact, it's an act of mercy to share good news with anyone who's on the road to eternal separation from God, which will ultimately lead them to hell.

There's Always a Price to Pay

Sharing the gospel message will take your time and put you in a place of vulnerability. However, you only need to think about the ransom price that the Father paid to redeem your soul to get a glimpse of what vulnerability really means. It's time to put your comfort zone aside, because this is a real part of what it means to be a follower of Jesus Christ:

> If any of you wants to be my follower, you
> must turn from your selfish ways, take up your
> cross daily, and follow me. (Luke 9:23)

Taking time to show mercy to another person in their time of need is the theme of the parable of the good Samaritan. It's ironic, but this parable starts with the expert in the law trying to test Jesus by asking Him to define the word *neighbor*.

When Jesus told the parable, He was using the Word of God as a mirror to allow the lawyer to see things from God's perspective rather than from his religious tradition or misconceptions.

Although the lawyer would have readily identified with either of the religious participants and therefore excused their inaction, there was only one correct answer to this question of life and death. The one who shows mercy is the one who proves to be a neighbor.

In like manner, the Word of God will move from head knowledge to faith only when it finds practical expression in our lives.

By answering his own rhetorical question, the lawyer discovered that his faith had to be activated for it to produce fruit for the kingdom of God. In this case, the fruit was mercy.

This is exactly what John that Baptist meant in Matthew 3:4-10 when he told the Pharisees and Sadducees to "produce fruit in keeping with repentance" or face being cut off by the axe (which speaks of judgment by God) that was already laid at the root of the trees (their lives), and being thrown into the fire of hell.

Trees that bear no fruit in their natural state are said to be barren and are fit only for the fire. This principle also applies to the spiritual realm, and it culminates with the stark reality that spiritual barrenness that goes on unremedied will eventually lead to eternal separation from God.

We need to realize that the heart of mankind was totally corrupted in the garden of Eden, and it simply cannot produce good fruit that will last and have eternal value unless it's regenerated by the Spirit of Christ.

Despite the witness of unmatched wisdom from above, teaching with great authority, incredible miracles that were undeniable, and signs and wonders that hadn't been seen since the beginning of creation, the gospel message of Jesus and its fruit were largely ignored by the Jewish religious leaders of His time. They appeared more interested in protecting their temple-based worship and external forms of religious activity than in pursuing the way of righteousness.

Throughout this book, I've laid many challenges before you to think more deeply about the question of personal faith. If you profess a belief in Christ, it's essential that your actions reflect your beliefs.

With this in mind, it's not surprising that Jesus chose someone like the good Samaritan to demonstrate that there's no practical divide between sacred and secular when it comes to doing the works of God.

What matters most is bringing the Father's heart of love and mercy to our generation, many of whom are either lost, abandoned, or wounded by life's dealings. They're lying on the side of their own Jericho road, waiting to be found.

For a time-poor business person, being a credible witness for Jesus Christ may mean stepping into the shoes of the good Samaritan and taking time to speak into the life of another business person or co-worker who's struggling with the issues of life. It may also mean taking a stand for a righteous cause on a social justice matter when it involves a heavenly cause. This is where Christians in the market place can make a difference.

In the same way that Jesus caused the expert in the law to take a moment and think more deeply about his faith, I've attempted to share some of my personal encounters and experiences to hopefully convey a greater level of understanding about how faith can be activated in the market place and beyond.

There are many times in life when we simply need to take that step of faith and trust God, no matter what trials or seasons of adversity we might be facing. Finding the peace and presence of God in the midst of our most difficult times is what allows our character to be built and forged to withstand the next season of our faith journey.

On this journey, we're no different from the children of Israel leaving Egypt in pursuit of their Promised Land. It's the choices we make along the way that ultimately determine our destiny. The successful journey can take place only through a walk of obedience. The alternative is to prepare ourselves for further wandering in the desert before we can enter. The choice of pathway belongs to us.

The children of Israel had to wander forty years in the desert because they failed to learn from their past mistakes and to activate their faith. There's little doubt that the apostle Paul was reflecting upon this aspect of Israel's history as he penned 1 Corinthians 10:1-13. There was so much worldliness in the fledgling Corinthian church, and the apostle was appealing to them to learn from Israel's mistakes, when an entire generation failed to enter the Promised Land because their faith was never able to displace their fear and unbelief.

In the same way, and while we still have breath, we can impact our generation for Jesus Christ. It's time to leave behind our past, our mistakes, and our excuses.

There's much work to do to bring in the end-time harvest—and more workers are urgently needed.

24

Our Commission

Many professing believers may not realize this, but the Great Commission is actually a *command* to all believers to go into all their world and to make a difference by sharing the gospel message with the expectation that signs and wonders will follow the message, as evidence of their belief or faith (Matthew 28:16-20; Mark 16:15-20).

To this end, the church of Jesus Christ is meant to be a vibrant expression of what God is doing among His people on a daily basis.

At an individual level, the gospel message includes our personal testimony, which carries within it a witness to the power of God to transform lives, and every believer should have a story to tell about their own encounter with God.

Believe me when I say that our testimony can change lives, especially in the market place. I've shared my testimony in many market places, work places, boardrooms, restaurants, and homes; I've shared it on park benches and on the streets; I've shared it while riding in cars, boats, and airplanes; and I've shared it on foreign mission fields.

I know for sure that people everywhere are looking for purpose and identity, and they generally live in the hope of finding a better place in life for themselves, their families, and their friends. If we desire to connect with these people, we first need to let them see Christ in us.

This means consistently living our lives in reverence toward God as a reflection of our faith in Jesus Christ to a world that's lost and separated from God. If we want people to be drawn to the Lord, we need to be salt-of-the-earth people in our market places and beyond, just as Jesus called us to be.

As the time of our Lord's return draws closer, God's people need to arise and let their light shine before men as never before. We need to step into God's purpose and plan for our lives with the understanding that God has already given us everything we need to accomplish His work in our day.

We need to continually seek fresh revelation from Him who is able to do immeasurably more than all we ask or imagine, according to the resurrection power that is within us (Ephesians 3:20).

As we step out in faith into the destiny He has planned for us, we do so in the belief that "the steps of a good man (or woman) are ordered by the LORD" (Psalm 27:23).

As we reach out to help others, we extend the hands of Jesus to a world that needs to be introduced to the Savior.

The fields are indeed ripe, but effectively entering the harvest as a worker will depend on our answer to this question: *How do I see my world?*

Jesus saw the same fields of lost people in His generation that we're seeing in ours. They're all around us, wherever we go.

Into the harvest field, Jesus called twelve men, who soon became 72, then 120, then 500, then 3,000—and then the total went off the Richter scale to the point that Christianity became—and remains—the world's largest religion.

The gospel message contains within it the power of God unto salvation (Romans 1:16), but it must be spoken and lived before men and women in order for it to be seen, aspired to, and believed.

When Christ lives in us, He will impact our life. Our hearts cannot be the same. He becomes the reason we live and move and have our being (Acts 17:28).

This love we experience from God is meant to impact our world. If this is not your experience, then you may need a fresh encounter with God— perhaps your first real encounter with Him. If you humble yourself before the Lord and pray with a sincere and repentant heart, this can be your reality right now as you pause from reading this book.

Jesus is coming again, and His bride (the church) needs to be ready and waiting for His return.

At the time of His first coming, it was the religious people who resisted Him most because they were comfortable with their beliefs and genuinely thought they had all the answers and were in right relationship with God.

For those who hold to the same view at the present time, a parable Jesus gave (in Matthew 24:45-51) about a wise steward speaks prophetically to the time in which we're now living. This parable speaks about our steward-ship of our Master's household while He is away, and it provides a warning to religious people about being ready for the return of Christ. In particular, the warning is given to those servants who aren't found to be faithful and wise in stewarding our Master's household (the church). The result for the unfaithful is their being assigned a place with hypocrites in hell.

While this might seem harsh to some, it's no different from the type of warnings the prophets gave to the early generations of Jews. The tragedy is that few took to heart the declarations of the prophets, and the Jewish nation is yet to wake up to the reality that the promised Messiah has already come and fulfilled all that the prophets had spoken.

The promised Messiah died a sacrificial death on a cross, rose from the dead, and will remain seated at the right hand of the Father until all His enemies are put under His feet (Matthew 22:44). And then the time of the end will come.

It was the failure of the Jewish religious leaders to realize their visitation from God (through the Messiah) that ultimately brought judgment upon their nation. When the temple was destroyed and Jerusalem devastated by the Romans in A.D. 70, this led to more than a million deaths, according to the estimate of the Jewish historian Josephus. Now listen to the prophetic words of Jesus Christ as He entered Jerusalem and wept over the city, because He could foresee this coming devastation of the Jewish people:

> For the days will come upon you when your enemies
> will barricade you and surround you and hem you in
> on every side. They will level you to the ground—you
> and the children within your walls. They will not leave
> one stone on another, because you did not recognize the
> time of your visitation from God. (Luke 19:43-44)

In the same way, if our generation neglects the warnings of the prophets and the Word of God, including the words spoken by the Messiah, Jesus Christ, we'll also risk missing out on the greatest visitation from God in the history of this planet.

The signs of the times mentioned in Matthew 24 are happening all around us, and they're foreshadowing the second coming of Christ. It's time for the church of Jesus Christ to arise and take its rightful place in loving God with all our heart, soul, mind, and strength, and to love one another just as Jesus loved and gave Himself for us.

In doing so, we can fulfill God's promises for our lives, and we can actually speed His return: "You ought to live holy and godly lives as you look forward to the day of God and speed its coming" (2 Peter 3:11-12).

Jesus Is Lord of the Market Place

Jesus had an incredible impact every time He stepped into a market place, because it was where people from every walk of life would gather together.

It goes without saying but Zacchaeus is one of my heroes when it comes to market place ministry. This man had built his life around his great wealth and his position of power within the local community, yet after a single encounter with the Messiah, all this no longer seemed to matter.

Zacchaeus just like so many today—a seemingly insignificant person in a crowd of many, just waiting to be discovered by a harvest worker. All it took was a flicker of faith, and this outcast, despised by society, was ready to connect with his God and to forsake all other gods.

When we see a crowd of people in our market place the task of winning them to Christ can often seem daunting. Yet when Jesus saw a crowd of people, He positioned Himself as a sower of the Word and always looked for an opportunity to share the good news with anyone who would listen. In fact, Jesus doggedly pursued every opportunity to make His Father known and to share what the kingdom of God was really like.

Before He ascended into heaven, Jesus gave the Great Commission to all believers because He wanted us to follow in His footsteps by going into all our world and to continue bringing the kingdom of God into our circumstances until we begin to experience heaven on earth.

To Jesus, the crowd was made up of individual people who all mattered to His Father, and no one was meant to be excluded. The religious leaders of His day showed contempt for Jesus simply because He reached out to "tax gatherers and sinners" who were lost.

Today, the market place—like all of society—has many people who could easily be identified as "sinners" and "lost." My question to you is this: Has it been your practice to simply pass by on the other side of the road and leave to others the task of reaching these people? Or do you choose to make a difference to your world by taking part in a lost person's encounter with God?

This concept is not about performing works of service (Ephesians 4:12) inside the church. I fully support such works, and I've had active personal involvement with this vital aspect of ministry for many years. But I'm speaking here about professing believers taking seriously the Great Commission given by Jesus Christ to take the good news to those outside the church. This is about going out into your world, wherever that might be.

For me, it's the market place. For others it might be a work place, a mothers' group, a sports group, or just a group of friends.

Regardless of individuals we meet, one thing I know for sure is that they can all benefit eternally from being reconnected to their Creator.

It's by our going into the highways and byways of life and being a good Samaritan to someone in need that the kingdom of God continues to grow and expand.

That's precisely how Tony Wyman and I first met. Tony was searching and looking for deeper meaning to his life. He could see something different in me, and he simply wanted to know more. When I revealed my faith in Jesus Christ as the source of my apparent business success, this ignited a search by Tony until he had his own personal encounter with Jesus Christ, and the rest is history.

Jesus frequently demonstrated the same principle of discipleship through what I describe as the power of one. In the midst of a crowd,

Jesus would have an encounter with one person like Zacchaeus (Luke 19:1-10), or a Roman centurion (Matthew 8:5-13), or a synagogue ruler named Jairus (Mark 5:21-24, 5:35-43), or an unnamed woman with an issue of blood (Mark 5:25-34)—and their entire world was changed in a moment of time as the kingdom of God was released into their lives.

At other times, Jesus would go to one person who was alone and lost on their life journey, like the woman at the well at Sychar (John 4:1-42), and her world—her home town—was changed from that day forward.

Jesus was led by the Spirit of God, and unless He was directed to address the crowd, He concentrated on meeting with individuals. The Gospels give many eyewitness accounts of the power of one ultimately becoming the power of many, as the good news about the Messiah spread among the people of His day.

This is how the early church was able propel the gospel message, as it was breathed on and empowered by the Holy Spirit to bring the kingdom of God to all nations of the world (Acts 1:8).

As was true with the early church apostles and disciples, we also are called to be ambassadors of the Lord and to reach out one by one to those in our market places and beyond—with a readiness to show mercy to those in need, as we too are led and empowered by the Holy Spirit.

There's no great secret to this. Just about any person will respond to genuine love and care, especially when they have a specific need or could simply do with a word of encouragement. The love of God being manifest through His people is probably the most powerful and yet most under-rated weapon that the church of Jesus Christ has available in abundance to impact this world. It radically changed the fabric of society during the days of the early church, and it has continued to do so over the centuries ever since.

The love of God working through His people creates a natural bridge of relationship with outsiders to allow the gospel message to be shared with them in due season.

Our Faith Must Be Real and Consistent

Because today's society is filled with so many different belief systems, ideologies, religions, and cults, people will generally want to see if our faith is being motivated by genuine love before they'll ever believe any message we try to convey.

Market place business people who claim to be serious about their faith in Jesus Christ also need to realize that building bridges and earning the right to speak into people's lives takes both time and commitment.

Seeking first the kingdom of God and His righteousness (Matthew 6:33) is a key principle that Jesus taught about living a faith-filled and abundant life. It effectively tells us to make the kingdom of God our absolute priority (as an outworking of our faith), and then God will take care of every element of our life, including our business.

God's kingdom poses an upside-down paradigm to the kingdom of this world, because it's based on faith (our "sixth sense"). Then in faith, by reading and meditating on God's Word, we can allow our minds to be transformed so we can partake of the supernatural life that comes through relationship with Jesus Christ.

For business people in particular, I would like to suggest that if you want to measure the depth of your love for Christ, have a good look at your work diary first, and next at your credit card statement. Although this may be a reality check to some people, how we spend our time and money are probably two of the best barometers of our true passions and priorities.

If we neglect our commission, the harvest fields around us will still be waiting for the workers to arrive, right up until the time that Jesus returns to the earth. In the same way that the door to the ark was shut by God in Noah's day, leaving behind an unbelieving world, so the door will also be shut to the wedding banquet, with only those who are ready and prepared allowed inside to join the Bridegroom (Jesus Christ).

As this chapter of my journey draws to a close, here are my greatest encouragements to God's people in the market place:

- Recognize the call of God upon your life—and the Great Commission that Jesus gave to every professing believer—to share the good news.

- Become the salt of the earth and the light of the world people that Jesus spoke about. Although we may be far from perfect, let the world see your love for your fellow man as a reflection of the nature and character of God.

- Determine to see our world differently. The fields of people are always ripe for harvest, but there's still a shortage of workers prepared to show mercy and give people a helping hand to get to a better place.

- Realize that the strength of our personal relationship with God will ultimately determine our effectiveness as harvest workers. For this reason, it's essential that we abide in Him if we wish to bear much fruit, because the Lord delights to answer our Spirit-led prayers, and to bring glory to the Father.

- Recognize that God orders our footsteps, and if we're prepared to ask, He will bring *kairos* God encounters across our path.

- Be prepared to share your testimony and to shape the Word at every opportunity, and lasting fruit will be the outcome. This fruit will endure into eternity, because it represents people's lives being impacted by the good news of Jesus Christ.

- Remember that God has gifted every person. Our challenge is to discover and then use our talents for building God's kingdom and not just our own. In this way we will store up treasures in heaven.
- Never forget that mercy is the heartbeat of God. Jesus came to seek and to save that which was lost. He did not judge or condemn; He simply showed the lost a better way to live their lives, based on a righteousness that's by faith rather than obeying a set of rules.
- Make it your goal in life to seek first the kingdom of God and His righteousness, and He will look after and prosper your life and business in ways that go beyond your wildest dreams.
- Stay hungry and thirsty for the things of God. "Blessed are those who hunger and thirst for righteousness, for they will be filled" (Matthew 5:6).
- Make a start with one person, just as Jesus did—and be ready for your world to change!

Faithfulness Rewarded

A few years ago, Carmel and I visited Omni Parker House in Boston. This hotel abounds with history, including the restaurant table where it's said that John F. Kennedy proposed to Jacqueline Bouvier.

The hotel's corporate insignia really caught my attention. It features the motto *Fideli Merces Certa* which means "To the faithful, there is certain reward."

All professing believers should be aware that the message behind this insignia is a central theme of the book of Revelation as well as an underlying theme of the sheep-and-goats parable (in Matthew 25:31-46) concerning the end-time judgment of all nations when Christ returns.

How we live our life matters to God, but it's the choices we make that will ultimately determine our eternal destiny. Any faith profession we make will be of little worth if it isn't practiced, since judgment is based on evidence, not on beliefs or intentions.

As we go into our world each day, we're meant to activate our faith and become salt and light to those around us. Who we are is meant to reflect the nature and character of the God we serve.

The market place is the focus of this book, primarily because it's where Jesus chose to spend much of His time, like many of us today.

The commission that Jesus set before professing believers is indeed a great task—which is why He also sent the Holy Spirit (Acts 1:8) to empower us to carry out the work.

The question that remains is this: Will you take up the challenge to go into your world and make a difference for Christ?

If you're prepared to take up this challenge, you'll have to step out of your religious comfort zone into a place where your activated faith will conquer your fears and have actions to match.

While the unwritten journals of the book of Acts are still being written, this is *your* time to sign up as a worker. All around you, the fields are ripe and ready for harvest—*right now!*

ABOUT THE AUTHOR

Ross Walker is a professional Economist with an extensive background in both public and private sector environments. Ross left the public sector in 1994 to establish Roscar Management Consulting Pty Ltd and has consulted extensively to the bus and coach and other industries in Australia ever since. Ross graduated from full time ministry training in 1997 but always felt drawn to the market place rather than the pulpit.

Since then, Roscar has established itself as a multi-award winning brand and recognised market leader in the field of logistics and project management having successfully delivered some of the largest transport events in Australia over the last two decades.

Ross is the principal of Roscar Group of Companies which specialise in project management of major transport events. It also operates technology and management consultancy businesses.

Ross is an entrepreneur and philanthropist and supporter of numerous Christian based ministries and charities. He has also had active involvement in market place ministry for almost four decades.

Ross is happily married to Carmel (41 years) and they have 3 children and 3 grand children. The family have dual residences on the Sunshine Coast in Queensland and in Port Melbourne, Victoria.

www.ingramcontent.com/pod-product-compliance
Lightning Source LLC
Chambersburg PA
CBHW062358090426
42740CB00010B/1322